GARF ASSESSMENT SOURCEBOOK

GARF ASSESSMENT SOURCEBOOK:
Using the DSM-IV Global Assessment of Relational Functioning

Lynelle C. Yingling, Ph.D.
William E. Miller, Jr., Ed.D.
Alice L. McDonald, M.S.
Susan T. Galewaler, M.S.

BRUNNER/MAZEL, *Publishers*
A member of the Taylor & Francis Group

USA	Publishing Office:	Taylor & Francis 1101 Vermont Avenue, N.W., Suite 200 Washington, DC 20005-3521 Tel: (202) 289-2174 Fax: (202) 289-3665
	Distribution Center:	Taylor & Francis 1900 Frost Road, Suite 101 Bristol, PA 19007-1598 Tel: (215) 785-5800 Fax: (215) 785-5515
UK		Taylor & Francis Ltd. 1 Gunpowder Square London EC4A 3DE Tel: 171 583 0490 Fax: 171 583 0581

GARF ASSESSMENT SOURCEBOOK: Using the DSM-IV Global Assessment of Relational Functioning

1 2 3 4 5 6 7 8 9 0   E B E B   9 0 9 8 7

This book was set in Palatino. The editors were Kathleen A. Savadel and Laura Haefner. Cover design by Curtis Tow, Curtis Tow Graphics.

A CIP catalog record for this book is available from the British Library.

∞ The paper in this publication meets the requirements of the ANSI Standard Z39.48-1984 (Permanence of Paper)

Library of Congress Cataloging-in-Publication Data
GARF assessment sourcebook : using the DSM-IV global assessment of
    relational functioning / by Lynelle C. Yingling . . . [et al.].
        p.   cm.
    Includes bibliographical references and index.
    ISBN 0-87630-864-7 (case : alk. paper)
    1. Family assessment—Handbooks, manuals, etc.   2. Diagnostic and
statistical manual of mental disorders—Handbooks, manuals, etc.
RC488.53.G37   1997
616.89'156—dc21   97-22610
                                                                        CIP

ISBN 0-87630-864-7 (case)

Contents

Foreword

The history of family therapy has been packed with innovative concepts, claims about new paradigms and models, and dramatic demonstrations of charismatic wizardry. In contrast, there has been only a modest number of proposals for methods of assessing the quality of therapy and evaluating treatment outcome. In addition, the field has conspicuously lacked consensus about principles.

In this book, Lynelle Yingling and colleagues have made the first major effort to describe in detail, and to evaluate, a family assessment method that has achieved sufficient recognition, both within and beyond the field of family therapy, so that a considerable number of clinics, training programs, and research projects have agreed to incorporate this method into their work. This method, the Global Assessment of Relational Functioning (GARF) scale, is presented by the authors, not as a final or fully confirmed approach, but as a feasible means of starting to share something across the highly diverse varieties of relationships, treatment approaches, and contexts that crowd the terrain of the family therapy field.

It is interesting to consider why family assessment, including this particular method of assessment, is being actively tried out at this time. Many, if not most, leading family therapists continue to be preoccupied with teaching, supervision, and clinical practice, not with research-based methods. Indeed, there continues to be a considerable number of therapy theoreticians who challenge the very idea that research on the "art" of therapy can be meaningful or relevant. However, as Yingling and colleagues show, the GARF is rooted in some of the best-established concepts and models for family therapy and can be used in teaching these concepts. Having members of trainee groups observe, independently rate, and discuss their rating discrepancies is an excellent teaching device, helping instructors to identify trainees who misunderstand certain concepts, fail to make on-target clinical observations, or, at times, who do make observations that others have missed. Thus, the GARF ratings can have a training function, even for instructors who are phobic or disdainful of formal research.

But the time has come when documented, preferably quantitative, evidence is being demanded of all forms of healthcare services, especially those, such as family therapy, that are not well established as reimbursable components of the healthcare repertory. At present, the GARF is certainly not a complete or definitive answer to these demands. However, it has the special merit of being practical—that is, suitable for routine and quick inclusion in clinical records—and is capable, the growing evidence indicates, of quite reliably making distinctions among various levels of relational dysfunction and changes in level of dysfunction during the course of therapy. As Yingling and colleagues sensibly discuss, this is the kind of evidence that managed care organizations are increasingly looking for. The GARF is the only family-oriented measure included in the pages of the DSM–IV—to be sure, in the Appendix for "Criteria Sets and Axes Provided for Further Study." This can only be viewed as a foot in the door controlled by the mental healthcare establishment. However, it seems to be an appropriate status for the GARF at this stage. This volume by Yingling and colleagues is a highly noteworthy effort to carry out the "further study" that is, in fact, needed.

In addition to presenting copies in full of the forms used in constructing GARF profiles, the work with the GARF reported here includes many ingredients of research programs that should be replicated and expanded. Here is a sample of such studies reported with varying degrees of confirmation in this book.

1 Comparison of the GARF as a single global rating and both separately and as a composite of ratings in the three major domains that have been identified—Problem Solving/Communication, Organization, and Emotional Climate.

2 Comparison of the GARF ratings with those from more complicated multidimensional scales such as those originated by Beavers, Epstein, and Olson, both in their observational forms and questionnaire self-report forms. Yingling and colleagues also include new scales they have devised that will help illuminate overall relational functioning beyond what can be suggested by GARF ratings.

3 Evaluation of the amount and kind of training needed to make reliable GARF ratings. (As with any clinical skill, the training needs to be gauged in relation to the experience of raters with a wide range of relational problems and mental disorders and in relation to their experience with couples and families. Earlier estimates that training could be very brief were misleading.)

4 Evaluation of change in GARF ratings from the initial session through the processes of later therapy. (The findings reported here indicate that GARF ratings do significantly improve in a substantial portion of clients, but that the poorest level of functioning quite often is not rated as evident in the initial session but, instead, two or three sessions later, perhaps as trust and self-disclosure have progressed.)

In summary, this book includes and also goes beyond the development of the GARF as a measure of relational functioning that has wide applicability for facilitating and evaluating clinical practice with families and other relational systems, for enhancing family therapy education and supervision, and for opening up new opportunities for clinical research that will be of interest both to family therapists and to many others in the current mental healthcare environment.

Lyman C. Wynne, M.D.

Preface

The compilation of this book has been a developmental journey. It began many years ago with the seed of interest in family systems being planted in each of us individually. We came together at a moment in time that supported the creation of a diversified writing team. However, we did not create this book in isolation. The entire context of our professional experiences provided the nurturing environment.

First, being in a doctoral program with a strong training emphasis in marriage and family therapy unified us. When the request for volunteers for GARF DSM–IV research field sites was announced in the Brown University newsletter, the enthusiastically naïve Texas A&M University training director volunteered the staff. Our enthusiasm for in-depth GARF research was encouraged and supported by Dr. Keith McFarland, Dean of Graduate Studies and Research at Texas A&M University–Commerce (formerly East Texas State University).

Perhaps our biggest debt of gratitude is owed to Dr. Lyman Wynne. His many years of work in the field, which led to the development of the GARF, made this book possible. But more than providing scientific expertise, he provided a kind and gentle spirit of a true founding father. Working with such a man of distinction over the past five years has been a lifetime highlight experience.

Other leaders in the field contributed generous amounts of time in reviewing materials describing their work and in providing permission to include those materials in this book. We are especially grateful to Dr. David Olson and Dr. Robert Hampson.

There are other members of the team whose names do not appear as authors. Many doctoral students contributed greatly to the research and theoretical understanding of the GARF. But the most important contributors are the families with whom we work. The real reason for this book being written is the families who were, are, and will be willing to work collaboratively with family therapists for family system change. In the case studies (altered to protect client identity), families who courageously shared personal stories for the benefit of others inspired us to focus on assessing family strengths. Hopefully, this book will provide some useful tools for improving the therapeutic relationship with clients to evoke more effective and efficient change.

As we progressed through the development of this book, each of our families offered unique involvement and nurtured this process. A special thanks to Isaac Fuller, Janet Fuller, and Susan Vaughn for artistic depiction of family functioning metaphors, and to Todd Smith for Spanish translation of the SAFE. For that, we are grateful.

CHAPTER 1

A Multi-Systems Approach: Collaborating for Health Through Systems Theory

Purpose and readers' guide
Marriage and family therapy (MFT) evolution
Futuristic partnering with systemic business principles

PURPOSE AND READERS' GUIDE

The purpose of this book is to present the Global Assessment of Relational Functioning (GARF) as a practical tool for integrating family assessment in ways that meet the needs of the client, the therapist, managed care, and contractual payers. This "why" and "how" book is designed as a sourcebook for therapists incorporating the *Diagnostic and Statistical Manual of Mental Disorders* (4th edition; DSM–IV; American Psychiatric Association, 1994) GARF to improve the quality of their clinical work. When effectively used, the GARF may provide therapists with assessment data for guiding their clinical work and outcome data for verifying treatment success to outside evaluators. Further exploratory and confirmatory research, as well as research-based application, will provide needed refinement of this new family systems DSM–IV tool.

The basic elements of the GARF described in the DSM–IV are:

A. *Problem solving*—skills in negotiating goals, rules, and routines; adaptability to stress; communication skills; ability to resolve conflict
B. *Organization*—maintenance of interpersonal roles and subsystem boundaries; hierarchical functioning; coalitions and distribution of power, control, and responsibility
C. *Emotional climate*—tone and range of feelings; quality of caring, empathy, involvement, and attachment/commitment; sharing of values; mutual affective responsiveness, respect, and regard; quality of sexual functioning (American Psychiatric Association, 1994, p. 758).

1

Our author team has translated these concepts into (a) interactional processes, (b) organizational structure, and (c) emotional climate/developmental nurturing output of the client family system. We have also extended these applications to broader cybernetic therapeutic/supervision/training/societal systems.

To achieve our goals, the necessary tools of *structural* knowledge, *process* charts, and *growth-producing environmental* proposals are included. Graphic language is used throughout to facilitate efficient communication in this busy world of the reader. Each chapter includes an outline of topics covered under the chapter title. Achieving our sourcebook goals with a tentative attitude of encouraging further research is perhaps the "miracle" goal for which we strive. Different readers may take slightly different paths in proceeding through this sourcebook to meet their specific interests and needs.

Goal-Based Reader's Guide

The *clinician* will likely be most interested in finding a quick understanding of the GARF and how it can direct treatment interventions to produce effective outcomes. For the therapist who has a clear understanding of family systems theory and how assessment is foundational to the therapeutic process, we suggest that Chapter 2, Chapter 4, and the Appendixes will serve as the "getting started" manual. Focusing on Chapter 2 will give a comprehensive theoretical understanding of the GARF. Chapter 4 will then illustrate how to put those concepts into practice following ethical guidelines. The forms included in the Appendixes will supply ready-to-use resources for implementation. As the clinician begins to partner more with managed care to produce the best outcome research procedures possible, reading Chapters 5 and 6 will be useful in formulating research plans. A good review of theory in Chapters 1 and 3 may be helpful reminders.

As a supplemental or required assessment textbook for family therapy training, the *academic* will likely want to cover the entire book in sequential order. Chapter 1 and Chapter 3 will provide basic theory review for students. Chapter 5 compares major family assessment tools and summarizes key information on instruments helpful in expanding our perspective that comprehensive training in family assessment is essential. Chapter 2 will provide the practical understanding of the GARF, as well as its historical development and limited verifying research. Chapter 6 will be future-directed for students, orienting them toward practice in the real world.

Parts of the book are especially useful to *managed care* quality assurance staff focusing on improvements in using outcome data for planning and implementing quantifiable measures of performance. Chapter 1 will provide the theoretical explanation of how systemic assessment is so compatible with quality assurance management. The research section in Chapter 2 describes verifying studies available at this time that empirically support the use of the GARF. Chapter 6 will provide a blueprint to implementing family system assessment outcome studies using the GARF.

Summarizing the reader's guide, a plan might look something like the following:

- Clinicians: Chapter 2, Chapter 4, Appendixes; followed by Chapter 5 and Chapter 6; supplemented by review of Chapter 1 and Chapter 3.
- Academics: Chapters 1–6 sequentially; emphasizing the family systems theory in Chapters 1, 3, and 5; emphasizing the research in Chapter 2; emphasizing the application in Chapters 4 and 6.
- Managed care planners: Chapters 1, 2, and 6.

To prepare the reader for this venture, an overview of systemic thinking, both in the family therapy field and in the business field, is our first stop.

MARRIAGE AND FAMILY THERAPY (MFT) EVOLUTION

The field of family therapy has matured since its beginnings in the 1950s. At that early time, the Batesonian double bind hypothesis highlighted the impact interactional processes within the basic social unit have on the psychological health of individual members within that unit (Bateson, Jackson, Haley, & Weakland, 1956). Becvar and Becvar (1996) trace the development of the field by identifying simultaneous happenings that formulated the connection (called *systems theory* or *cybernetics*) between the scientific world and the family relations world. This unique way of understanding human problems was built by "human relations engineers" who took scientific theory and applied it to therapeutic intervention to solve human problems.

Using a life cycle development metaphor, the field of family therapy could be considered to be in a leaving-home or young adult stage. Licensure for the independent practice of marriage and family therapy (MFT) designates the legal age of majority and has been achieved in the majority of states. However, some discipline-of-origin parents have been reluctant to allow MFT a separate independent identity, resulting in the typical enmeshed system struggles common at this stage of development. Perhaps another decade of maturity will bring a recognition of this new identity. But can the older generation step aside and allow the younger ideas to be recognized as generative? And can the younger generation appreciate and learn from the older generation's struggles? James Framo's article (1996) provides a stimulating review of the development of the MFT field.

Whatever the result of the extended family struggles, the new family of MFT is crystallizing a set of family rules distinct from the disciplines of origin. Continuing the metaphor of family development, perhaps the two adult partners forming this new family unit could be identified as traditional structural assumptions and postmodern interpretations of family systems. With the new generation of children about to emerge, whose belief systems will they be taught? Will they gain from the strengths of both parents so that the apparent conflicting rules can be reconciled into a balanced whole? Or will this new marriage suffer such difficulties in forming a union that they turn over the parenting functions to grandparents? What appears to be happening is the beginnings of conflict resolution between the two young marrieds, giving hope for the next generation of healthy children who experience clear communication and confident parental hierarchy, resulting in a balanced growth-promoting nurturing system.

What are the belief systems of this new family unit? A variety of models explaining how to intervene therapeutically in family functioning have been developed. These models will be explored briefly in Chapter 3. Generally speaking, systemic therapeutic intervention includes (a) assessing family system functioning data, (b) conceptualizing that data into a treatment plan, and (c) using MFT intervention techniques to implement the treatment plan. Some form of assessment seems to be foundational. Models identify specific methods and seem to adopt at least one of three focus areas for the intervention process:

- Organizational structure of the family system, paying particular attention to hierarchy and boundaries;

- Interactional processes of the family system, paying particular attention to dyadic interactions of the marital/parental subsystem as marital partners attempt to solve problems; and
- Differentiation from family-of-origin rules and processes that developmentally interfere with clear-thinking problem solving in the nuclear family, thereby promoting a nurturing environment for member growth.

Though models vary in the assumptions they adopt, most models accept the following systemic functioning assumptions as valid and useful:

1 Problems are *contextually based,* meaning they are the result of ineffective interactional and organizational rules in the primary social environment versus the result of individual psychopathology.

2 Assessment focuses on *circular versus linear causality.* Linear causality looks at an isolated segment of the problem: for example, "An angry wife tries to get revenge by prolonging the divorce settlement with a contested divorce trial." A circular causality assessment broadens the focus on the problem to sound like this: "The wife grew up in a family where money was very hard to come by and the children often went without necessary food and clothing because the father irresponsibly spent family income on alcohol. The wife's relationship with her husband has been one in which she tried to play the child role so that she could make her husband play the role of the responsible father she wished she had as a child. The husband resented being coerced into this 'fathering' role and began separating from his wife by retreating to the bars. The wife became increasingly frustrated with the lack of connectedness with her husband and demonstrated more dependency in an attempt to gain his support. The husband reacted to this attempt at connectedness by withdrawing even more. Both parents, fearful of losing all aspects of 'family,' have turned to the children as sources of affirmation. A prolonged divorce trial seems to be the only way either spouse knows to protect him/herself from horrifying isolation."

3 Troubled families are *stuck in a phase of the family development life cycle* because of lack of resources needed for adjusting to the transition or inability to access the resources available. These resources include the appropriate amount of glue [cohesion] and bounce [adaptability] to respond effectively to stress. The rules for communicating with each other determine the glue and bounce levels.

4 *Symptoms are metaphorical* of the system functioning problems. Therefore, presenting problems are clues that lead to the underlying difficulties in the family's communication rules that create organizational boundaries.

5 Because *symptoms are system maintained and system maintaining,* they are difficult to give up. In other words, the presenting problems are a result of family rules that are an ineffective way of dealing with stress, but are the only way the family knows at this time. The ineffectiveness of the approach increases the stress level for the family; therefore, the family members try even harder to use the only way they know, and thus increase the stress more, resulting in their increased anxious efforts to use what they know, and so on.

6 Change in the family's interactional patterns (that are a result of communication rules that constitute organizational boundaries) results in a *second-order change* and is necessary to achieve lasting symptom relief.

7 Structural organizations that generally promote healthy system functioning and improved relationship nurturance for growth are on three levels: (a) the adults in the nuclear family need an *egalitarian relationship* to diminish power struggles, (b) a child

needs a *parental hierarchy* to provide safety for the child's developmental process, and (c) parents need to be on a *peer-type adult relationship* with their "former parents" in order to achieve intimacy and empowering support versus intrusion. Regardless of whether the family structure is married or divorced, children need the security of parent/s being in charge of the family functioning. Parenting is a demanding responsibility and generally requires the resources of more than one adult; ideally, both biological parents can work together to maintain a balanced parental hierarchy, though substitute resources for either parent can be used.

Mills and Sprenkle (1995) describe the first- versus second-order cybernetics debate with illustrations of intervention techniques. Is it necessary to give up family system functioning assumptions in order to treat families respectfully and own one's own part in shaping the therapeutic system? The postmodern contribution seems to be adding a more future-oriented, optimistic process focus to the more static traditional content focus. A focus on process has resulted in a more egalitarian multi-systems level perspective in viewing the intervention system as well as the client system.

The challenging postmodern perspective seems to create a balanced MFT theory. The traditional structural systemic identification of the field, blended with the lowered hierarchy collaborative postmodern focus on process, results in a healthy nurturing theoretical system. Preparing competent family therapists today includes combining theory and skill development from both traditional and postmodern perspectives into a smooth integrative approach that is flexible enough to meet the needs of the clients (M. Nichols & Schwartz, 1995; Ratliff & Yingling, 1996). Perhaps it is time to move from adolescent squabbling to take on adult responsibility for what we do.

Regardless of model biases, the foundation to the practice of MFT is legalistically defined as systemic thinking (Licensed Marriage and Family Therapist Act, 1991; American Association for Marriage and Family Therapy [AAMFT], 1993). Perhaps we can reflect on our roots of understanding systems from the field of physics and see our philosophical compatibility with the current societal understanding of human systems in all types of organizations.

Part of being accountable/adult is being scientific enough to defend what we do. With increased competition in the field and tightening budgets everywhere, the payers of our services demand justification for their expenditure. Without assessment, scientific accountability is an impossible challenge. With too rigid a scientific approach, growth is stifled. Can we integrate assessment of the family system in a practical way clinically and still respond to the accountability demands of those who keep our doors open for business?

FUTURISTIC PARTNERING WITH SYSTEMIC BUSINESS PRINCIPLES

Partnering with managed care in some form of relationship seems to be the future picture for mental health providers. Managed care companies for outpatient behavioral health are competing under the criteria of the National Committee for Quality Assurance (NCQA), which are to be implemented for accreditation reviews in 1997 ("NCQA Develops Standards," 1996). The NCQA is a private, not-for-profit organization using accreditation and performance measurement to assess and report on the quality of managed care plans. Although it has no regulatory authority, the NCQA is seen as the industry standard by many business payers. Its annual Public Call for Measures invites professional provider feedback on the HEDIS (Health Employer and Information Set) performance measurement set. This invitation is an opportunity for MFTs to be heard (Jennings & Towers, 1996). The NCQA can be contacted either by calling (202) 628-5788 or (800) 274-2237, or by visiting its website at http://www.ncqa.org. The first standard for NCQA is quality management and improvement ("NCQA releases," 1996).

Incorporating the terms *quality* and *system* in company titles and slogans seems to be a trend. Total Quality Management (TQM) has been identified as the way for American business to survive. But do we truly understand how the quality assurance concepts from TQM are parallel to the concepts in systemic family therapy and how they can be applied in the successful practice of family therapy?

Paralleling the development of family therapy, Dr. W. Edwards Deming, a statistician with a degree in mathematical physics, began revolutionizing the field of manufacturing and service organization management with his 1950 work in Japan (Deming, 1993). These principles laid the foundation for what later became known as TQM, which has been defined as "a systemic organizational philosophy that concentrates on meeting and exceeding the customer needs by constant improvement of the system, involvement of all people in the organization, and using statistics [objective data] as a tool for enlightenment" (Yingling, 1994, p. 5). TQM seems to be the systemic approach to management much as MFT is the systemic approach to therapy.

In this management approach, a *system* is defined as "a network of interdependent components that work together to try to accomplish the aim of the system" (Deming, 1993, p. 50). People are viewed as the foundation of any business system, even manufacturing. Transformation (second-order change) is seen as essential for our economy to survive. The leadership for this transformation has to be based on profound knowledge about system functioning, variation within the system, perpetual testing of predictive hypotheses for system improvement, and human relationships.

Deming's (1986) famous 14 points for management include a strong focus on a collaborative, supportive interactional process within a relatively flattened hierarchical structure in order to create a smooth functioning system that produces quality outputs, whose consistency can be measured with objective statistical tools. Another important concept is to first assess the system functioning before making a symptomatic relief change. This allows for special causes of excessive system variation to be identified and corrected before focusing on improving quality through reducing the in-control variation. Special causes are definable stressors separate from the normal system variation. Changing a symptom without understanding the impact on the system, a first-order change, can lead to throwing the system out of balance, a second-order change, in a way that creates worse symptoms. Assessing the system functioning first and making any necessary adjustments to system functioning will generally relieve symptoms in a permanent way. With much recent criticism of TQM not delivering what it promised, Brown, Hitchcock, and Willard (1994) have described the short-sighted focus on linear output versus the humanistic focus on systemic functioning predicting failure. They emphasize that our society needs valid implementation of TQM systemic beliefs and principles now more than ever. Perhaps the focus on linear output is a part of the quandary the mental health profession is currently encountering.

Family therapists are already trained to conceptualize in systemic functioning terms. We understand the importance of assessing and possibly intervening in the organizational structure and the interactional processes of the family-therapeutic system in order to produce quality outputs—symptom-free members of the system who develop in a healthy way, drawing from the nurturance provided by the healthy system.

Applying systemic principles to the business practice of MFT challenges our objective analytical skills. As the practice of MFT matures and is recognized as an "adult" in the business world, we will be expected to compete under quality-assurance standards. The GARF is one systemic family functioning assessment tool that can be useful in this competitive marketplace.

In what way will NCQA standards influence managed care's selection of providers and demands on providers for outcome data? A draft copy of accreditation standards for managed behavioral health care organizations was developed in April 1996 (NCQA, 1996). These standards incorporate many external criteria according to which managed care companies will be judged in order to achieve NCQA accreditation. However, the first principles documented are the quality-improvement standards. These standards state that "Quality management is an integrative process that links knowledge, structure, and processes together throughout the MBHO [Managed Behavioral Healthcare Organization] to assess and improve quality " (NCQA, 1996, p. 2). These words seem to be very compatible with Deming's writings describing systems, as well as with the GARF's description of a relational system as emotional climate (nurturing output similar to Deming's knowledge), organizational structure, and problem-solving skills (interactional processes). Perhaps these three variables are the essence of life that permeate the sciences and the humanities.

CHAPTER 2

DSM–IV: GARF

Defining the GARF
Historical development
Collecting and analyzing GARF data
Summary

The intent of this chapter is to familiarize the reader with the GARF and its origins and to delineate the problems and solutions with which the clinical research team grappled while undertaking our GARF study. Results of this and other studies that establish the GARF as a reliable, useable clinical instrument are discussed. This chapter will hopefully reduce stress for those using the GARF in either formal or informal research settings.

DEFINING THE GARF

DSM–IV Description

Now that the GARF has been born and named in the DSM–IV appendix, what are the identifying characteristics of this newborn? First, it is an assessment tool that is designed for relationship system functioning rather than individual functioning. Therefore, the focus of the assessor must be on more than one person. Because the family system is the primary relationship system affecting mental health, the GARF is designed to be used primarily with a family system. However, the components are systemic in nature and can be adapted to use with any ongoing relationship system, such as organizational families in the work-place, as well as with any designated subsystems within the expanded family system.

Second, the GARF is designed as a clinical rating scale rather than a self-report instrument. The assessment is made by an outside observer of the system, such as the therapist, the treatment team, observing therapist/s, or neutral researcher/s uninvolved with the therapy relationship. Alice L. McDonald, one of the present authors, has adapted the five-level GARF scale into a global self-report instrument (see Appendix C) using fairy tale metaphors.

Third, the time frame for rating is generally the present as you observe it. The use of present ratings lends itself well to doing session-by-session assessments and easily tracking change over time. Jacob's (1995) findings with self-report assessment supports the assumption that time-frame directions in the assessment model are important for treatment outcome studies. GARF correlations with family crises and therapeutic interventions identified in session case notes can be helpful in understanding the change process.

The GARF scale contains a progressive rating of family relational functioning that ranges from a low of 1 to a high of 100. This scale system parallels the DSM–IV's Global Assessment of Functioning (GAF) rating for individuals. In addition, this ratio scale is divided into five categories:

  1–20 = chaotic
21–40 = rarely satisfactory
41–60 = predominantly unsatisfactory
61–80 = somewhat unsatisfactory
81–100 = satisfactory

Raters are to assign specific intermediate codes within the cutting-point categories whenever possible. If specific numerical ratings are not possible, the rater is asked to select the midpoint for the appropriate category. The DSM–IV's instructions are to "rate the degree to which a family or other ongoing relational unit meets the affective and/or instrumental needs of its members" (American Psychiatric Association, 1994, p. 758). Raters are to consider the family's affective and instrumental functioning in the three defined areas:

A. *Problem solving*—Skills in negotiating goals, rules, and routines; adaptability to stress; communication skills; ability to resolve conflict
B. *Organization*—Maintenance of interpersonal roles and subsystem boundaries; hierarchical functioning; coalitions and distribution of power, control, and responsibility
C. *Emotional climate*—Tone and range of feelings; quality of caring, empathy, involvement, and attachment/commitment; sharing of values; mutual affective responsiveness, respect, and regard; quality of sexual functioning (American Psychiatric Association, 1994, p. 758)

Table 2.1 presents the descriptors of the GARF by delineating the numerical rating scale, the DSM–IV overall description of each category, comparable metaphorical story, and the graphic depiction of the metaphorical story.

Clinical Use Enhancements

To expand the clinical usefulness of the GARF, the East Texas State University clinic teams, who field-tested the GARF, developed two supplemental tools: (1) the GARF Profile Chart (Appendix B) and (2) the GARF Self-Report for Families (Appendix C). The charting form was developed in order to follow a family's progress in therapy and to identify patterns of congruence and divergence among the three variables throughout the course of therapy. The bottom half of the page contains a dated session-by-session recording of four scores: Interactional Processes (I), Organizational Structure (O), Emotional Climate/Developmental Nurturance (E), and the global GARF. In each session column, a place is provided for recording who attends the session. If the therapist is working with a treatment team, the

Table 2.1
GARF Levels of Family Functioning

Level	DSM–IV Description	Metaphorical story	Metaphorical drawing*
5 (81–100)	Relational unit is functioning satisfactorily from self-report of participants and from perspectives of observers	*The Three Bears*	
4 (61–80)	Functioning of relational unit is somewhat unsatisfactory. Over a period of time, many but not all difficulties are resolved without complaints	*Little Red Riding Hood*	
3 (41–60)	Relational unit has occasional times of satisfying and competent functioning together but clearly dysfunctional, unsatisfying relationships tend to predominate	*Cinderella*	
2 (21–40)	Relational unit is obviously and seriously dysfunctional; forms and time periods of satisfactory relating are rare	*Hansel and Gretel*	
1 (1–20)	Relational unit has become too dysfunctional to retain continuity of contact and attachment	*The Ugly Duckling*	

*Drawings by Janet and Isaac Fuller

therapist may record the family's average global GARF as rated by the treatment team. The top half of the page contains directions for using the form, the DSM–IV definition for each of the variables, and a chart for plotting the I, O, and E scores for each session, up to 10 therapy sessions per page. Marking the three dimensions with different colored pens provides a very clear picture of the way this system is changing during therapy. This data form is attached to the inside front of the client folder to make recording and analyzing scores after each session easier and to provide a one-page data summary for easy computer entry. To reduce the risk that a therapist's rating bias would inflate and distort the assessment (e.g., an upward curve that did not faithfully represent the family's functioning), the GARF scores are first recorded on the individual session Case Notes form, then transferred to the summary GARF Profile Chart. Treatment team global ratings are averaged and recorded on the back of the team message, which is given to the therapist during supervision after the therapist assigns a rating. We were pleased that this recording plan resulted in unpredictable patterns of change, which encouraged us about the validity of the process.

The second adaptation, the self-report fairy tale metaphor tool developed by McDonald (Appendix C), is very useful in clinical settings. According to the directions, family members are asked to identify jointly or separately which metaphor reminds them most of their family. The family's process of consensus building or sharing different views can be a very helpful task for the outside rater to observe in order to make a more valid GARF assessment. Metaphorical language is nonthreatening to adult family members and can be understood by children. Descriptions of the fairy tales were carefully worded to incorporate characteristics described in the DSM–IV. Therefore, the GARF can be used as more than a clinical rating scale, blending the assessment and intervention functions of therapy. The self-report dimension may add valuable clarity when the family is assessed through collective insights of both the family and therapist. By combining the results of the family's self-report with the therapist's clinical evaluation, a collaborative intervention strategy can be planned.

Training Perceptions

The GARF was intended to require very little training in order to use. The Group for the Advancement of Psychiatry (GAP) Committee on the Family (1996) recommends approximately 1.5 to 2 hr of preparatory time in order to use the GARF clinically; research training would be longer. They recommend the following steps:

1 Study the GARF instructions and scale anchor points for 20–30 min.
2 Clarify any questions about concepts with an MFT (marriage and family therapy) teacher/mentor for 10–15 min.
3 Read or view practice materials (e.g., written vignettes in the June 1996 issue of *Family Process*) and make a tentative GARF rating; allow at least an hour.
4 Discuss your ratings with the MFT teacher to identify points of uncertainty or confusion.

We have developed a more specific training process that included the following:

- Each therapist read through the descriptions of each level (see Appendix B) that are now incorporated in DSM–IV.
- We created a table based on the DSM–IV statements about the GARF. This table separated the variable statements into three parallel columns, thus encouraging treatment team therapists to learn how to distinguish among these variables (Appendix B). This table of GARF variables was posted in clinic observation rooms as a reminder for the treatment team therapists.
- We practiced assigning the GARF global ratings as a therapist in the room, and a treatment team member for one semester, and recording GARF ratings on each session's case notes.
- We developed the charting form (Appendix B) and have used that form for cases since the summer of 1991, modifying and improving it as we gained further experience.
- During group supervision, we began informally noting patterns of change on the charting form and the individual symptoms associated with these changes.
- We analyzed data collected on the charting form for 2 years to better understand the GARF's implications for interventions. Our conceptualization of the GARF has clarified during frequent discussions of (a) initial research findings and (b) future plans for data analysis.
- Later, we found McDonald's fairy tale metaphors and companion graphics very useful in training other therapists to use the GARF. As these materials were presented, the therapists learned to quickly and clearly distinguish the discrete five-level systemic

characteristics of the GARF categories of functioning (Table 2.1 and Appendix C) and to identify corresponding Axis I and II individual symptoms with each.

Research on the GARF that is currently underway at Southern Methodist University seeks to develop a written training manual for using the GARF (R. Hampson, personal communication, September 30, 1996).

Intervention Implications

Training in understanding the components of the GARF and using GARF assessment to plan intervention strategies was enhanced when the three variables were identified with structural, strategic, and family-of-origin models of family therapy. A GARF assessment that describes the family as having a strong organizational structure and weak problem-solving skills seems to imply a behavioral skill-training intervention. However, if the total GARF rating in all three areas is weak, this seems to warrant a strategic intervention to influence behavioral interactions in a way that shifts the structure to a healthier organizational level. This combined structural and interactional strengthening would then likely result in an improved emotional climate that nurtures development of members and reduces individual symptoms/Axis I diagnoses. Depression would be relieved by the ability to effectively verbalize one's fears/anger; anxiety would be relieved by the safety of a well-organized family structure. If the individual diagnoses were of the Axis II type, then developmental delays from family-of-origin experiences would likely need to be addressed before the emotional climate assessment would improve. In order for any therapy to produce long-lasting results, a thorough assessment of the system must occur. In order for managed care to predict how long treatment will take to eliminate symptoms, assessment must include system as well as symptom (Axis I and II diagnoses) functioning.

Training of providers and managed care utilization review staff in family systems assessment seems timely. One colleague (B. Watts, personal communication, March 12, 1997) shared his use of the GARF and the related self-report Systemic Assessment of the Family Environment (Appendix D) in computerized treatment planning. By adding the GARF language into Therascribe's (Jongsma, Peterson, & McInnis, 1997) problem definitions, short-term treatment goals, long-term objectives, and therapeutic interventions, he is able to meet the demands of managed care with a comprehensive family systems method of working. Dennis (personal communication, March 17, 1997) has developed a computerized scoring program for the Child Well-Being Scale (1996), which is programmed to produce a GARF score. Courts in his Minnesota county are using the GARF scores as significant factors in decisions involving child removal and juvenile offenders. His computerized program is also being used in Orange County, California. The potential for innovative use, and possible misuse, of the GARF is only beginning to be realized. Inclusion in the DSM–IV, if only in the appendix at this time, gives the GARF a powerful level of legitimacy. Continued improvement through research is critical.

Systemic assessment of the broader system functioning (second-order cybernetics) including the therapist, treatment team, and supervision systems can be enhanced by using the GARF constructs. This approach to assessment is becoming increasingly important to understanding systemic functioning.

Our defining new ways to use the GARF for outcome research is just beginning. More forms are needed for (a) tracking individual diagnoses of a family member with family system change, (b) correlating intervention strategies with system change and symptom relief, (c) assessing the therapeutic system with the GARF, (d) refining a parallel self-report instrument, and (e) integrating GARF definitions into standard computerized treatment planning programs.

HISTORICAL DEVELOPMENT

How did the GARF get into the DSM–IV, and why is that so important to clinicians? The theoretical roots of the GARF reach deep to the beginnings of the family therapy movement. The unifying effect of a diagnostic protocol for mental disorders in the widely accepted *Diagnostic and Statistical Manuals of Mental Disorders* (DSMs) of the American Psychiatric Association provided a parallel development that would come to limit the practice of family therapy.

The DSM–IV introduction provides a detailed history of DSM development in parallel with the World Health Organization's development of the *International Classification of Diseases* (ICD). A classification of mental disorders developed from the need to collect statistical information. The 1840 U.S. census included one mental illness category, called idiocy/insanity. The 1880 census expanded to seven categories: mania, melancholia, monomania, paresis, dementia, dipsomania, and epilepsy. In 1917 the American Psychiatric Association formulated a plan to incorporate more attention to clinical utility, especially in mental hospitals, rather than to purely statistical gathering. Later, the U.S. Army and Veterans Administration (VA) expanded the nomenclature to incorporate more outpatient presentations of World War II servicemen and veterans; simultaneously, the World Health Organization incorporated a section for 26 mental disorders in the ICD–6, being highly influenced by the VA nomenclature. DSM–I was published in 1952 as a clinical parallel of the ICD–6; DSM–II paralleled ICD–8. The 1980 publication of DSM–III was based on ICD–9, with the goal of providing a nomenclature more for clinicians and researchers than for statisticians. Specific diagnostic criteria, a multiaxial system, and a theory-neutral approach were introduced. This first attempt contained a number of inconsistencies and was revised in 1987.

So what did the DSM–IV Task Force hope to add? The 27-member task force with 13 work groups comprising 5–8 members each was appointed in 1988. One goal was to facilitate communication and collaboration between the DSM–IV and ICD–10 developers to stay in compliance with the U.S. treaty obligation with the World Health Organization for consistency with ICD (ICD–10 was published in 1992 but not yet implemented). The second goal was to compile the best and most user-friendly diagnostic system possible, based on user input and making only documented changes. To accomplish this second goal, the task force conducted 150 comprehensive and systematic reviews of literature, 40 analyses of collected but not analyzed data, and 12 field trials before making any changes. Results of this extensive review are recorded in the *DSM–IV Sourcebook*, to be published in five volumes by the American Psychiatric Association (1994, 1995, 1996); three volumes have been released as of this writing. Stringent criteria for field trials included (a) 5–10 diverse sites with approximately 100 subjects at each; (b) comparison of DSM–III, DSM–III–R, ICD–10, and proposed DSM–IV criteria; and (c) data collection on reliability, performance characteristics, demographics of clients and family history, associated clinical features, and onset, level of impairment, complications, and course of disorder. The guiding criteria for change were clinical utility, reliability, performance characteristics of individual criteria, and validity measures (American Psychiatric Association, 1994).

How did the GARF fit into this broad scheme of mental health classification and clinical diagnosis? Reviewing the multi-system complexities of the DSM development generates amazement and gratitude for inclusion of the GARF in the DSM–IV appendix. In 1983 Lyman Wynne, a founding theorist, clinician, and researcher in the family therapy field, reported on the weaknesses of the DSM–III for working effectively with family systems (GAP, 1996). The year 1986 marked the beginnings of formal work on the GARF by the GAP Committee on the Family. The GAP Committee on the Family (1989) then wrote a challenging article in the *American Journal of Psychiatry* for broadening the systemic view of human problems.

Serious work began in 1987 to construct two new classification schemas for family functioning: one that dimensionalizes and one that categorizes. Encouragement came for further development of categories, especially for such problems as family violence, which would not be completed in time for DSM–IV. However, the GAP Committee on the Family (1989) did publish the Classification of Relational Diagnoses (CORD) for future categorical research.

More encouragement came from the DSM–IV Task Force chair Allen Frances and the Multiaxial Issues Work Group chair Janet Williams to develop a dimensionalized global scale based on Axis IV. This encouragement sparked the development of the GARF. In 1989 Robert Beavers was simultaneously a member of the GAP Committee on the Family, President of the American Association for Marriage and Family Therapy, and on the Board of Directors of American Family Therapy Association. He convened an interorganizational meeting that resulted in the Coalition on Family Diagnosis, co-chaired by Herta Guttman and Florence Kaslow. The GAP and the Coalition on Family Diagnosis then worked together to create the GARF. Two goals marked the development of the GARF: (a) a simple instrument that was sophisticated enough for both clinicians and researchers to find useful and (b) a dimensionalized relational instrument worthy of becoming Axis IV in future versions of DSM, benefiting the family therapy field and the larger mental health establishment (GAP, 1996).

The final version of the DSM–IV was somewhat disappointing because the GARF did not appear as a major axis. It was placed in the appendix under the category "Criteria Sets and Axes Provided for Further Study." But the GARF is the first explicit DSM recognition of a criteria set for interpersonal relationships. We have much work to complete in testing, verifying, and refining the GARF before the DSM–V begins to be developed.

How did this team of authors become involved? In the fall of 1990 Lynelle C. Yingling was directing a family therapy clinic at East Texas State University (now Texas A&M University—Commerce) and read a call for pilot study participants in testing the GARF. Having been a supervisee of Robert Beavers in 1988 and being familiar with the GAP plans, Yingling volunteered the clinic to participate. In the spring 1991 semester, nine therapists served on treatment teams and used the GARF with 35 families to test for interrater and interfamily reliability. All therapists were trained with a minimum of one doctoral-level course in family therapy; most had at least two courses and were simultaneously enrolled in others. Usable results from this effort were included in the Coalition on Family Diagnosis report to the Multiaxial Work Group and in later writings (GAP, 1996). Our team was encouraged by the consistent same-family ratings between team members and the effective discrimination between families exhibiting very different levels of individual symptoms.

However, we believed the instrument could be more clinically useful if the variables could be rated separately, as the different variables imply intervention techniques from discrete models of family therapy. We also suspected that the emotional climate dimension of the GARF might be distorting the global rating because of therapist reactions from personal biases, or perhaps because of the directions provided for the ratings. Timing of the assessment seemed to make a critical difference, so rating over time might be very important clinically. We developed a simplified graph form (See Appendix B) to track the three variables over each session, using a numerical rating at the bottom and a plotted profile at the top. This form also included room for identifying the date and the family members present at each session. During the summer 1991 semester, six therapists used the GARF profile form with 37 families to evaluate the simplified graph form's clinical utility, track change over time, and analyze the three scale factors separately. We were so pleased with this form that we adopted it as a required procedure in the clinic. Several of the authors continue to use the form in private practice work. Attaching the form to the inside of each client folder provides a wealth of easily accessed information for treatment planning and outcome data entry.

Gaining great fondness for the GARF, we continued experimenting by comparing the GARF results with Beavers' Self-report Family Inventory (SFI) (Beavers & Hampson, 1990), Olson's Family Adaptability and Cohesion Evaluation Scale (FACES) (Olson, Portner, & Lavee, 1985), and Yingling's Systematic Assessment of the Family Environment (Appendix D). We also began tracking DSM–III Axes I and II diagnoses with the GARF. However, our therapist team kept changing, and the original 1991 team was not there in 1992. So the original team decided to focus on analyzing the mass of data we had accumulated. The results of this analysis are reported later in this chapter. As Program Director at the Southwest Family Institute 1993–1994, Yingling incorporated the GARF into the required clinical procedures for the clinical interns from a variety of disciplines of origin, though lack of consistent teamwork and uniform degree program training did not produce the same exciting GARF attachment as had the doctoral program. The authors from the original project have presented our results at state and national family therapy conferences, as well as at several in-house agency trainings. Our enthusiasm over the past five years has continued to grow, apparently because of the basic solidarity of the GARF model and the heuristic possibilities it generates.

COLLECTING AND ANALYZING GARF DATA

Challenges to Overcome

As we planned our research design, we became aware that there were numerous practical and theoretical dilemmas. In our eagerness to learn about GARF and about our client population, we had initially asked too many research questions to effectively collect and analyze data. Other practical concerns included choosing instruments and forms that the clinical staff would routinely complete, motivating staff to consistently participate in the research, training and integrating new staff into the team, deciding what data to measure and how to code that data, and obtaining reliable computer hardware and software. We also struggled with developing forms to report the results and training the ancillary office staff to routinely and accurately input the data. Theoretical problems arose concerning whether we would view the data from a "therapist-accurate" or "client-accurate" stance. We had hoped to compare technical interventions and client outcome but found this task would be overwhelming to both staff and design.

This project began with the clinical staff that came to the Marriage, Family and Child Consultation Center (MFCCC) in the summer and fall of 1991. We were excited and ambitious and hoped to compare both Beavers' and Olson's instruments with the GARF. We had many questions we wanted to answer about assessment and family work and thus posed far too many research questions. As the reality of pursuing both clinical and academic work settled on us, we had to revamp our design. Many of the research questions, including extensive comparison of other assessment models with the GARF, were reduced or eliminated. Ultimately our work refocused on evaluating reliability of the GARF and examining its potential as a clinical instrument to inform process and ascertain outcome.

Because we were in a university doctoral program, new staff were added as each semester changed. Staff had to be encouraged to learn the assessment process on their own. The clinic uses a team training model, and new members often appeared intimidated by lack of experience. New staff were tempted to confirm their ratings before assigning them on paper. More seasoned team members had to refrain from coaching new members in "GARF ratings" so as not to bias the results to the older members' ways of thinking and using the instrument. Comparisons were frequently made after each team member had written his or her ratings on the team form, and team interest, cohesion, and learning process were facilitated by the lively discussions about rating differences and consistencies.

We became aware that one of the biggest challenges in using the GARF is learning the subscales so that they can be used consistently by the staff. We invited each new therapist-in-training to rate his or her own family as a means of becoming personally acquainted with the scales. It is essential that the therapist learns how the subscales are broken down internally. Comprehending that there are organizational, interactional, and emotional components eases the analysis of family functioning. McDonald, one team member, used fairy tales to facilitate the new team members' comprehension of the quintiles. *The Three Bears* was used to represent 81–100, *Little Red Riding Hood* for 61–80, *Cinderella* for 41–60, *Hansel and Gretel* for 21–40, and *The Ugly Duckling* for 1–20. This association was later elaborated into a self-report version for client use (Appendix C). Another recommended training tool is to watch a video of family therapy or a movie such as *Moonstruck* or *Ordinary People*. Each person in training would make an assessment rating of the family and then compare ratings with others.

Another aspect of working with therapists-in-training was motivating them to remain current with the assessment process. Our supervisor developed forms that made immediate recording more palatable; again, the team approach promoted an eagerness to compare ratings. These forms are included in the appendices.

We did not initially develop forms to facilitate the computer encoding process of the data. When we began reviewing client ratings and were preparing to enter data, we found that there was no descriptive coding language developed for the variables we wished to use. We set about developing this language to represent family members present at each session, family structure, and presenting problem. These are presented in Figure 2.1. Several unexpected dilemmas immediately appeared. We had anticipated there would be 5 basic types of families that the clinic routinely treated. However, we found that 12 categories were needed to accurately describe our client population. Fifteen "family members present" codes were needed to describe the client configurations who appeared for therapy. We also began with 9 presenting-problem categories that rapidly expanded to 44 descriptive codes. These codes did not all really relate to "family" concerns, so 5 categories were created to address these differences: marital, individual, parent–child, extended family, and other concerns. We developed codes to track the therapist of record and referenced the semester in which this person started so that we could track team composition.

Clarifying these categories was helpful, but it was only a beginning. Immediately, more pressing concerns arose based on these codes. We struggled with whether to take the therapist or the client as the "authority" on the presenting problem. We pondered "How many presenting problems can we allow?" and "How does one designate only one problem as primary in a systemic perspective?" We concluded that initially what the family termed

Marital Concerns *Presenting Problem* Code		Individual Concerns *Presenting Problem* Code		Parent-child Concerns *Presenting Problem* Code		Extended Family Concerns *Presenting Problem* Code		Other Concerns* *Presenting Problem* Code	
Marital	1	Chemical abuse	6	Incest-child	5	Incest-adult	4	Other	9
Divorce	2	School problems	8	Incest-child &		Incest-adult &		Suicide threat	39
Domestic violence	3	Rape	43*	other	13	disability	12	Family death	40
Divorce & divorce				Divorce & school		Marital, domestic		Premarital	
violence	10			problems	14	violence, &		communication	41
Marital & other	11			Marital & school		incest-adult	21	Child behavioral	
Divorce & other	17			problems	15	Incest-adult & other	23	problems	42
Marital & divorce	18			Divorce, domestic		Marital &		Launching	44
Marital & domestic				violence, &		incest-adult	30		
Violence	19			incest-child	16	Incest-adult &			
Chemical & other	27*			Domestic violence		school problems	33		
Marital, divorce, &				& incest-child	20	Incest-adult, disability,			
chemical abuse	28			Incest-child &		& other	38		
Marital, divorce,				incest-adult	22				
domestic violence,				School problems					
& other	29			& other	24				
Marital & chemical				Marital, domestic					
abuse	31			violence, &					
Marital, domestic				school problems	25				
violence, &				Marital, school					
disability	32			problems, &					
Marital, domestic				other	26				
violence, &									
chemical abuse	34								
Marital, incest-adult,									
incest-child, &									
school problems	35								
Marital, incest-child	36								
Marital, domestic									
violence, & other	37								

*Assign by subsystem evaluation

Family Structure Code		Family Members Present Code	
Married	1	Extended family system	1
Separated	2	Nuclear family system	2
Divorced	3	Marital subsystem	3
Remarried	4	Parent-child subsystem	4
Never married	5	Parent-former parent subsystem	5
Never married living with	6	Sibling subsystem	6
Divorced living with	8	Mother only	7
Premarital	10	Father only	8
Grandparent & child	11	Child only	9
Married & remarried	12	Grandmother only	10
		Other	12
		Parent-former parent subsystem,	
		& sibling subsystem	13
		Remarried & adult stepchildren	14
		Grandparents	15

Figure 2.1 MFCCC Study. Coding of presenting problems, family structure, and family members present at each session.

the presenting problem was often a smoke screen for the later "real" concern. To be consistent, we switched to a more collaborative perspective and began using the Goal Attainment Scale (see Appendix C) to facilitate and clarify our descriptions.

Other questions arose regarding the family structure variables. We found that it was difficult to be clear whether one was assessing the individual or the family, especially when only one member of the family routinely came to therapy. We began to question how differing subsystem session attendance influenced the assessment process. Basically, we confronted the design problems that clinical field research faces. We could not predict which members of a family would consistently attend therapy sessions. Thus, we attempted to track on the variables that arose on a session-by-session basis. Because we were testing for interrater reliability and evaluating the instrument, perhaps these factors were not critical. However, more work is needed to ascertain how these variables influence the effectiveness of family assessment.

We also noted differences between the therapist and team assessment using the GARF. It became apparent that the team tended to assess more objectively. The therapist as a "member of the family" in the therapy room tended perhaps to rate more intuitively, comprehending the emotional climate of the family from a different perspective than the team. The therapist is with the family, yet not a part of the family. We wanted to compare insider and outsider ratings. We also hoped to compare self-report perceptions among different family members. Some of these thoughts gave rise to our use of graphing for reporting each session. We initially began tracking global ratings, comparing therapist and team. Later we began breaking the therapist ratings into the interactional, structural, and emotional components and began to hypothesize how this could delineate assessment as process in therapy. It seemed that we might begin to pick up trends with individual families that might indicate whether a family responded to structural, strategic, or family-of-origin approaches as we examined the GARF as process. We also thought it was interesting and important to evaluate if a therapist's theoretical stance as to intervention biased subscale reporting on the GARF. Although this may be true to some degree, our team and therapist in the room global ratings were quite comparable. Team member subscale ratings were also often within 1–2 points of each other, despite different theoretical biases. This recording process will be further delineated in Chapter 4's case illustration.

Another consideration that is critical in using the GARF is understanding the cultural/ethnic orientation of the family. Responsible assessment requires an understanding of cultural norms and differences. Our study did not track on this factor, but it is one that requires discussion. The language of the GARF is relatively clear and bias free. In general, it does not dictate a norm for structure, interaction, or emotion, but allows for collaborative interpretation of functionality between therapist and client. What remains, then, is for the therapist to know and understand cultural models should he or she take on the evaluator role. This is an educational and training concern in assessment as well as the general training of therapists. Pare (1995, 1996) addresses these concerns, as does Falicov (1995). Considering culture as context and knowing the norms of that context appears to be the solution. The GARF can be used in a more collaborative, social constructivist manner, with the therapist consulting the family as to its understandings of family functioning and then assigning the scale evaluations. This approach follows the suggestions of exploring cultural differences with curiosity given by Dyche and Zayas (1995).

Larger system involvement also is a factor in assessment formulation. Often families come to therapy and are involved with court, social agency, or other outsider systems. It is important to evaluate this component of family influence thoroughly. Such an investigation includes the relationship of the system to the presenting problem and other family concerns. It is also important to note the boundaries between the family and the system and to examine the alignments of the external system and family. Family and system perceptions about these relationships are important to explore. It is also important to examine past impact, binds, and movement in the larger system components. An awareness of the larger system's impact on family openness is essential (Imber-Black, 1988).

Pederson (1991) points out that even people from the same cultural group may have experiences that differ from one another. Culture is not dictating of experience. Speight, Myers, Cox, and Highlen (1991) emphasize the importance of training counselors to be aware of their own uniqueness; as they have that experience, they will be able to recognize their clients' worldview. Their challenge to multiculturalism is to treat differences as a "gift to enjoy" rather than "a problem in need of a solution." Culture need not be seen as a barrier to counseling. It can be an asset in exploring differences. There are several benefits of looking at multiculturalism with a wide lens rather than looking at culture in exotic, narrow terms (Pederson, 1991). Doing so helps the counselor be aware of one's own mindset with regard to the client's outcome. It keeps the counselor from expecting simplistic answers to complicated patterns emerging from ethnicity and nationality. Lastly, it helps counselors track a client as he or she moves from one identifiable feature of one's culture to another.

Multiculturalism is a part of every counselor's experience. If we look at each encounter with a client as a unique experience showing us the interconnectedness of all life, we can appreciate the diversity of human beings and the client's desire for solutions.

Research and the GARF

The GARF was developed to provide a valid, reliable, and practical measure of current family functioning for alerting therapists and screening clients (GAP, 1996; Wynne, 1992). If the GARF could validly and reliably measure current family functioning, then perhaps it also could be used periodically during the course of therapy as a measure of incremental improvement. Similarly, the difference between a pretreatment GARF score and a post-treatment GARF score might demonstrate promise as a measure of therapy outcome. Pike-Urlacher, Mackinnon, and Piercy (1996) noted that "It is essential that family therapists be able to demonstrate which family interventions with which populations, in which contexts are not only effective but also cost-effective" (p. 365). The reality of the 1990s is that therapists face both (a) shrinking private and public funds for mental health treatment and (b) increasing demands by the public, state and federal government, peers, managed care organizations, and professional ethics for accountability and proof of treatment effectiveness. A valid and reliable measure of family functioning must be established before family therapists can demonstrate the effectiveness and cost-effectiveness of treatment. The following summarizes research that examined the validity and feasibility of the GARF and the GARF's utility as a clinical measure of treatment outcome, and compared the GARF with other assessment instruments such as the Beavers SFI (Beavers & Hampson, 1990) and the Systemic Assessment of the Family Environment (SAFE) (Appendix D).

MFCCC and Rochester

Two recent research efforts (Wynne, 1992; Yingling, Miller, McDonald, & Galewaler, 1994a, 1994b) sought empirical evidence of the GARF's practicality and reliability. Both studies were conducted at marriage and family training centers; however, each had a different research focus. Wynne's field trial study (1992) examined the feasibility and interrater reliability of the GARF. Yingling et al. (1994a, 1994b) studied the GARF interrater reliability (therapist vs. team) and the utility of the GARF as a longitudinal clinical measure of family therapy outcome.

Rochester. After a pilot test at the University of Rochester, Wynne (1992) slightly revised the GARF and its instructions, then began collecting data to examine the GARF's interrater reliability. The Family and Marriage Clinic at the University of Rochester and the MFCCC (now the Community Counseling Center at Texas A&M University—Commerce) were among the five participating centers that contributed interrater data. A total of 93 raters evaluated a total of 59 couples or families (Wynne, 1992). Two of the centers, the Family and Marriage Clinic at the University of Rochester and the MFCCC, provided enough data to statistically test the GARF's interrater reliability and differentiation between families. At the MFCCC (28 families, 9 raters, and 80 ratings), the families' presenting problems were frequently sexual abuse or physical abuse. Perhaps it is not surprising that the GARF scores ($M = 42.0$, $SD = 10.2$) for the families seen at the MFCCC were lower than the scores ($M = 61.3$, $SD = 11.0$) found at the Family and Marriage Clinic (20 families, 20 raters, and 106 ratings), where the families usually presented marital discord or disciplinary problems with children (GAP, 1996; Wynne, 1992). Wynne (1992) noted that even though the presenting problems and treatment centers were different, the standard deviation of the GARF score was nearly the same at the MFCCC and the Family and Marriage Clinic. Furthermore, a two-way analysis of variance (ANOVA) detected a significant difference between families ($p = .0000$) and raters ($p = .02$); therefore, Wynne found that the GARF had satisfactory reliability and differentiation between families. Further support of the GARF's interrater reliability has been reported by other researchers (Dausch, Miklowitz, & Richards, 1996; Guttman, cited in GAP, 1996; Johnston, 1992).

MFCCC.   From June 1991 to September 1992, the GARF was used in outcome research (Yingling et al., 1994a, 1994b) conducted at the MFCCC. The MFCCC provided a primary regional resource for family therapy referrals. The diverse client population included students, faculty, and nonuniversity families from the surrounding rural Texas area. The MFCCC was staffed by doctoral intern therapists enrolled in advanced clinical training in marriage and family therapy. The interns were instructed in the use of the GARF and required to use the GARF during the research period.

The Yingling et al. study (1994a, 1994b) began in June 1991 as an unfunded effort to field test the GARF's utility as a clinical measure of family functioning. In late 1992 this research continued under mini-grant funding from East Texas State University (now Texas A&M University—Commerce) to analyze the data collected during the GARF field test. The study sought to answer the following research questions:

1   What is the interrater reliability of the GARF?
2   Which of the three subscales in the GARF most accurately predicts the overall rating of the client?
3   What is the correlation of ratings using various clinical rating scales and self-report assessment instruments commonly used in the field, such as the GARF, Beavers' Systems Model clinical rating scale, Beavers' SFI, Olson's Circumplex Model clinical rating scale, Olson's FACES, and Yingling's SAFE?
4   What length of treatment time is required to make a significant change in the GARF, and how is the time factor related to the types of presenting problems?
5   What are the most common DSM–III–R diagnoses of incest-recovering clients?
6   Is there a correlational relationship between the GARF changes and the level of DSM–III–R symptomatology?
7   What intervention strategies seem to predict quicker GARF changes and with what issues?

Data were collected from families who had given written permission to voluntarily participate in research. The study included only those families ($N = 93$) who had begun and completed therapy at the MFCCC from June 1991 to September 1992. Closer examination of the GARF field test data soon revealed incomplete and nonstandardized records that made the data analysis phase of the research much more complex and time consuming. In part because of the duration of the field study (June 1991–September 1992), data were collected from both active cases, in which the family was still in therapy, and nonactive terminated cases. A standard coding scheme that reflected major categories of family structure (see Figure 2.1) was developed because no suitable and universally accepted data coding approach was found in prior studies. Additional forms were developed to simplify data entry from archival records once the coding scheme was established.

During the development of the coding scheme, it became clear that collected data were insufficient to examine many of the original research questions. The Yingling et al. (1994a, 1994b) study was modified to include collecting descriptive data on client families (e.g., the presenting problem, who attended therapy, and the number of sessions). More specifically, the study sought to answer the following research questions: (a) what are the characteristics of client families, and what services do they seek?; (b) is there a significant correlation between GARF scores recorded by observing teams and the score reported by the therapist? and (c) is the GARF score assigned at the final therapy session significantly different from the GARF score assigned at the first therapy session?

Yingling et al. (1994a, 1994b) found (a) several interesting characteristics about the client families, (b) a statistically significant correlation between the GARF scores assigned by observing teams and the ones assigned by the therapist, (c) the families' GARF scores often increased by the end of treatment and (d) families' GARF scores sometimes dropped during the course of therapy. These findings and their possible implications will be discussed in more detail.

As can be seen in Figure 2.2 and Figure 2.3, marital structure was the most frequent family structure attending the first session: 54 (or 58%) of the families were married, and 12 (or 13%) were divorced. Similarly, presenting problems (see Figure 2.4) also reflected predominantly marital issues: 61 (or 66%) marital, 15 (or 16%) parental, and 14 (or 15%) extended family.

Families in this study were not members of a managed care program, and such programs typically limit the length of therapy; however, the families averaged only six sessions of therapy before terminating, which may indicate that clients expect both rapid and measurable improvement. Similar treatment duration has been reported among individuals in outpatient treatment at a clinical psychology and social work training facility (Kadera, Lambert, & Andrews, 1996). In the Kadera et al. study, therapy outcome was measured with a self-report instrument that the patients ($N = 21$) completed before each session. Figure 2.5 compares the cumulative treatment outcome in the Yingling et al. study with the cumulative treatment outcome reported in the Kadera et al. study. It is interesting that the graphs of treatment outcome are similar for individual therapy and for marriage and family therapy. The graph in Figure 2.5 appears to generally support a therapy dosage model, in which the log of the number of sessions is linearly related to the normalized probability of client improvement (Howard et al., 1986; Howard, Orlinsky, & Lueger, 1994).

Family Structure	Marital Concerns	Individual Concerns	Parental Concerns	Extended Family Concerns	Total
Married	39	1	7	7	54
Separated	6	-	1	1	8
Divorced	4	2	5	1	12
Remarried	4	-	1	3	8
Never married	7	-	1	2	10
Grandparent and child	1	-	-	-	1
Total	61	3	15	14	93

Figure 2.2   MFCCC Study: family structure attending the first therapy session by presenting problem concerns. $n = 93$.

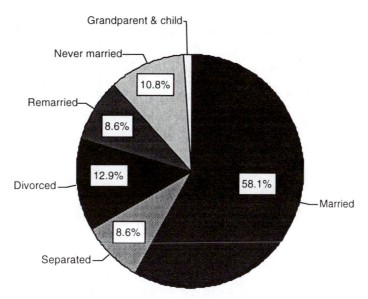

Figure 2.3   Family structure attending therapy. *n* = 93 cases.

Two other findings provided empirical support for the GARF as an assessment instrument. The family overall GARF score reported by the observing team was found to be correlated ($r = .80$, $p < .001$) with the family overall GARF score reported by the therapist; thus, this indicates a relatively high consensus among trained therapists who used the GARF. Furthermore, the overall GARF score assigned to the family at the end of therapy ($M = 41.1$, $SEM = 1.5$, $SD = 14.0$, Mdn = 40.0, and mode = 30.0) was generally higher ($p < .001$) than the overall GARF score ($M = 34.8$, $SEM = 1.3$, $SD = 12.1$, Mdn = 34.5, and mode = 30.0) assigned at the beginning of family therapy. This last finding appears consistent with the higher levels of family functioning that are desired on completion of therapy; however, as will be discussed below, not all families achieved this desired improvement.

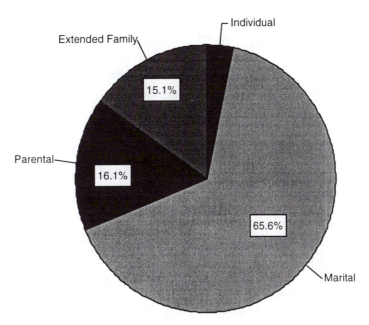

Figure 2.4   Presenting problems of family attending family therapy. *n* = 93 cases.

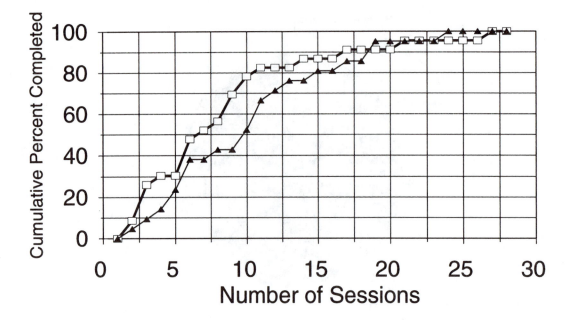

Figure 2.5 Comparative analysis of therapy completion trends. Data for individuals are from ''How Much Therapy is Really Enough: A Session-by-Session Analysis of the Psychotherapy Dose–Effect Relationship,'' by S.W. Kadera, M. J. Lambert, and A. A. Andrews, 1996, *Journal of Psychotherapy Practice and Research, 5(2),* p. 141. Copyright 1996 by American Psychiatric Press, Inc.

As noted above, the total GARF scores assigned during the families' final session were significantly higher than the GARF scores assigned in the initial session; therefore, the GARF appeared to detect higher functioning on completion of family therapy. When comparing these two scores, it is important to consider the reliability and errors of measurement (Anastasi, 1988; Lambert & Hill, 1994). Previous authors (Dickey, 1996; Jacob, 1995; Lambert & Cattani-Thompson, 1996; Lambert & Hill, 1994; Snyder & Rice, 1996) have further cautioned researchers to remember that an instrument with low reliability may distort the measurement of therapeutic change. To examine whether instrument reliability and errors of measurement had distorted the therapeutic change measured by the GARF, the change in GARF scores was tested with the reliable change index (RC) method reported by Jacobson and Truax (1991). The RC is calculated by dividing the difference in scores by the standard error of the difference between two scores. GARF scores were recorded at the beginning and end of therapy for 89 of the 93 families who participated in this study. Then the RC formula was used to examine differences between these GARF scores. Results of this evaluation revealed the following: 23 families had significantly higher ($p < .05$) GARF scores on terminating therapy; GARF scores for 25 of the families were higher, but not significantly ($p > .05$) higher; GARF scores were unchanged for 27 of the families; and the remaining 14 families had lower GARF scores on terminating therapy. Of the 14 families that had lower GARF scores at termination, it was interesting that the only clients with a significantly ($p < .05$) lower GARF score were as follows: 1 couple that sought therapy for divorce issues, 2 couples with a presenting problem of domestic violence, and a child in individual therapy for school behavior problems. The finding that some families had lower or no increase in GARF scores after therapy may be due to several factors and appears worthy of further examination. An earlier study by Mohr et al. (1990) attempted to identify those persons at risk for nonresponse or negative outcome in individual psychotherapy. Wesley and Waring (1996) noted that "research has consistently found that severely distressed couples are less likely to benefit from therapy" (p. 426).

The lowest GARF score was not always assigned at the beginning session of therapy. In about one third (33 of 91) of the cases in this study, the family's assigned GARF score was lower in the second or later sessions; however, this occurred as late as the ninth session when the presenting problem was marital with incest-adult (see Figure 2.6). Thus, the family functioning was viewed as lower (at least temporarily) than when therapy began. The reasons for this apparent drop in family functioning are unclear but may have significant implications for assessment and treatment planning. As Figure 2.6 illustrates, most of these cases were marital, and the GARF dropped during the second session of therapy. The GARF dropped from the initial score in cases where the presenting problems frequently included divorce, domestic violence, chemical abuse, incest of a child or of an adult, or a combination of the above. Thus, some families with more complex presenting problems tended to be assessed at an initial GARF score that was higher than in subsequent sessions. To investigate this further, the number of cases in which the GARF dropped below the first GARF was compared to the total number of cases for each presenting problem (see Figure 2.7).

For families who presented marital problems, one third (6 of 18) were assigned their lowest GARF scores in their second or later therapy sessions (see Figure 2.7). Moreover, this occurrence appeared to be more frequent when the marital issues involved more severe presenting problems, such as divorce with domestic violence (2 out of 3 cases), domestic violence (3 out of 5 cases), and marital presenting problems with domestic violence (2 out of 4 cases). The reason for such a drop in a family's GARF scores during therapy is not yet known, and there appear to be several possible factors to investigate. Perhaps the clinicians had assigned a lower GARF because of a more accurate assessment based on observing the family interaction over a longer period of time. The lower GARF might reflect the family's response when a "family secret" was revealed in session. It also is possible that some family members gained confidence in the process of therapy and became more candid and more authentic during later sessions. In addition, treatment intervention or factors outside of therapy may contribute to a lowered level of family functioning. Further research may be necessary to determine the reasons for these lower GARF scores. Managed care organizations and clinicians may also consider whether some client families are better served by diagnosis and treatment plans that have been based on later (possibly lower) GARF scores rather than the initial-session GARF scores. This raises an interesting question of *whether therapy progress should be measured on the basis of the initial or lowest level of functioning.* Furthermore, it appears that different patterns of GARF scores through the treatment process may be associated with different presenting problems.

The MFCCC study examined possible longitudinal applications of the GARF; however, the reader is cautioned that the following trends are based on a limited number of clients attending therapy at the MFCCC as described above and may not be representative of other clients seen in other mental health settings. Figure 2.8 illustrates the average session-by-session GARF scores for families seeking therapy for problems in each of the major structural categories: Individual Problems, Marital Problems, Parental Problems, and Extended Family Problems. More detailed graphs were plotted for each of the above categories (Figures 2.9, 2.10, 2.11, and 2.12, respectively). The pattern (see Figure 2.9) of average GARF scores appeared to be essentially flat at 35 for clients ($n = 3$) with Individual problems, perhaps because of only 4 or fewer sessions of treatment. From Figure 2.10, it may be noted that average GARF scores increased for the families ($n = 61$) presenting Marital problems and remained above 50 by the 12th therapy session. When the session-by-session GARF

System Category of Presenting Concern	Presenting Concern	Session Number						TOTALS
		2	3	4	5	7	9	
Individual	Child behavior	1	-	-	-	-	-	1
	Subtotal	1	-	-	-	-	-	1
Marital	Marital	3	2	1	-	-	-	6
	Divorce	2	-	-	-	-	-	2
	Domestic violence	1	1	1	-	-	-	3
	Chemical	1	-	-	-	-	-	1
	Divorce & divorce violence	2	-	-	-	-	-	2
	Marital & school problems	1	-	-	-	-	-	1
	Divorce & other problems	1	-	-	-	1	-	2
	Marital & domestic violence	2	-	-	-	-	-	2
	Incest-adult, other problems	1	-	-	-	-	-	1
	Chemical & other problems	1	-	-	-	-	-	1
	Marital, divorce, domestic violence, and other problems	-	-	1	-	-	-	1
	Marital & chemical	-	-	1	-	-	-	1
	Marital, domestic violence, & disability	-	-	-	-	1	-	1
	Marital, domestic violence, & other problems	1	-	-	-	-	-	1
	Premarital communications	-	-	-	1	-	-	1
	Subtotal	16	3	4	1	2	-	26
Parental	Incest-child	-	1	-	-	-	-	1
	School problems	1	-	-	-	1	-	2
	Child behavior	1	-	-	-	-	-	1
	Subtotal	2	1	-	-	1	-	4
Extended Family	Divorce	-	1	-	-	-	-	1
	Marital & incest-adult	-	-	-	-	-	1	1
	Subtotal	-	1	-	-	-	1	2
	TOTALS	19	5	4	1	3	1	33

Figure 2.6   Presenting problems and session number in which GARF was lower than initial GARF.

Detailed Problems	Individual Problems	Marital Problems	Parental Problems	Extended Family Problems	Total
Marital		6 of 18			6 of 18
Divorce		2 of 9	0 of 2	1 of 2	3 of 13
Domestic Violence		3 of 5			3 of 5
Incest-Adult				0 of 1	0 of 1
Incest-Child	0 of 1	0 of 1	1 of 2		1 of 4
Chemical Abuse		1 of 1			1 of 1
School Problems	0 of 1		2 of 2		2 of 3
Divorce, Domestic Violence		2 of 3	0 of 1		2 of 4
Marital, Other Problems			0 of 1	0 of 1	0 of 2
Incest-Child, Other Problems			0 of 1		0 of 1
Divorce, School Problems				0 of 1	0 of 1
Marital, School Problems		1 of 1		0 of 1	1 of 2
Divorce, Other Problems		2 of 2			2 of 2
Marital, Divorce Problems		0 of 3			0 of 3
Marital, Domestic Violence		2 of 4			2 of 4
Domestic Violence, Incest-Child		0 of 1			0 of 1
Incest-Adult, Other Problems		1 of 2			1 of 2
Chemical Abuse, Other Problems		1 of 1			1 of 1
Marital, Divorce, Domestic Violence, & Other Problems		1 of 1			1 of 1
Marital, Incest-Adult				1 of 1	1 of 1
Marital, Chemical Abuse		1 of 2			1 of 2
Marital, Domestic Violence, & Disability		1 of 1			1 of 1
Marital, Incest-Child		0 of 1			0 of 1
Marital, Domestic Violence, & Other Problems		1 of 1			1 of 1
Suicide Threat		0 of 1	0 of 1	0 of 1	0 of 3
Family Death			0 of 1	0 of 2	0 of 3
Premarital Communication		1 of 2			1 of 2
Child Behavioral Problems	1 of 1		1 of 4	0 of 1	2 of 6
Rape		0 of 1			0 of 1
Launching				0 of 3	0 of 3
Totals	1 of 3	26 of 61	4 of 15	2 of 14	33 of 93

Figure 2.7 Number of cases by presenting problem where the GARF score was lower in second or later sessions of therapy than in first session.

scores for families who presented Parental problems were averaged, the pattern (see Figure 2.11) was fluctuating and took 16 therapy sessions to first reach a GARF score of 50. The average GARF scores for families presenting Extended Family problems was also quite variable (see Figure 2.12), perhaps because of the variety of presenting problems that were consolidated into this structural category. It was anticipated that graphs of the average GARF scores for families with similar presenting problems may reveal additional patterns of clinical interest.

In this study, many families presented multiple problems for treatment. The coding scheme (Figure 2.1) was primarily organized by structural categories. Within each structural category, a more detailed coding was used to identify specific presenting problems. Yingling et al. then grouped these specific presenting problems into one of these summary catego-

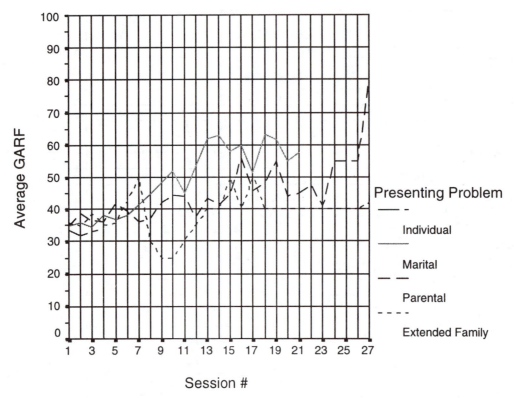

Figure 2.8   Average GARF by presenting problem.

ries: divorce, incest, or violence. The researchers hoped to compare GARF scores for families that presented divorce-related problems with those who presented incest-related problems or who presented violence-related problems. Unfortunately, many families faced multiple problems that overlapped two or more summary categories; hence, these summary categories were not exclusive. In other words, a family that presented incest-related problems and violence-related problems would be included in those two summary cate-

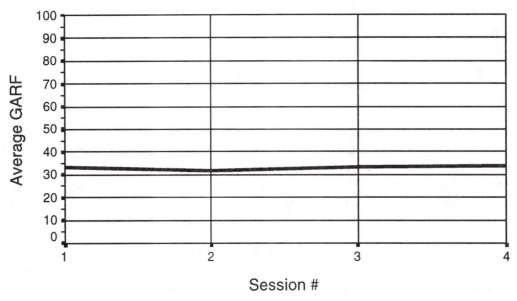

Figure 2.9   Average GARF individual problems presented at MFCCC. $n = 3$.

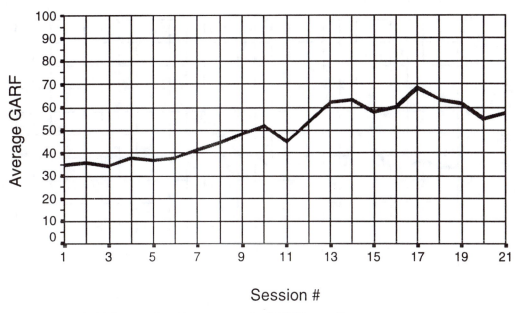

Figure 2.10 Average GARF for marital problems presented at MFCCC. *n* = 61.

gories. Despite this limitation, the researchers believed that graphing the average session-by-session GARF scores for each summary category may reveal some important patterns. The reader is cautioned that many of the cases appear in two or three of these summary categories; however, general trends are discussed with recommendations for future studies.

Figure 2.13 represents the session-by-session average GARF scores for 24 families who sought therapy to address issues that included divorce. Although Figure 2.13 consolidates six different presenting problems, all of which included divorce, the graph indicates average GARF scores below 50 until the ninth session. The lowest GARF scores for families who presented problems that included divorce ranged from 15 to 55 (*M* = 32.9, *SD* = 11.4, mode = 25).

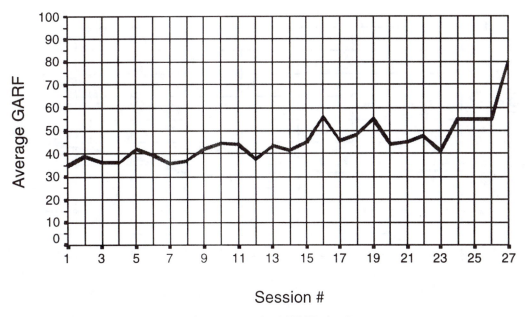

Figure 2.11 Average GARF for parental problems presented at MFCCC. *n* = 15.

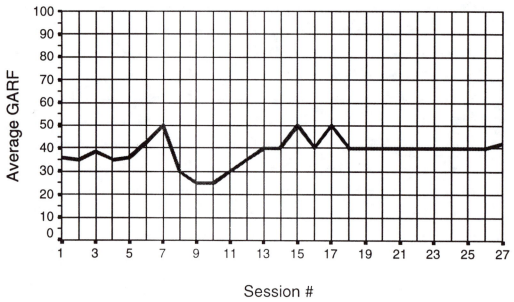

Figure 2.12   Average GARF for extended family problems presented at MFCCC. $n = 14$.

Average GARF scores graphed on Figure 2.14 combine seven presenting problems for the 11 families whose problems included incest. The low GARF scores shown on Figure 2.14 are perhaps indicative of long duration in treating a variety of presenting problems, all of which included incest. Lowest GARF scores for these families ranged from 20 to 55 ($M = 29.6$, $SD = 10.4$, mode = 30). Although two sessions (Numbers 15 and 17) show average GARF scores that temporarily reach 50, the families' average scores remained at or below 40 for almost 27 sessions.

GARF scores for the 17 families whose presenting problems included violence were averaged and graphed on Figure 2.15. Average GARF scores for families with one of seven different presenting problems, all of which included violence, were consistently below 40

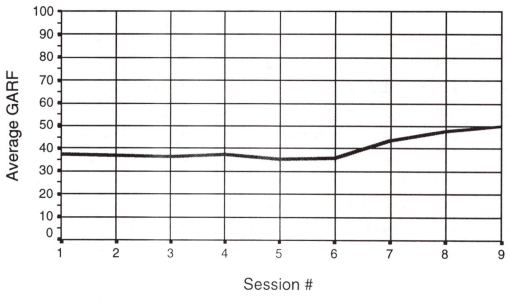

Figure 2.13   Average GARF for problems including divorce presented at MFCCC. $n = 24$.

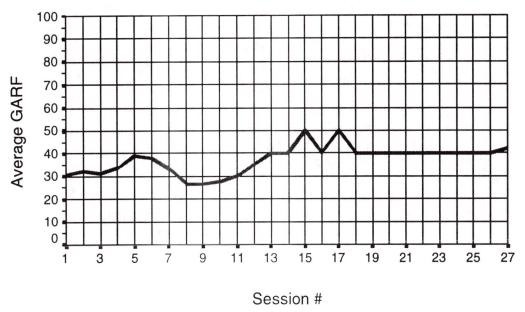

Figure 2.14 Average GARF for problems including incest presented at MFCCC. *n* = 11.

through seven sessions of therapy. The lowest GARF scores ($M = 28.9$, $SD = 9.3$, mode $= 20$) ranged from 15 to 50.

In summary, the Yingling et al. study supports the GARF's utility as a practical instrument to assess family functioning in clinical settings. The research questions were "what are the characteristics of client families and what services do they seek?"; "is there a significant correlation between GARF scores recorded by observing teams and the scores reported by the therapist?"; and "is the GARF score assigned at the final therapy session significantly different from the GARF score assigned at the first therapy session?" Regarding the first research question, the study found that the majority of clients initially attending family therapy were families rather than individuals and that the average attendance was six sessions. Therefore, therapists might consider using a family assessment instrument

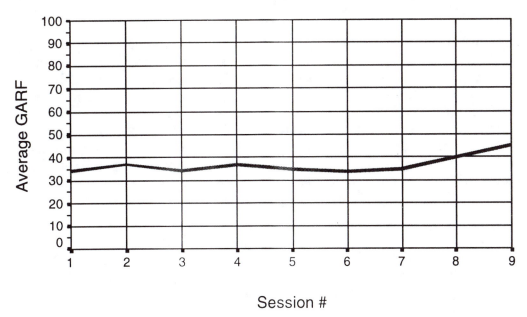

Figure 2.15 Average GARF for problems including violence presented at MFCCC. *n* = 17.

such as the GARF during the first session and begin planning for six or fewer treatment sessions. With respect to the second research question, a statistically significant correlation was found between the GARF scores assigned by the observing team and the ones assigned by the therapist; therefore, it appears that a single therapist can be trained to assign GARF scores that are comparable to those assigned by a trained observation team. Regarding the third research question, this study found that the final GARF score was frequently higher than the initial GARF score; however, the initial GARF score may not always be the minimum score. Furthermore, the Yingling et al. study found tentative indication that families addressing problems related to divorce, incest, or violence may have somewhat predictable patterns in their GARF scores.

When interpreting the above findings, the reader is cautioned that the Yingling et al. study was limited to clients and families who were voluntary participants receiving marriage and family therapy from doctoral interns at a university training center. The results of the study are further limited by the number of families who participated ($N = 93$) who were primarily Caucasian, lived in a rural Southern community, and voluntarily sought family therapy. Therefore, the above findings may possibly not generalize to larger samples, involuntary clients, more ethnically diverse clients, or other treatment settings. Despite these limitations, the Yingling et al. study appears to support the utility of the GARF as a clinical instrument to assess families and measure treatment progress.

Hampson's Data

Concurrent validity of the GARF has been supported by three recent studies (Gordon, 1997; Hampson, 1997; Pierce, 1993) that compared the ratings of families who were assessed on both the Beavers scales and on the GARF scale. In a study of families ($N = 59$) consisting of two or more persons, Pierce found a correlation ($r = -.48, p = .001$) between the GARF scale and the Beavers Competence global scale and a correlation ($r = -.54, p = .001$) between the GARF scale and the Beavers Competence computed subscale. The scaling (low to high) for the Beavers instrument is directionally reversed from that on the GARF (high to low). In other words, higher scores on the Beavers scale indicates less family competence, as do lower scores on the GARF. Thus, the negative Pearson product–moment correlation between the Beavers scales and the GARF scale indicated congruence between these instruments.

Hampson, Henney, and Beavers (1996) compared the GARF with the Beavers Systems Model clinical rating scale, the SFI, and treatment outcome. They found a moderate significant correlation between the first-session GARF score and Beavers' Global Health subscale. Although the first-session GARF appeared to be a significant predictor of treatment outcome, treatment outcome was not significantly related to high changes in a family's GARF score. Results of an ANOVA indicated a significant relationship between the GARF and categorical ratings on the Beavers scales. No significant correlation was found between the SFI and GARF. A subsequent study (Gordon, 1997) supports Hampson et al.'s finding of a moderately high significant correlation between the first-session GARF score and Beavers' Global Health subscale.

Adolescent Symposium Data

In a symposium for mental health professionals, a family therapy training videotape was used to examine (a) the interrater reliability of the GARF, (b) interrater reliability of the SAFE, and (c) whether rater education or experience was related to either GARF or SAFE scores (Yingling, 1996b). Most of the 39 participants had completed a bachelor's degree ($n = 11$) or a master's degree ($n = 23$) in one of a variety of mental health disciplines. The participants had training backgrounds in counseling ($n = 11$), social work ($n = 10$), psychology ($n = 8$), or related disciplines ($n = 2$). Only 7 of the participants had completed at least three graduate courses in marriage and family therapy; similarly, only 9 participants had completed four or more such graduate courses. Most of the participants did not hold licenses in their respective disciplines.

The participants viewed a videotape (Yingling, 1996a) of a family, rated the observed family on the GARF, completed the SAFE as if they were a member of the family, and then completed a brief demographic questionnaire. Only 35 of the 39 participants rated the family with the GARF, and those scores ranged from a low of 10 to an impossible 155, indicating that some participants had difficulty rating the family and perhaps did not understand the GARF. When the erroneously high score of 155 was excluded from further analysis, the scores ($M = 39.5$, $SD = 12.9$, $SEM = 2.2$) supported high interrater reliability of the GARF. It was noted that the GARF standard deviation between raters was somewhat higher than previously reported by Wynne (1992) or Yingling et al. (1994a, 1994b), perhaps indicating that these raters had less training and experience than those in the aforementioned studies. An ANOVA indicated a relationship between GARF ratings assigned and amount of graduate MFT education, $F(14) = 4.1$, $p < .05$; however, this finding must be considered very tentative because of the small sample size. The SAFE was completed by 32 of the participants with total scores that ranged from 13 to 34 ($M = 23.0$, $SD = 4.6$, $SEM = 0.8$). These results supported the interrater reliability of the SAFE, because two thirds of the scores lay between 19 and 26. Using 0.05 as the criterion for significance (alpha) and a sample size of 32, this study had an 89% power to detect a significant correlation between the number of graduate courses completed and the two SAFE scales; however, no such correlation was detected.

Clinical Practice Database Utility

One present author has incorporated GARF ratings into a clinical record of private practice clients ($N = 70$) over the past 2 years. The Excel 97 spreadsheet record keeping system included the GARF ratings for the first session, lowest rating, and final rating. SAFE scores and Beck Depression Inventory (BDI) scores also were recorded, along with the number of sessions, date and source of referral, and beginning and ending session dates. When each client file was closed, remaining data were entered into the database. This system of data entry was manageable to keep up with and provided a readily analyzed record.

The families seen in private practice had first-session GARF scores ($M = 46.5$, $SD = 14.3$, $SEM = 1.8$), lowest GARF scores ($M = 41.1$, $SD = 13.4$, $SEM = 1.7$), and ending GARF scores ($M = 56.4$, $SD = 16.1$, $SEM = 2.1$) that were higher ($p < .000$) than corresponding scores found at the MFCCC. The families seen in private practice also attended significantly ($p < .05$) fewer sessions ($M = 4.6$, $SD = 3.1$, $SEM = 0.4$) than the families seen at the MFCCC ($M = 6.1$, $SD = 5.7$, $SEM = 0.6$). In fact, 17% (12) of the families seen in private practice attended only one session.

Sufficient data were collected for 45 of the 70 families to examine whether their GARF scores were correlated with either their mean SAFE (I + O) or BDI scores. Calculation of the Pearson product–moment indicated that the GARF scores were not correlated with either the SAFE ($r = -.21$, $p < .15$) or BDI ($r = .06$, $p < .69$) scores. With this sample size and a criterion for significance (alpha) of 0.05, the study had a power of 97% to detect a 0.50 correlation. Thus no significant correlation between the GARF and SAFE or between the GARF and BDI is likely, even if the study were repeated with a much larger sample.

In 21 (49%) of the 49 families who attended three or more sessions, the lowest GARF score was recorded during the second or later session. The RC change index (see above) was computed to examine whether the families' GARF scores at the ending therapy session were different from their scores in the first session. Of the 49 families who attended more than one session of therapy, the RC index indicated ($p < .05$) higher family functioning for 18 families and lower family functioning for 2 families, as measured by their GARF scores.

This pilot project in a solo practice setting indicated that using the GARF in clinical private practice is manageable and useful. This research also raised an interesting question regarding the GARF, SAFE, and BDI. No significant correlation was found between GARF scores and scores for the SAFE or the BDI; therefore, it would appear these instruments are not redundant. If the GARF, SAFE, and BDI are not redundant, then perhaps these three instruments measure different constructs, and further research might examine whether the three should be included for a comprehensive family assessment.

SUMMARY

The above discussion has presented recent studies that have examined the validity, reliability, and practicality of the GARF in clinical settings. On the basis of the above studies, the GARF appears to have considerable potential both as an instrument to screen/identify and as a measure of therapy progress. The finding that the level of family functioning as measured by the GARF sometimes drops after the first therapy session deserves additional exploration. Further research with larger samples is needed to confirm whether these findings apply in a variety of settings with diverse clients. The work of Dausch et al. (1996) using the GARF with recently episodic bipolar patients shows promising results and procedures for working in specialized populations. Longitudinal studies might evaluate the family therapy GARF patterns for treatment of specific presenting problems that correspond to specific DSM–IV diagnoses.

With all the demands on clinicians today, one questions why research is so important to clinical practice. But today is the age of efficiency and economy. To survive in practice, one must be able to document that one's clinical work is effective. All payers for service are demanding accountability through data. So clinicians must become researchers. But even more important than the external pressure to document with numbers is the clinician's understanding of how assessment drives treatment and treatment drives outcome. Research data help us constantly improve our process.

CHAPTER 3

Systemic Assessment Tools

Assessment in the therapeutic process
MFT models distinguished
Value added: Providing quality clinical services
Skills summary for MFT clinicians: A quality assessment tool

Assessment is fundamental in ascertaining efficacy and effectiveness. This chapter explores the interrelationship of theory, assessment, and the role of the therapist in the intervention process. Brief synopses of several major theoretical approaches are given with respect to assessment. We have attempted to delineate one systemic process that incorporates many of the varied theoretical tenets. We have included a systemic skill development scale that can serve as a self-evaluation or be used in supervision and training of new therapists.

ASSESSMENT IN THE THERAPEUTIC PROCESS

In the field of marital and family therapy, there are numerous diverse approaches to treatment. Some of these approaches emphasize assessment, others do not. From the outset, marriage and family therapy has been an enterprise that was seen as solution-finding. Its origins are rooted in the search for solutions to difficult problems, such as schizophrenia research and aid to impoverished and troubled families. The pioneers in the field were innovators who were astute observers and clinicians willing to implement divergent approaches. These creative methods have allowed vast expansion and growth of ideas related to the field. Initially, there was a rapid proliferation of theory and technique, often with the developer claiming unsubstantiated success and perhaps even maintaining to have found a panacea. Because of this diversity, there is no agreed-on underlying taxonomy or nosology. Each school of thought has a theoretical stance regarding which variables are most related to function or dysfunction.

A uniform method of assessment is difficult if not impossible in such an environment. Equally complicated is obtaining meaningful process and outcome research. We appear to have come to a time now when a more integrative approach will facilitate clearer understanding of the factors and dynamics involved in relational functioning. Clarifying the therapeutic process and involving the clinical community in ongoing clinical research is an essential step to validating the effectiveness of marital and family therapy as an entity in the mental health care contingent. Perhaps we would be wise to take note of science's view of theory as provisional. As new theories about physical realities are developed, they are in fact really an extension of previous theory. Theories are made to be supported, unsupported, or refined. They are actually hypotheses. Ideally, a unified approach may be derived but, realistically, several approaches coexist and explain perceived reality in a manner that facilitates further research and movement (Hawking, 1988).

Currently, efforts to promulgate a more uniform system of relational diagnosis have taken a bifurcating, but mutually agreeable, pathway. Work has been underway since the mid-1980s. Specifically, the GAP Committee on the Family has been laboring to introduce relational concepts into the DSM publications. The committee's efforts have resulted in the formulation of two proposals. One, which is dimensionalized, is the basis for the GARF discussed herein. The other, the CORD, is a typological approach that is more reflective of diagnositic categories for individual disorders now found on Axis I of the DSM manuals. The two approaches are not mutually exclusive and both offer a wealth of opportunity for research. Thoughts about the CORD methodology are well illuminated in *Relational Diagnosis and Dysfunctional Family Patterns*, edited by Kaslow (1996). They are meant to be used in conjunction with individual diagnostic methodologies to provide a basis for evaluation of relationships in mental health and dysfunction.

The process of therapy can be conceptualized as having many stages or phases. Most approaches have an initial "joining" phase during which time assessment begins. Because measurement implies a static state, historically, assessment has been viewed as a static measure of factors underlying health or pathology. However, assessment in a therapeutic situation is by its nature an ongoing process. The therapist and client are always noting, evaluating, responding, or reacting to the transactions of therapy, each person using his own internal process to interpret and comprehend what has transpired. It is difficult, therefore, to comprehend any form of assessment as truly static or objective. Assessment is multisided. Three basic observational positions are recognized in formal, structured assessment. *Outsider* evaluation is described as the use of a clinical rating scale by an observer/therapist/team or researcher. *Insider* methods use client self-report about his or her experience of system functioning. *Insider–outsider* methods use a more collaborative process whereby the client and therapist develop criteria delineating desired change in a well-defined manner. These stances are explored in greater detail in Chapter 5.

Inherently there is a reciprocal relationship between theory, assessment, the role of the therapist, and intervention. Differences in theoretical orientation regarding the role of the therapist influence the assessment process. The data observed in assessment are used in intervention. Interventions are developed after a therapist or the therapist/client team defines symptoms and consider how they "fit" into the "problem." Interventions are based on this assessment and relate to the theoretical hypotheses held to facilitate change. Hypothesizing again varies with theoretical orientation. There is a plethora of hypotheses regarding symptom "role" within the various paradigms. For example, symptoms can be viewed as functional, as indications of structural or transactional deficits, as need-based and reactive signs, or as projective responses, to enumerate a few of the conceptualizations. When a hypothesis is developed, a strategy for intervention follows. Even hypothesis development itself is a strategy and intervention, because evaluation can produce enough clarification with the client to begin the change process. Assessment, hypothesizing, and strategizing are interrelated and at the core of therapeutic process.

Because each approach to family therapy has a theory about families and family functioning, each places different emphasis on factors underlying a presented problem. These differences also influence the manner in which hypothesizing and intervention ensue. Evaluation of theory tenets and therapeutic outcome varies with the orientation. The following discussion highlights differences among major models as to factors seen as underlying dysfunction, the role of the therapist, aspects of assessment, hypothesizing, and strategizing as well as brief comments regarding outcome research for that model.

MFT MODELS DISTINGUISHED

Behavioral family therapists use assessment more intensively than most other schools of thought. Assessment is a critical initial phase of therapy as well as an endpoint in this process. The family's capacity for adaptability, flexibility, and change are regarded as underlying factors of marital success. Verbal, physiological, and behavioral variables are evaluated to elucidate strengths and weaknesses as well as feelings about the relationship (Jacobsen, 1981). Reinforcement patterns are seen as causal in problem situations. Behavioral assessment uses interview methods, self-report measures, and spousal observations in the home, as well as direct observation of the couple in problem-solving and communication tasks. Because of the structured nature of assessment, the therapist is generally regarded as being outside of the family system. Assessment is regarded as a critical part of the initial process of therapy as well as an endpoint to evaluate interventions. It is not directly incorporated into the process of therapy. Hypothesizing is done from a more directive stance, and the therapist is placed in the role of teacher in many of the behavioral approaches. Data about therapy outcomes are often included on a case basis. Outcome studies are generally based on observers' ratings and self-report instruments.

Structural family therapists also use assessment but it is more incorporated into the therapeutic process and becomes a part of intervention. Enactment is used to assess transactional sequences that exist at present within the family system. After joining with the family system, the therapist wants to experience these structures and intervene directly in these patterns. Aponte (1981) writes,

> Conceptually, the process of assessment can be broken down into identifying the *problem*, determining its *locus* in the ecosystem, and defining the system's *structures* that sustain the problem. Identifying the *problem* means looking for where in the operationalization of the structure the system fails to carry out its function. . . . Identifying the problem also involves seeing a problem in relation to the other problems to which it is structurally related . . . problems do not appear in isolation (pp. 318–319).

Assessment is made in terms of a structural diagnosis that incorporates the "problem" in the context of the family structural dynamics. Observation and experience of the transactions are the primary diagnostic tools. Interaction with the family will provide more information. These interactions will be based on the hypothesis (or hypotheses) that the therapist formulates from observation and experience with the family. Goals are derived from this hypothesis, intervention is implemented, and feedback in the form of nonverbal and verbal transactions completes the loop, which ends and restarts the process. Thus assessment becomes an integral part of process in structural family therapy. Outcome research (Minuchin et al., 1975; Minuchin, Rosman, & Baker, 1978) has supported the efficacy of this modality with psychosomatic children, anorexic treatment, and psychosomatic asthmatics and diabetics. A study presented by Minuchin in *Families of the Slums* (Minuchin, Montalvo, Guerney, Rosman, & Schumer, 1967) supports the effectiveness of this mode of family therapy with this population.

Strategic family therapists conceptualize symptoms as being derived from failed attempts to resolve problems. These problems must be seen in the context of the family and with regard to a function that the symptom serves. Remediation of the dysfunctional sequence of behavior becomes a clear therapeutic goal. Assessment in this modality often begins with intervention by the therapist in order to observe the system's response. Behavioral/interactional responsive sequences are observed and used in further assessment. Thus each action and interaction informs the process of therapy. Diagnostic labels are avoided, because labeling would disattribute the systemic perspective and possibly convey a concept of permanency to the problem. The strategic therapist maintains a position of responsiveness and responsibility in therapy. It is an active directive stance, and assessment is based on therapist evaluation of the emerging patterns from client responses to interventions. Hypotheses are continuously generated, and strategies may come directly from the therapist, or from team members, depending on the particular school of thought being used. Thus assessment is from an outsider stance. Outcome information is most frequently contained in the form of case report. The Mental Research Institute group has generated more systematic outcome data than other groups. The paucity of studies about this model makes it difficult to establish its efficacy. Several strategic approaches and little overall consistency to approach also cause difficulty.

Bowenian, or family systems, therapy brought the extended family into the assessment picture. Kerr and Bowen (1988) conceptualize symptoms as reflecting anxiety in the relationship, which in turn is related to the degree of differentiation of family members. Therapeutic questions are intended to promote thinking about emotional patterns in the family, differentiation, anxiety, and emotional reactivity. The evaluation process is divided into several components: the history of the presenting problem; a history of the nuclear family with an evaluation of stress and anxiety; a history of the extended family systems, including an elaboration of their degree of involvement in the presenting system; and finally, definition of the problem to be addressed. A family diagram is used to conceptualize the emotional patterns generationally. This theoretical approach is based on clinical observations. It does not lend itself to rigorous evaluation. There have been a few studies that tracked responses indicating differentiation references. Its outcome is best measured by reports of successful treatment.

The *experiential* family therapies are more focused on "being" or awareness of the self, emotion, and personal growth. Functional communication and interactions are emphasized also. The hypothesis that underlies most of these approaches is that a healthy family promotes individual growth and change through encouragement and working together. The therapist is regarded as a model. Assessment is a natural part of the therapy process. It is accomplished through information given by the family as the therapist becomes acquainted with them as a group and individually. Formal assessment and history taking are not generally a part of therapy. In some ways, the therapist takes an insider–outsider stance as he or she learns about the family and experiences with it.

Satir (1983) recommended four concepts that she regarded as "measuring tools": (1) analyzing the techniques used by each member of the family for handling the presence of "differentness," (2) role function analysis, (3) "self-manifestation analysis," and (4) the preparation of a "model analysis," which explores early life impact on family members (pp. 133–134). As of 1994, there are no empirical studies of this modality. One practitioner, Alvin Mahrer, recommends examining "in therapy outcomes" as the reference (M. Nichols & Schwartz, 1995).

Solution-focused therapy is a recent innovation that draws heavily from the strategic school of thought but emphasizes the interactions around problems and what solutions have worked in the past. O'Hanlon and Weiner-Davis (1989) envision assessment and assessment questions as intervention. Hypothesis, strategy, and assessment combine as therapy centers on past solutions and questions and tasks around them that allow the client/family to recognize strength and resources. This alters the narrow focus on the "problem" and facilitates change. Outcome research has not been rigorously applied in evaluating this approach, but some follow-up studies indicate that clients met treatment goals about 77% of the time, and 51% indicated that the presenting problem was not active at the 18-month follow-up (Wylie, 1990, pp. 34–35).

Collaborative approaches have evolved in the 1990s. This philosophically oriented model propounds that human interaction is learned and shaped in conversation and that change occurs from that place. Egalitarian conversations are the goal in this approach as the client and therapist discuss life situations and explore old meanings as well as create new ones. Harlene Anderson (1997) advises that the therapist listens from a "not knowing" uninformed stance that attempts to hear and facilitate interactive listening and communication. Outcome research with this model might best evaluate efficacy in relation to the therapist. Recent studies have shown that therapeutic efficacy is as much related to the therapist as to technique (Wylie, 1990).

In light of this variety of approaches, it is not surprising that process and outcome research for family therapy as a field is sparse. Formal assessment methods are difficult at best to apply across such a diverse terrain. Assessment from a structured stance changes the atmosphere of the therapeutic relationship and poses problems in regard to how clients and therapists view their relationship hierarchically. Observational assessment may impede the family's ability to react naturally. Insider evaluation reflects individual stances and biases. These factors complicate clinical research for the independent therapist as well as for the researcher in a facility where several modalities are used.

Changes in research approaches are allowing for a convergence of clinical and research endeavors. With the advent of qualitative methodology, many of the conundrums of investigation have been alleviated. More collaborative efforts between therapist and clients are possible, and major objections to hierarchical boundaries that dominated quantitative methodology are removed. It is now possible to use both methodologies and enhance understanding of process and outcome.

VALUE ADDED: PROVIDING QUALITY CLINICAL SERVICES

The pioneers of the family therapy field were both researchers and clinicians who spent much of their time reviewing and analyzing their own and others' works. Frequently they operated through research funding of the National Institute of Mental Health or educational institutions. Today there are many practitioners in the field who have chosen this as a career and a way to sustain their livelihood. Fewer practitioners engage in research activities, and more engage in private practice in nonaffiliated clinical settings. Clinical practice and research are not common associates in today's milieu. Conferences are the major resource for communicating about new approaches and research findings. Managed care organizations and their protocols seem to dictate therapeutic direction and process. There are numerous external pressures that shape clinical intervention and detract from research time. More than ever, knowing how to measure efficacy and effectiveness is an imperative professional and personal goal as well as an ethical mandate. Such evaluation is difficult without a consensual base. As yet, a comprehensive, reliable relational diagnosis system has not been elaborated. Unlike medicine, which has in many ways reached a "scientific" stance, the variables that we as therapists confront are myriad and diverse. It is both fortunate and difficult that at this time in the development of our profession, we must validate and maintain credibility as health care providers. Assessment as a beginning and an end to the therapeutic process is implicit.

In addition to aiding us in complying with professional standards, assessment is a tool for professional and personal development, process formulation, and a marketing tool. Assessment of our professional interventions is a vehicle through which we can grow both personally and professionally. It facilitates the provider's determination of strengths and weaknesses, allowing for both enhancement of one's self-view as well as professional and personal remediation. Ethically we are constrained to evaluate ourselves, our process, and findings, and report the latter in a professional manner to facilitate client care for others. Additionally, therapists in solo or small group practices often do not have the opportunity to staff or process cases as routinely as is done in larger clinical or educational situations. Professional development is difficult for such practitioners.

Effective assessment is helpful in encouraging and validating the work done in isolation and a helpful adjunct when consultation and supervision are used. It is a professional language base and allows for communication of process and results without breaching more tender confidentialities. Client feedback at the end of therapy is a system check to compare and contrast therapist perceptions of the progress and movement. Personal growth and development are enhanced as therapists inform themselves individually and through supervision/consultation about their interaction with clients. Personal evaluation by objective process and interaction consideration promotes personal change and growth in relation to self and others. Assessment is more than a label or diagnosis; it drives and informs the action and interaction of therapy. The therapeutic relationship begins with assessment. Each consequent session also begins with evaluation of progress between meetings and ends with consideration of the movement within the session itself. Thus assessment is a marker of beginning, middle, and end of process. Effective therapy notes this.

Additionally, in this competitive market and time, effective outcome assessment is a marketing asset. Insurance boards, both open and managed, expect quality care to be available to their patrons. Clients are encouraged when they have an awareness that their endeavors are producing change and that change has happened for others. Delivery of quality services promotes a practice through satisfaction of both the therapist and client. Therapists who are certain of their credibility and efficacy can target specific areas of strength and foster growth in those markets. There is more advantage to effective assessment than initially is evident.

The GARF was developed as a tool that could be used with minimal training and has proven to be effective and reliable when used under variable conditions by both highly skilled clinicians and people who were given brief introduction to the concepts (GAP, 1996). However, there are some skills that are rudimentary and thus beneficial to highlight herein. The Systemic MFT Skill Development Scale is meant to be used as a skill development and assessment guide for clinicians at all levels of experience who wish to do either self- or other evaluation. (See Appendix A.) Being familiar with the concepts expressed in these skills seems to facilitate more rapid and specific use of the GARF.

SKILLS SUMMARY FOR MFT CLINICIANS: A QUALITY ASSESSMENT TOOL

The Systemic MFT Skill Development Scale (hereafter referred to as the "Skill Scale") is a listing of therapeutic skills based on the above models and assumptions, which can be used for evaluation of MFT trainees' developing competence as MFTs. It can also be used by experienced practitioners to perform a routine checkup and reminder. The evaluator can rate on a 1–10 scale the competence level in each skill; then goals for improvement can be identified for specific growth focus over a specified time frame and reevaluated periodically.

Table 3.1 identifies the non-theory-based skills necessary for any clinical work. The Skill Scale is divided into sequential areas, beginning with basic administrative business skills (section A) of the therapist used outside of the therapy room and forming the environmental context for therapy. Moving a little closer to the therapy session, the focus is on team functioning (section B). Today more than ever, therapists must be able to work effectively with colleagues. As one moves the focus into the therapy room, the person of the therapist attributes (section C) form the basic context for the therapeutic relationship and consequent therapy process. As the therapist begins the therapy process, joining skills (section D) initiate and sustain the therapeutic relationship system. All of the above skills seem to be necessary requirements for any theoretical orientation applied with clients.

The intervention process, including assessment (section E), hypothesis formulation (section F), and strategizing (section G) skills, are then classified according to theory models in a general way in Table 3.2. Strategic, structural, and family-of-origin skills are described using a camera lens metaphor to define the depth of field focus. These theory focus skills seem to be loosely parallel with the three variables of the GARF: interactional processes, organizational structure, and emotional climate.

The foundational skill area is assessment. Effective assessment will likely encompass all three dimensions simultaneously but will focus primarily on one dimension when planning the intervention strategy. The strategic focus is on interactional processes, observing the patterns system members use to communicate in order to solve problems. Assessment data are then formulated, consciously or subconsciously, into a hypothesis about strengths and barriers evident in the communication style/s observed. The intervention strategy is de-

Table 3.1
Generic Skills in the Systemic MFT Skill Development Scale Applicable to All Models

A. Administrative Functions
    1. Keeping up with paperwork
    2. Keeping on schedule in sessions
    3. Organizing any special materials needed for sessions
    4. Taping sessions routinely and reviewing as needed
    5. Working effectively with office staff

B. Team Functioning
    1. Paying full attention to the case in progress
    2. Developing messages based on current assessment
    3. Sharing ideas during consultation and supervision
    4. Processing conflicts appropriately with team members
    5. Providing support for team members that facilitates their growth

C. Person of the Therapist Attributes
    1. Aware of own issues that could influence relationship with clients
    2. Sufficient resolution of own issues or appropriate use of referral, team, or supervision to protect clients
    3. Appropriate sensitivity to gender and ethnic issues in self that could interfere with effective client services
    4. Monitors all interactions with clients to set appropriate sexual boundaries

D. Joining Skills
    1. Confirm family members with empathic responses
    2. Absolve individuals from personal responsibility for the problem
    3. Track information as a neutral listener
    4. Understand and use the family's language
    5. Emphasize the expert position to create a therapeutic context and engender hope

Table 3.2
Model-Related Therapeutic Skills in the Systemic MFT Skill Development Scale

E. Assessment Skills

Strategic (macro lens) = tracking interactional patterns around the symptom/presenting problem that are a result of the family's attempts to get fundamental needs met by responding to the stress of the necessary change

    1. Problem-solving enactment/reenactment
    2. Circular questioning
    3. Clinical rating scale family assessment models (GARF/Circumplex Model/Beavers Systems Model)

Structural (50-mm lens) = defining how the family structure maintains the ineffective patterns by identifying the family rules about boundaries that define power bases/decision-making authority and consequently inhibit the system's ability to use more effective interactional patterns for meeting the family's needs

    4. Sculpting/choreographing
    5. Listing family rules
    6. Self-report family assessment written instruments (FACES/SFI/SAFE)

Family-of-Origin (wide-angle lens) = identifying loyalties that inconspicuously lock in the ineffective family structure that supports the interactional patterns that perpetuate the symptom and rigidify the patterns

    7. Genogram construction
    8. Listing family-of-origin rules
    9. Tracking reactions to "parent firing" assignments

F. Hypothesis Formulation Skills: conceptualizing/writing on the basis of one key dimension or an integration of dimensions

    1. Interactional = identifying interactional patterns around the symptom until a structural identification begins to emerge
    2. Organizational = identifying ineffective dyadic, nuclear, and extended family rules that establish boundaries around subsystems and designate power bases

G. Strategizing Skills: formulating, executing, and evaluating interventions based on the hypothesis

Strategic

    1. Focus on solution of the presenting problem in a way that will provide a systemic change that will strengthen future problem-solving capabilities
    2. Reframe the motives of the interactional patterns as an attempt to make the structure more functional
    3. Reframe the stuckness into hopefulness through metaphor
    4. Use paradoxical/straightforward directives to help the family experience new interactional patterns
    5. Reduce anxiety about change by giving "go slow" directives
    6. Coach the family on improving problem-solving skills

Structural

    7. Join effectively before beginning stroke-kick approach to facilitate restructuring
    8. Interrupt and redirect communication interchanges to redirect power bases/alliances
    9. Use rearranging of family member seatings to imply alliance shifts
    10. Affirm all efforts at positive structural changes
    11. Facilitate family bringing about positive structural changes:

        a. Strengthened egalitarian marital subsystem
        b. Strengthened parental hierarchy
        c. Strengthened sibling support subsystem
        d. Strengthened adult relationship with former parents

Family of Origin

    12. Use genogram construction to help family identify family-of-origin (FOO) patterns consciously
    13. Refer to FOO members by given names versus role names in session
    14. Use practice exercises (unmailed letters, etc.) to help client identify desired changes in relationship with FOO member/s
    15. Give assignments to begin changing the interaction patterns with FOO to adult–adult interaction, using the nuclear family as the support resource to help protect from regression to child–adult interactions
    16. Invite FOO members into session and coach a renegotiation of interactional rules for an adult–adult relationship; include the spouse as cotherapist if possible

signed to empower the strengths assessed and sidestep the barriers to effectiveness. The enactment/reenactment technique demonstrates the interactional processes live for the assessor. Strengths and weaknesses can be identified in a manner as near real as possible for the therapist. Circular questioning, a technique developed by the Milan Team (Boscolo, Cecchin, Hoffman, & Penn, 1987), is an extremely powerful reframing intervention tool that also provides excellent information about family members' abilities to view the problem systemically. The GARF, along with the Beavers Systems Model and the Circumplex Model clinical rating scales, are somewhat arbitrarily placed under strategic assessment skills in the Skill Scale. The assessment models include all dimensions of the family system functioning; however, the clinical rating scale assessment process is more dynamic and interactional in nature.

The collected structural assessment data indicate how the structure is organized by family rules about boundaries. These rules define power bases and decision-making authority, thus controlling the possibilities for communicating effectively. Appropriate hierarchies can be assessed by the graphic technique of sculpting. One picture is worth a thousand words in describing power and connectedness. Sculpting can be done using Satir's traditional model (Satir & Baldwin, 1983). Adaptations can be developed using empty chairs, paper dolls, stacking dolls, wooden blocks, and so on, as representative family members. A more direct approach is to ask family members to tell you what the family rules are and to write them down on the board. Definition of roles can be categorized into any area of family functioning that appears to be problematic. Self-report written scales, such as the Systemic Assessment of the Family Environment (SAFE), the Self-report Family Inventory (SFI), and the Family Adaptability and Cohesion Evaluation Scale (FACES), are listed under structural assessment skills. Administering, scoring, and interpreting these multidimensional assessment tools creates a more fixed structural profile of the family system, hence, the categorization as structural.

Finding primarily strengths in the structure can possibly lead the therapist to focusing only on behavioral communication skills. However, few clients seem to come into our offices needing only to learn how to express their needs. Generally, new skills in communication must be used to realign relationship roles and boundaries that have been skewed, resulting in power-struggle marriages, parentified/scared children, or "fettered parental hands" (a concept from Satir's *Peoplemaking* that implies that parents who are developmentally still children to their parents cannot function well as parents to their own children). A competent family therapist must be able to assess these structural blocks in order to provide effective second-order change interventions that eliminate symptoms long term. If communication blocks and organizational distortions are evident, a combination of strategic and structural skills will be necessary.

When symptoms persist despite apparent success in improving communication and appropriate role definition, looking to wide-angle focus of extended family may be the key. Developmental blocks caused by inconspicuous loyalties to ineffective/developmentally inappropriate family structure and interactional rules modeled from childhood may be perpetuating the current symptom into a rigidified pattern. The emotional development into adulthood may be blocked for adult members of the nuclear family system. Until the underlying emotional issues are identified and resolved, strategic and structural interventions will not result in long-term symptom relief, that is, a second-order change in the system functioning. The basic skill in this area is construction of a genogram (McGoldrick & Gerson, 1985). The genogram can then serve as a session-by-session resource for paying attention to patterns and rules about family functioning. Mapping relationships in the prior generations can lead to defining relationship rules that are subconsciously being carried over into the current family in ineffective ways. Using Williamson's (1991) restructuring intervention process of "parent firing" can provide clear assessment information. As preparation for the renegotiation of peer roles between the adults and their parents proceeds, the level of anxiety in the client will clearly demonstrate to the assessor how rigidly the extended family clings to the rule of "I will *always* be your mother." When these rules are firmly entrenched, therapy to free the nuclear family client to develop into adulthood so the client can then function as a mature spouse and parent will be slow and tedious. The family-of-origin intervention techniques identified in the Skill Scale are tools from which to choose. The message of longer treatment is not welcomed by managed care but is a necessary truth to speak. This extended family level of assessment will make it possible for therapists and managed care to work together to effectively meet the true needs of the customer in a case-specific manner, incorporating a preventive dimension for future treatment need.

Thus, assessment skills in all three focus areas of the system are essential to provide competent systemic therapy. As in any system change, the process of skill development is dynamic. Assessing one's skills periodically can help the therapist keep a balance in systemic skill development.

CHAPTER 4

Putting GARF Assessment into Clinical Context

Rating initial session GARFs
GARF as an outcome and process instrument
GARF self-report instrument as a process/outcome tool
Other applications of the GARF as an outcome/process tool
Expanded case example—The Rodriguez Family
Ethical guidelines for use of the GARF
Summary

The GARF is a flexible tool that can be used as an outcome or process measure as well as an initial assessment device. It also can be used in supervision. The intent of this chapter is to illustrate how to use the GARF as both a global and a subscale assessment instrument. When sessions are routinely scored and plotted in graph form, session outcome is seen globally. Therapeutic process can also be elucidated by including subscale plotting by session. Examples to highlight these applications are included. Then, a complete case study using the skills summary format and other tools contained in this book is presented. To that end, cases from our practices and supervision experiences have been selected. Informed consent was obtained in all cases after clients read the proposed summaries. Although client cases are drawn from actual files, some aspects have been altered, and pseudonyms have been used to protect the clients.

Initially, sessions will be depicted representing the five GARF scoring categories. These cases will depict both global and subscale rating analyses. The first four examples illustrate presenting sessions. The last vignette is of an ending session. Then, cases illustrating the GARF as a process instrument will be detailed. This is followed by a discussion of the GARF as an outcome instrument in conjunction with the Goal Attainment Scale and Client Satisfaction tools. Finally, there will be a complete case study using many of the forms and instruments that are employed in our practices.

RATING INITIAL SESSION GARFS

In assessing relational functioning as a new GARF user, it is helpful to keep a copy of the GARF descriptors (see Appendix B) in front of you. Initially, it is helpful to make an overall rating based on the descriptors from the quintiles. This overall rating can then be refined, if that is desired, into subscale ratings. The case illustrations will be analyzed with a format that presents the overall rating descriptors for the quintile, followed by case information. A brief discussion of subscale evaluation concludes the description of the illustrated GARF category.

Category 1. Overall rating of 1–20. Relational unit has become too dysfunctional to retain continuity of contact and attachment.

Jennifer, Joe, and their children, Debbie, age 13, and Barbara, age 5, came to therapy after Jennifer had gone to a woman's shelter. There had been a fight, and Joe had torn the telephone from the wall and beaten Jennifer. The daughters contacted the police. This had occurred a week before, and now the couple wanted to "work things out." This type of violence occurred frequently in the family, generally at least one to two times per month. Jennifer had returned home with the stipulation that they would find someone who could help them. As they talked, each overspoke the other, disagreeing frequently about petty details. Joe had not worked for some time and had historically been unable to maintain a job for more than a few months. He had not looked for employment for some time. Jennifer was a university student, struggling to make ends meet and still attend classes. She had a part-time job as well as carrying a full course load. Joe did not like the fact that she was gone much of the time and that he was to be responsible for the children. He cleaned house sporadically and fixed meals when he was hungry. The children fended for themselves the majority of the time. When home, Jennifer would attempt to institute some routine, but this was quickly discarded in her absence. Joe saw no benefit to rules. He also believed that a man is to be in charge and that his family was not allowing this to happen. In session, the children were clinging and withdrawn. Each vied for Jennifer's attention and were despondent when they could not monopolize her. Jennifer tried to respond to them as well as to Joe but was clearly overwhelmed.

Initially, a global rating of 12 was assigned. Clearly, this family lacked even daily maintenance routines and had little ability to communicate in order to set goals or routine. Conflict appeared to be the outgrowth of irresolvable stress. Problem solving was marked at 10. Personal and generational responsibility was not clearly defined. The children were in charge of their own mealtimes as well as bedtime. There was no agreed-on distribution of power, control, or responsibility. Organization was scored at 8. Little evidence of mutual involvement, caring, commitment, or empathy was apparent here. There was significant physical danger present in the family. Although the children wish to be affectionate, neither parent has the resources for this. Even the sibling system is discordant. The emotional climate was evaluated to be at 8. If using the subscales, the global can be recomputed to reflect them as their mean, which would give this family a subscale mean of 9.

Category 2. Overall rating 21–40. Relational unit is obviously and seriously dysfunctional; forms and time periods of satisfactory relating are rare.

Martha and Bill came to therapy at Bill's insistence. At first glance this couple appeared to be relatively well functioning, at least as individuals. Martha was a successful nurse, and Bill was a computer specialist who owned his own firm. Bill began the session, explaining that he was concerned about their 30-year marriage. There had been no sexual intimacy for more than 5 years, and he had looked at his consulting business as a means of separating from the marriage without divorcing. He discussed concerns about Martha's health. When asked to list their goals for coming to therapy, Martha listed that she wanted to be heard and wanted to be treated like an adult. As she spoke, she detailed the manner in which she felt ignored and was openly hostile toward Bill, explaining that she had to go to bed early just to get peace. She perceived that he was always criticizing her and that she could never do anything correctly. Bill took defensive stances as he was attacked and attempted to explain his concerns, which included the fact that their younger daughter, age 22, reported to him that Martha drank in quantity nightly and could not be roused until morning.

Bill spoke fondly of this daughter as well as her older sibling. Martha saw the daughter's presence as troublesome and unwelcome. She spoke more fondly of the older daughter, who no longer resided in the home. When queried if there was any time that they enjoyed together, they indicated that they did well when traveling as a couple. Martha, however, indicated that Bill was generally critical of her demeanor and dress at these times and that this frequently spoiled the fun.

This couple evidenced being locked in avoidance and in a seriously dysfunctional position. The global rating was 26. Although there are routines present, they are more related to professional, not couple, life. Life cycle changes create discordance and few attempts are made to resolve the conflict. Avoidance predominates. Problem solving was rated at 26. Organizationally, decisions for the family are made by default. Bill might initiate action, but Martha tends to ignore any request. Solutions are not forthcoming. There appears to be some alignment between parent and child that confuses interpersonal roles and subsystem boundaries. Power is not shared or negotiated. A rating of 25 was given. Emotionally, this couple does admit to some good times. Distancing and hostility do predominate, and there has been no sexual relationship for some time. An emotional climate rating of 28 was given. In this case, the initial global and the subscale mean were approximately equal.

Category 3. Overall rating 41–60. Relational unit has occasional times of satisfying and competent functioning together, but clearly dysfunctional, unsatisfying relationships tend to predominate.

Mark, age 30, and Bridget, age 32, came to therapy after Bridget locked Mark out of the house. Both had been drinking, and an argument had ensued because Bridget believed that all Mark wanted was her mother's money. As they talked about their frequent fighting and other marital concerns, both cried openly. Bridget took Mark's hand and patted it, explaining that he had many therapeutic issues to work through and that she was already in therapy with another person. Bridget did all of the talking for Mark about his "problems" and detailed how she maintained the family finances, paying the bills and allotting Mark $20.00 for lunch and other expenses weekly. She monopolized all responses even when directed to her partner. Mark was able to speak openly only when the couple was separated for individual assessment. He discussed how their life focused on partying on the weekend or going to be with Bridget's mother, who frequently spent large sums of money on Bridget's house. He perceived that most of the couple's problems arose from his refusal to immediately follow his wife's directions—such as taking out the trash when asked. He did note that their arguments seemed to occur when both were drinking heavily. Their sexual relationship had been discontinued for over a year, beginning shortly after their marriage.

A global score of 44 was given. This family does have some routines, albeit not negotiated ones. There does not appear to be effective communication, and problem-solving skills are limited. A problem-solving rating of 45 was assigned. Organizationally, this family does not share power. The central role of Bridget's mother in the family compromises appropriate hierarchy as well as control and responsibility. Bridget and her mother maintain a powerful coalition. Mark seems to allow this. A rating of 42 was assigned. This couple does enjoy life together in ways that are outside the normal parameters of this rating. There is some evidence of warmth and support between them, although it is unequally distributed. An emotional climate rating of 46 was given.

Category 4. Overall rating 61–80. Functioning of the relational unit is somewhat unsatisfactory. Over a period of time, many but not all difficulties are resolved without complaints.

Beverly and Beth seemed to represent a typical mother and teen-age daughter. Beth, a bouncy 16-year-old, could alternate between smiles and sulks quickly when her wishes were not granted. Beverly was an elementary school teacher who was still struggling from a divorce from Beth's father that had occurred several years previously. Beverly had struggled to become a parent who could say no and still felt the effects of Beth's disapproval when denied. Her greatest concern was to steer Beth safely through her teen years. To this end, she tended to be overly controlling, fearing that Beth could not make good decisions on her own. Beverly had a difficult time allowing Beth to learn from small mistakes and would discuss her concerns at length. This tended to negate Beth's good sense. At times, Beverly would remark that she feared Beth would create problems as her older brothers had. Although this created great dissonance in their relationship, it was evident that both mother and daughter cared for each other as they sat and discussed their differences. Beth could freely express her feelings as well as use them to manipulate her mother. This manipulation tended to frustrate Beverly, who would become more controlling, and a power imbalance would escalate.

This relational unit functioned well overall and was globally given a 71. Problem-solving skills were fairly strong; Beverly would listen to Beth in most instances, and they both knew what the rules were in their daily lives and responded to them in normative, age-related ways. A problem solving score of 79 was given. Organizationally, this family has more concerns. Beverly overfunctions with regard to power, control, and responsibility. The sibling subsystem seems to be depreciated. Because of the frequency of this, an organizational rating of 63 was given. Warmth and caring are present but are disrupted by Beverly's fears and Beth's manipulations. Beverly's affect is relatively changeable, probably because of stress and limited resources. An emotional subscale rating of 70 was given. The subscale mean and initial global are compatible.

Category 5. Overall rating 81–99. Relational unit is functioning satisfactorily from self-report of participants and from perspectives of observers.

Cliff and Nancy had been married for 3 years. Nancy had a young son, Eric, age 5, from her previous marriage. Both Cliff and Nancy had successful professional careers. Their presenting problems related to lack of skills in communication, according to their self-report. They were unable to adapt to Cliff's custodial problems with his 11-year-old son, Jeff, who had visitation on the weekends. Cliff could not relate well to his son and was still in conflict with his former spouse. Jeff was triangulated between his parents because of this, and visiting was difficult. On several occasions, he had injured Eric. Nancy was frightened for her son and wished for visitation to end. Cliff was adamant that he had to see his son and feared losing him totally if he did not maintain his custodial routine. When Eric was present, Cliff often relegated responsibility for his care to Nancy. She felt unheard and unsupported and retaliated by spending quantities of money, endangering the unit's long-term financial goals. Other power issues were also at play.

During the course of therapy, Nancy and Cliff learned how to set goals that were mutually satisfying and then seek resources and routines that allowed both of their children's needs to be met. They had been correct in noting a need for improved communication skills. There had also been a need for improving the sharing of power and responsibility. They discussed their shared values after learning to listen to each other. This increased their respect and regard, and they left therapy functioning well. Their problem-solving scores rose from a 45 to a 90. Organization had been low at 35 but rose to 85 because they understood and agreed on responsibilities with regard to child care as well as couple tasks and needs. They no longer subjugated their marriage to their children but balanced these areas well. Emotionally this couple had presented at a low of 41. At the end of therapy, there was an optimistic atmosphere present. All parties could express emotions and needs and generally feel supported. Sexual functioning had resumed and obtained a mutually satisfactory level. A rating of 87 was given. The subscale mean was 88.

GARF AS AN OUTCOME AND PROCESS INSTRUMENT

Outcome research has often been regarded as a necessary but unwelcome task by the therapeutic community. A focus on results rather than process has been anathema to family therapists. The need for resolution to this dilemma has been frequently discussed in journals and other writings (Framo, 1992; Pinsof, 1988). Wynne (1988) spoke to this dilemma and suggested that a "tentative solution. . .is to recommend that two primary baselines be given priority in family therapy research: (a) the multiple versions of the family members' 'initial' presenting problems, and (b) the problem identified by consensus of family and therapist" (p. 253).

In this section, outcome and process can be seen as intertwined when GARF is graphed as both a global and a subscale instrument. Using the GARF in conjunction with the Goal Attainment Scale, Self-Report GARF or SAFE, and Client Satisfaction tools provides insider–outsider dimensions to the assessment and outcome aspects of therapy. Additionally, discussing GARF parameters and charting progress with the client can enhance the therapeutic process. The GARF can also be used as a process research tool when combined with case notes that include therapeutic interventions and reflections. Case examples to illustrate this process and outcome duality follow.

The Davis Family—Communication Crisis

Ben and Mary had known each other more than 20 years when they decided to marry—each for the first time. They were convinced that the length and strength of their friendship provided a solid base for the union. Additionally, they shared many common values, being mutually active in a church wherein roles and boundaries were very clear. Each had viable careers, although neither was particularly content in their occupations. They came to therapy for a premarital "checkup" and presented well. The plans for the union were already made, and Ben was to move to Mary's state. They married, believing that there could be no problems.

Several months later, Ben and Mary returned. Ben had not been able to find new employment in the area and Mary disliked the prospect of supporting a husband, a position not well thought of by their church. Ben was chagrined but confident that he would find a position. In the meantime, Mary felt that she was being devalued. She wanted to go on vacation when her work allowed it, but Ben would not forego job hunting. When she broached the subject, he was unresponsive, referring to his "work ethic," which happened to be like hers. Mary, feeling defeated and out of line, would withdraw and fume. Eventually her anger would erupt, and the cycle would begin again. Ben's rigidity interfered with their ability to organize. Both needed to learn communication skills to convey their respective positions clearly and hear the other's position. In examining the first session ratings, it appeared that the interactional component was key to bringing both the emotional tone and power distribution into alignment. Ineffective communication was inhibit-

PROFILE CHART:

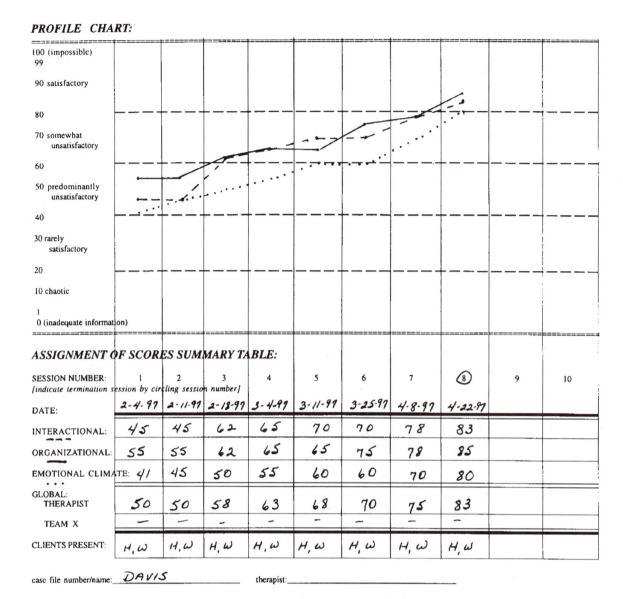

ASSIGNMENT OF SCORES SUMMARY TABLE:

SESSION NUMBER: *[indicate termination session by circling session number]*	1	2	3	4	5	6	7	(8)	9	10
DATE:	2-4-97	2-11-97	2-18-97	3-4-97	3-11-97	3-25-97	4-8-97	4-22-97		
INTERACTIONAL:	45	45	62	65	70	70	78	83		
ORGANIZATIONAL:	55	55	62	65	65	75	78	85		
EMOTIONAL CLIMATE:	41	45	50	55	60	60	70	80		
GLOBAL: THERAPIST	50	50	58	63	68	70	75	83		
TEAM X	—	—	—	—	—	—	—	—		
CLIENTS PRESENT:	H, W	H, W	H, W	H, W	H, W	H, W	H, W	H, W		

case file number/name: __DAVIS__   therapist:_____

Figure 4.1 GARF as process: the Davis family (see Appendix B for complete GARF Profile Chart).

ing negotiation and decision-making processes. The first and second sessions focused on developing listening skills and learning affective language. The next three sessions addressed the assertiveness component of communication. Both Ben and Mary needed to know how to make requests and not feel guilty. They each tended to mind-read and attempt to notice the other's emotional state before communication began. This promoted an organizational power imbalance and fed the emotional process. The interactional and organizational ratings improved, as did the emotional mark. The following sessions related to negotiating family routines by clearly stating wants and needs on a pad and then clarifying each partner's position. They progressed from this to direct communication. Figure 4.1 graphs the eight sessions. At the end, Ben and Mary negotiated vacation time as well as job search needs, and both were content that they could apply the process to other areas in their lives.

The Knight Family—A Case in Need of Organization

Martha, 39, a mother of three active teenagers, had experienced many personal and psychological problems since having thyroid surgery 5 years prior to coming to this office. She had been unable to perform normal household duties or hold a job. Her husband, John, 40, and she had been married for 20 years. He worked as a computer consultant for a large national firm and traveled often. Initially, Martha presented for therapy and complained about her marital and family situation. She was asked to bring the family for the next meeting. The children—Patrick, age 15; Phillip, age 13; and Elizabeth, age 11—all were experiencing educational and social problems. Patrick was a daydreamer, writing at his computer for long periods of time or watching super-hero programs on television. He was a large boy, and when he felt angered in social settings would throw furniture. He had thrown a fellow student through a plate glass window at school the previous year. Phillip was in difficulties with the legal system for drug usage, violating curfew, and shoplifting. Elizabeth had been diagnosed as having learning differences the previous spring. She was an attractive young girl who related many physical problems and was definitely overweight.

The parents were asked to discuss their goals for this family intervention in the presence of the children. Immediately, disruptions began. Patrick spoke over his father, negating his words. Phillip paced around the room and then abruptly left. Martha quickly followed him. Elizabeth immediately joined her father on the couch, taking her mother's place. A global rating in the first quintile was considered (15). There was little evidence of family or couple routine present. Martha would walk out without informing members of her destination or time of return. Phillip followed suit. The inability to communicate placed problem solving at a 15. Organization was lacking as most family members had no functionally defined roles. Martha joined with the children, disrupting the parenting and marital dyad routinely. She demonstrated regressive behavior when the tension level escalated. A rating of 8 was assigned because of the frequent emotional and physical outbursts from all three males in the family. Emotionally this family did want to work together but had no roles or rules established. At times they could watch television or go out together. Both Martha and John voiced concern about their family's problems. It was obvious that they cared for each other and the children despite the frequent distancing. An emotional climate rating of 15 was given. The subscale mean was 13.

John reassembled the family in the therapy room. The children continued to disrupt the session, speaking over the parents but not the therapist. John persisted in stating his wishes for the family—he wanted to implement some work responsibility in the home as he was overwhelmed by having to perform at work and then run the house also. He discussed his concerns about physical violence, and he and Martha agreed to take enforcing action when problems arose. A non-violence contract was negotiated and signed by all members (see Appendix F). Each person was asked what he or she would like to happen in the family, and his or her concerns were noted on a large pad. Being heard seemed to help, and the family left the session on a more positive note. Figure 4.2 charts their GARF ratings for the following sessions.

The couple was asked to return alone for the third session and, because the organizational component of the GARF was lower, boundaries around the parental and couple dyad were addressed. Each parent discussed perceptions of family roles and what he or she hoped would happen for them in therapy. The Goal Attainment Scale was used to delineate what they viewed as attainable individual and parental goals, which included reasonable family chores in the house for all the children and the hope that as a family they could go out at least biweekly and have an enjoyable family night. The objectives of the next family

PROFILE CHART:

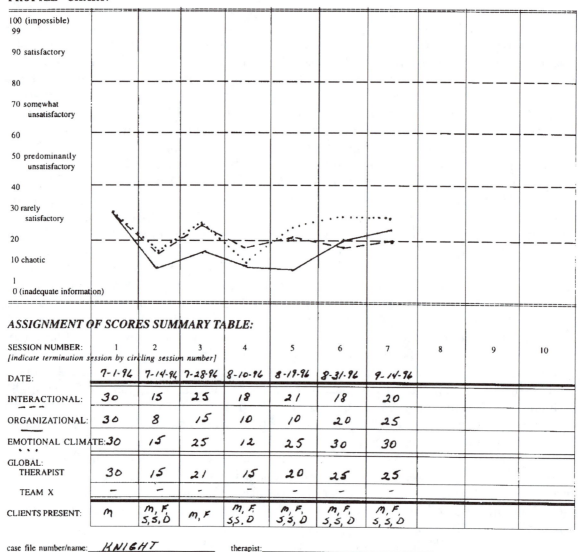

ASSIGNMENT OF SCORES SUMMARY TABLE:

SESSION NUMBER: *[indicate termination session by circling session number]*	1	2	3	4	5	6	7	8	9	10
DATE:	7-1-96	7-14-96	7-28-96	8-10-96	8-19-96	8-31-96	9-14-96			
INTERACTIONAL:	30	15	25	18	21	18	20			
ORGANIZATIONAL:	30	8	15	10	10	20	25			
EMOTIONAL CLIMATE:	30	15	25	12	25	30	30			
GLOBAL: THERAPIST	30	15	21	15	20	25	25			
TEAM X	–	–	–	–	–	–	–			
CLIENTS PRESENT:	m	m, F, S, S, D	m, F	m, F, S, S, D	m, F, S, S, D	m, F, S, S, D	m, F, S, S, D			

case file number/name: _KNIGHT_   therapist: _____

Figure 4.2 GARF as process: the Knight family.

session were then reclarified from this work. Without the presence of the children, this couple could negotiate and communicate relatively well. Each agreed on responsibilities, although John continued to view his role in an overfunctioning manner.

The fourth session was a conjoint session with all members present. The children again were disrespectful of the parents and restless. John introduced the topic of goals, and when the children objected, Martha quickly regressed into a childlike stance, joining the sibling subsystem. A discussion of this ensued, and she attempted to become a parent again. It was obvious that the children used her regressions to their advantage. Phillip even mimicked them, exhibiting similar regressive behavior, and was rewarded by her reaching out to him. Elizabeth regressed to an infantile inflection in response to this and was chastised for being a "baby" by her mother. In a comparison of the four sessions, it appeared that interaction and emotion were being impaired by inadequate maintenance of interpersonal roles and subsystem boundaries. There were frequent coalitions formed against John, who appeared to have all the responsibility but lacked power. He used anger as a means of control.

As therapy progressed, John and Martha were able to become more effective coparents. Several bimonthly sessions were needed to help Martha move into that parenting stance. She continued to sabotage John's effort, which she saw as control, by not enforcing consequences. It took legal intervention with Phillip to facilitate a more parental stance. The family began to learn to listen and express themselves with less disruption. This family remains in therapy at this writing.

The Smith Family—A Contest About Power and Values

Sarah, a bright and rebellious 12-year-old, was brought to therapy by her parents, Bob and Karen. Sarah had been sneaking out at night and visiting neighborhood boys. She had begun drinking and also was self-mutilating. Sarah was the youngest of the Smith's three daughters. Janis, age 18, and Dawn, age 14, also were bright girls. Janis was quiet and withdrawn, preparing to leave for college at a church institution. Dawn was equally intense, but prone to tears. She seemed to possess the nonangry emotions for the family. This family was in chaos, not knowing how to handle Sarah's behaviors and feeling blighted by them. The family was guided by their religious beliefs and adhered rigidly to what they believed to be appropriate routines that would provide happiness. Communication and negotiation skills were minimal, because they strictly adhered to what they knew to be right without question. Uniqueness was not acceptable here. Emotionally, the family spent time together in church or in front of the television. The girls spent much of their time alone in their rooms.

After physical safety was contracted, the first sessions focused on the family members' affective responses to the current situation. There was little ability to empathize with the identified patient (IP). She was seen as a problem, not a symptom. The family could not identify either familial or personal needs. This lack of responsiveness and connection negated the necessity for individuation, decision making, and communication. The emotional climate of the family was impairing interaction and organization. In the fourth session, summer was approaching. It was decided that work would be done on problem-solving skills by planning a vacation for the family. This changed the blaming focus and introduced a note of hope for relief, and the interactional and emotional ratings began to climb minutely. The family went on vacation and returned to therapy a week later. It appeared to the family that all was well, and so they withdrew from therapy.

The GARF ratings indicated that this was probably premature as the global rating was 32 (see Figure 4.3). At that time, Janis was preparing to leave for school. Sarah perceived that she was losing her only ally who understood her actions and became despondent and even more rebellious. Five weeks later, she ran away, and her parents, fearing that they could not keep her at home, agreed to a brief hospitalization. Her parents wanted time to find a foster home for her, believing that they were incompetent to handle her. Because the emotional climate of the family was a known focus of therapy, empathy work was done with the parents during the hospital stay, and Sarah was returned to her home. The parents began to perceive that there were problems in the family and initiated connection with Sarah, supporting her. Sarah returned to school but felt unacceptable to her classmates. Within 30 days, she engaged in a fight at school and ran away. After coaching, the parents agreed to acknowledge Sarah's problems. They chose to file charges against one of the young men who had been sexually involved with Sarah. When this occurred, Sarah felt supported, and the course of therapy dramatically changed. The family became emotionally

PROFILE CHART:

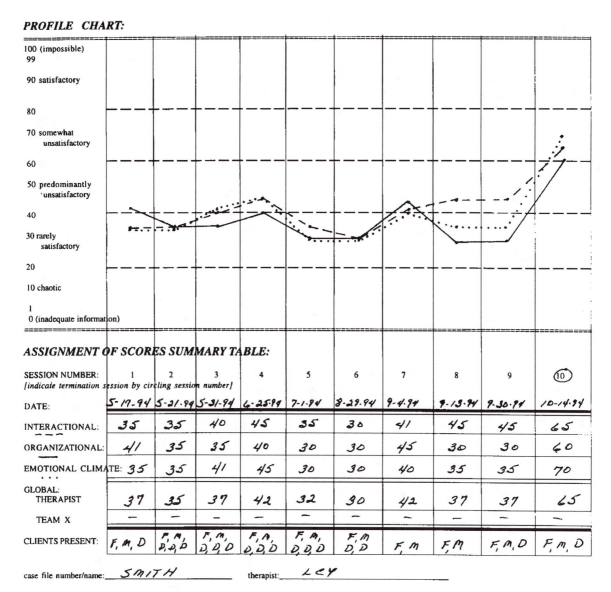

ASSIGNMENT OF SCORES SUMMARY TABLE:

SESSION NUMBER: [indicate termination session by circling session number]	1	2	3	4	5	6	7	8	9	⑩
DATE:	5-17-94	5-21-94	5-31-94	6-25-94	7-1-94	8-29-94	9-4-94	9-13-94	9-30-94	10-14-94
INTERACTIONAL:	35	35	40	45	35	30	41	45	45	65
ORGANIZATIONAL:	41	35	35	40	30	30	45	30	30	60
EMOTIONAL CLIMATE:	35	35	41	45	30	30	40	35	35	70
GLOBAL: THERAPIST	37	35	37	42	32	30	42	37	37	65
TEAM X	—	—	—	—	—	—	—	—	—	—
CLIENTS PRESENT:	F, M, D	F, M, D, D, D	F, M, D, D, D	F, M, D, D, D	F, M, D, D, D	F, M, D, D	F, M	F, M	F, M, D	F, M, D

case file number/name: ___SMITH___   therapist: ___LCY___

Figure 4.3   GARF as process: the Smith family.

responsive to Sarah's situtation, and all levels of the GARF continued to rise until therapy termination, when the ratings were in the upper fourth quintile. Figure 4.3 depicts the Smith family's GARF graph.

GARF in Extended-Family and Other Systems

Kelly, a 13-year-old 7th grade special education student, was referred to therapy by her school counselor. She resided with her maternal grandmother, Rose, who worked two minimum-wage jobs to survive. Rose also had difficulty with Kelly at home. Kelly had a history of several years of sexual abuse by a stepfather. Her mother had moved out of state to continue to live with the stepfather and had taken Kelly's two younger brothers with her. Kelly had frequent problems with impulse control and anger management. She would run away from school personnel and did not respond when called. Rose indicated that Kelly often looked like another person "took over" for her and wondered if she had multiple

PROFILE CHART:

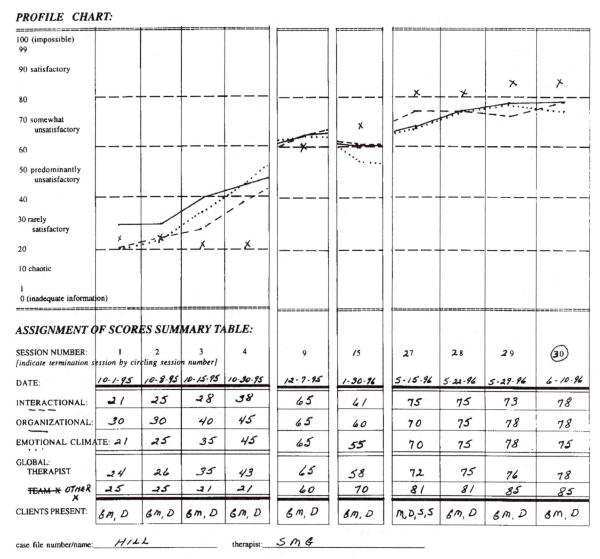

SESSION NUMBER: [indicate termination session by circling session number]	1	2	3	4	9	15	27	28	29	(30)
DATE:	10-1-95	10-8-95	10-15-95	10-30-95	12-7-95	1-30-96	5-15-96	5-22-96	5-29-96	6-10-96
INTERACTIONAL:	21	25	28	38	65	41	75	75	73	78
ORGANIZATIONAL:	30	30	40	45	65	60	70	75	78	78
EMOTIONAL CLIMATE:	21	25	35	45	65	55	70	75	78	75
GLOBAL: THERAPIST	24	26	35	43	65	58	72	75	76	78
TEAM ✗ OTHER ✗	25	25	21	21	60	70	81	81	85	85
CLIENTS PRESENT:	6m, D	6m, D	6m, D	6m, D	6m, D	6m, D	m,D,S,S	6m, D	6m, D	6m, D

ASSIGNMENT OF SCORES SUMMARY TABLE:

case file number/name: ___HILL___   therapist: ___SMG___

Figure 4.4   GARF as process: extended family.

personalities. At times, Kelly would strike out at Rose. The schoolteachers were at a loss as to how to handle her but were hoping to avoid institutionalization. She was on medication from the county mental health agency, but this did not seem to make a difference. Some of the teachers attempted to discuss her abuse history with her. This caused more confusion for Kelly, and she began sexually acting out on the bus and at church. Her church supervisors also intervened in an attempt to help the child and beleaguered grandmother.

When Rose and Kelly first presented, the GARF was especially low because of the intermittent violence and lack of attachment. The family had few routines except a routine bedtime. There was little communication, because Rose did bookkeeping for small companies when at home. All the subscales were in the second quintile (see Figure 4.4). The organizational component was noted as a strength to be nurtured therapeutically. Rose did maintain some semblance of the grandmother role. Focus in initial therapy sessions was on attachment and other emotional concerns and boundary making. Because of Kelly's intellectual limitations, game interventions were developed and generalized through Rose. This fostered connection and conversation in the family and improved both the emotional climate and organization.

During this time, Kelly was being challenged emotionally because of several situations in her school environment. One of her teachers became overly involved with her and continued to press her for information regarding her abuse. Rose attempted to intercede but was not effective. Finally, by Session 9, the school hierarchy took action. After this, there was considerably less disruption both at home and at school. The "Other" GARF ratings are represented by an "X" symbol on the chart to illustrate the interfacing of school and family functioning.

These interventions took some time, but by Session 4, Kelly and Rose were establishing routines and rules. They began to enjoy some activities together, and Kelly was responding better to authority. Sessions 5–8 were periods of stable GARF scores. By Session 9, it was time to address the emotions underlying Kelly's dissociative mechanisms and develop coping skills. Sessions 10–14 on the chart represent unchanged ratings. During this time, therapy addressed communication skills, especially those concerning assertiveness and negotiation.

Kelly's mother came to visit with Kelly's younger brothers. Usually, any contact with this part of the family triggered impulse problems because of Kelly's limitations in emotional expression. Arrangement was made for Kelly's mother, Karen, to come to therapy with her. As the time for the visit approached, Kelly began acting out again. Session 15 reflects that change, mostly noted in the alternation between anger and withdrawal that Kelly exhibited. Karen and Kelly's brothers came into Session 27 with Kelly. They began to discuss Kelly's sense of loss. Karen, who like Kelly is moderately mentally impaired, had gone to several months of therapy before coming to this session and was able to communicate her sense of loss to Kelly as well as her perceptions of being unable to leave her husband and support herself. For the first time, Kelly cried and discussed her grief about her mother's absence. Since that time, Kelly has been able to relate her affective experiences more openly in therapy. After the mother's visit, GARF ratings stabilized across the subscales in the upper 70s.

GARF SELF-REPORT INSTRUMENT AS A PROCESS/OUTCOME TOOL

The GARF Self-Report instrument (Appendix C) provides a way to use the GARF category constructs metaphorically as an assessment–intervention strategy. One example of its use is working on family-of-origin issues with premarital couples. The therapist can first work on topics such as communication skills, finances, in-laws, sex values, and parenting, and then have the couple read the GARF self-report. By then the therapist will have joined with the couple, and they will feel at ease, sharing honestly about where their family of origin fits in terms of the GARF self-report.

One woman who picked out the *Hansel and Gretel* model shared how her stepfather preferred her sister over her and gave expensive things to the sister while at the same time sexually abusing the sister. Her fiancé, on the other hand, chose *The Ugly Duckling* model because he felt ignored in the family and was given neither time nor material things. He grew up being very resilient but at the same time feeling unworthy of receiving anything from others. By using the GARF self-report at this time in therapy, the couple were able to face issues from their past that might have hindered a good relationship in married life.

The therapist can read the GARF self-report script for families with limited reading skills. In a session with a mother, two teenage daughters, and a bright teenage boy who was living with the family, the answers were very insightful. One daughter with the mental capacity of a 5-year-old talked about how she wished her family would play board games and play together like Little Red Riding Hood's family.

The mother of two girls chose Cinderella's story for her family of origin because she was treated as the not-so-smart one and was given many chores to do compared to her siblings. The mother chose *Hansel and Gretel* for her immediate family, because her husband had withdrawn from the family and spent as little time as possible interacting. The remaining teenage daughter felt like Gretel because at one time she felt very close to her father but felt abandoned when the teenage boy came to live with them. She made attempts to join others outside of the family but to no avail, and she blamed it on the fact that she was in special classes. Her biggest concern was that the teenage boy, to whom she had grown attached, would be taken away. The teenage boy who moved in with this family had no place to live. He had much difficulty with his stepmother and as a result, his father made him leave. The boy's mother was on drugs and did not provide a stable home, frequently switching relationships. The boy felt unloved and unwanted. He chose *The Ugly Duckling* as his GARF because he had just found out from an authority that he would have to leave this family. He would be going to a boys' ranch.

Another scenario was with a blended family. Two children, ages 11 and 12, identified with *Cinderella* for both their family-of-origin home and blended family. Only the stepmother was present with the children when the stories were read aloud. As the story of Cinderella was read, the two children looked at each other for confirmation and then commented on how they had been "used" in both families. The only comment the stepmother made was that she saw her blended family as similar to *Little Red Riding Hood* because she would send her children to her mother's house when she and her husband argued. She admitted in a later session that she had used one of her husband's children as a built-in babysitter for her younger children. Also, another stepchild, who had been sexually molested by one of her mother's live-in boyfriends, attended a later session. She was 9 years old when she came to live in this blended family. She molested the two younger half-sisters and a younger half-brother. This little girl saw herself as the Ugly Duckling because the family had isolated her by sending her to her stepgrandmother's house.

OTHER APPLICATIONS OF THE GARF AS AN OUTCOME/PROCESS TOOL

Using assessment as intervention (Bussell, Matsey, Reiss, & Hetherington, 1995) can be helpful. This fits well with the concept of the family as collaborator in evaluating goals and outcome. Lynelle Yingling developed a Global Attainment Scale (GAS) (see Appendix C) that stated GARF levels of functioning as suggested directions for movement in the family. This has been used briefly as of this writing, and positive results are in evidence. Using the combined tools, the family is given information about functional relationships in a goal-directed format and then is asked to clarify steps through which to attain these skills. Clients have responded well to these ideas and had a sense of concrete directions.

The GARF itself can also be used in intervention by consulting with the family during sessions about where they would rate themselves. As in the use with the GAS, this provides the family direction. Families are fascinated by the graphs and relate to this visual concept. It is important to use this as a mutual exercise, because some families become overly enthusiastic with their progress and overreport success. Underreporting also occurs, and either of these is a helpful clarifier when introduced as a point of confusion for the therapist.

The GARF can serve as a useful validation of therapeutic process and progress when submitting authorization requests to managed care. It is an easily understandable record when presented with reference to DSM–IV. The research from our study definitely challenges the six-session limit of managed care, because the GARF shows continuity and outcome. There is indication that only small increments of progress can be made in this time.

The GARF can also be used as a supervision instrument. Therapists-in-training biases appear on the graph, especially when compared with divergent team ratings. It is helpful to formulate treatment strategy by following the graph and discussing how certain interventions influence the subscales. To this same end, the GARF can become a process research tool when combined with a detailed case note form as shown in Appendix E.

EXPANDED CASE EXAMPLE—THE RODRIGUEZ FAMILY

This complete synopsis of a case with illustrated form completion is a walk-through of how we incorporate the GARF into our total clinical process. We hope that our process can be blended with the reader's preferred procedures for record keeping. We have also included necessary permission forms to remind the reader to comply with professional ethics.

Initial Contact

The case began when Mrs. Maria Rodriguez called and requested family counseling to help her and her husband, José, deal with family depression, which they believed was related to their daughter Cecilia's several recent suicide attempts. The office staff completed Section A of the Clinic Client Intake Form (Figure 4.5). After an intake session was scheduled with one of the intern therapists (Section B of Figure 4.5), the office staff prepared a new client folder containing the following forms:

- Clinic Client Intake Form (partially complete)
- Contact Summary Sheet
- Duty to Warn Form
- Parental Release Form
- Permission for Consultation/Taping/Research
- Consent for Release of Confidential Material
- Goal Attainment Scale
- GARF Self-Report Form
- Global Assessment of Relational Functioning
- Case Notes
- Therapist Periodic Assessment
- Termination Form
- Family Evaluation of Services

Intake Session

Maria, José, and their daughter, 14-year-old Cecilia, attended the intake session, which was conducted by Mary, the therapist assigned to their case. Mary explained her professional and ethical responsibilities as disclosed in the Duty to Warn form (Figure 4.6); then José

CLINIC CLIENT INTAKE FORM

A. Initial contact information collected by office staff:

Date of initial call/intake: 8/24/95   Staff doing intake: Kim

Name: Rodriguez, Maria   New Client( )   Former Client( )

Spouse: José   Home Phone: 972-680-6713

Address: 3900 Walnut   Work phone: (Her) 214-697-7100

Reno, TX 75044   (Him) 972-888-7921

Employment: (Her) Pediatrician at-PMC   Insurance: (Her) Prudential

(Him) Mechanic at Goodwin   (Him) Prudential

Social Security #: (Her) 447-97-0801   Combined annual income: $60,000 –

(Him) 419-62-3467   Assessed fee: $ 50 –

Date of birth: (Her) 5/2/47   1st appointment: 8/27/95

(Him) 5/27/47   Appointment written in book [√]

Referral source: Baylor Hospital   Appointment not scheduled because:

(probation officer: _____)

phone number: _____

Information reviewed with caller:

[√] 1st appointment arrival time   Ethnic Origin:

[√] Payment w/Services   ___ 1. Black

[√] Insurance statement   _√_ 2. Anglo

[√] 24-Hour statement   _√_ 3. Hispanic

                    ___ 4. Asian

                    ___ 5. Other:

Assigned file number: 1206

Family Members Attending 1st Session: Maria, Cecilia, José

B. Therapist assigned: M. Dobbs

C. Intake information collected by therapist at 1st session
(date: _____)

FAMILY STRUCTURE: [check one]

___ Married
___ Separated
_√_ Divorced
___ Remarried
___ Not married: living alone
___ Not married: living with extended family
___ Grandparent and child with absent parents
___ Cohabitation with unmarried partner

Total number of marriages of male head of household: 1
Total number of marriages of female head of household: 2

NAME OF ALL FAMILY MEMBERS	AGE/DOB	RELATION	IN HOUSEHOLD
1. Maria	5/47; 47	wife	√
2. Cecilia	7/82; 14	daughter	√
3. José	5/47; 47	husband	√
4. Alberto	24	stepson	no
5. Stefan	22	stepson	in/out

PREVIOUS EXPERIENCE WITH therapy:

_√_ NMC Hospital ____ date: 4/96 ____ outcome little change: same
_√_ other: outpt Hospital date: 9/94 outcome little change

PRESENT MEDICATIONS (WHO, WHAT, WHY, MONITORING PHYSICIAN):
Wellbutrin 50mg, Prozac kid   } Both Maria and Cecilia
Glucatrol kid

PROBLEM/S AS DESCRIBED BY FAMILY:
Concerns of all regarding Maria and Cecilia's depression and diabetes
Maria feels she is going crazy
José relates no personal problems

PRESENTING PROBLEM/S (identify session # in which each becomes known):
___ anxiety
___ chemical dependency
_√_ depression
___ divorce issues
___ disability stress
___ child abuse/neglect-rape
___ eating disorder
___ incest ___ child ___ adult survivor
___ grief
___ marital stress
___ school problem
___ parent-child conflict
___ suicide threat
___ sexual disorder
___ work stress
___ spousal abuse
_√_ other individual: obesity
___ other family:

FAMILY'S IDENTIFIED PATIENT: Cecilia

SUBSYSTEM FAMILY BELIEVES INVOLVED IN PRESENTING PROBLEM:
_√_ individual ___ marital ___ parental ___ extended

FAMILY'S ATTEMPTS TO SOLVE PROBLEM:
Medication and individual therapy. Some family
sessions at the hospital.

D. SUMMARY ASSESSMENT INFORMATION COLLECTED IN FILE:
[√] all relevant informed consent forms
[√] SAFE/GRRF SELF-EVAL?
[√] Beck Inventory
[√] 10-minute research videotape segment of what family wants to change
[√] Goal Attainment Scale completion and evaluation
[√] Genogram
[√] Therapist Periodic Assessment
[√] Casenotes for each session
[√] Contact Summary Sheet complete
[√] Family's Evaluation of Services

1996, LCN

Figure 4.5   Closed-File Intake Form.

59

DUTY TO WARN

Confidentiality and privileged communication remain rights of all clients according to state law. However, some courts have held that if a client intends to take harmful or dangerous action against another human being, or against himself/herself, a therapist has a DUTY TO WARN A) the person who is likely to suffer the result of harmful behavior, B) the person's family, or C) the family of the client who intends to harm himself/herself. In cases of suspected child or elder abuse, the therapist has a responsibility to notify the appropriate authorities of such allegations. Court orders, especially in cases involving children's safety, can sometimes require disclosure of records. Third-party payment from an insurance company will require some level of disclosure as covered by specialized release forms.

The therapist will, whenever possible, share with the client the intent to notify relatives or authorities. In cases of threatened homicide or suicide or exposure of a spouse to AIDS, every effort will be made to resolve the issue before such a breach of confidentiality takes place.

M. Dobbs
_____
Therapist

I have read the above and understand the therapist's professional responsibility to make such decisions where necessary.

Date 8·27·95   Client   Maria Rodriguez

Date 8·27·95   Client   José Rodriguez

Date 8·27·95   Client   Cecilia Rodriguez

Date _____   Client _____

Figure 4.6 Duty to Warn Form.

and Maria read and signed it. The state law required parental or guardian permission for the mental health treatment of minor children. Maria then read and signed the Parental Release form (Figure 4.7), granting permission for Cecilia to receive therapy services. Mary explained the Permission for Consultation/Taping/Research form (Figure 4.8); both José and Maria read and signed it. The family had been referred by another counselor who was

PARENTAL RELEASE FORM

Cecilia Rodriguez
Child/children names/s

has my permission to participate in the therapy services offered by ___*CHSD, INC.*___ .
It is my understanding that all client material is confidential and will not be released to any agency or person without the written permission of all family members participating in therapy, with some legal exceptions. Work with an individual child is generally more productive if parents voluntarily agree to not request information about the child's private session. The therapist agrees to share with the parent/s any information which is necessary for the safety of the child.

Maria Rodriguez
Parent's/legal custodian's signature

2910 Walnut
Plano Texas 75041
Parent's/legal custodian's address

_9 72-680-8713_
Parent's/legal custodian's telephone number

If divorced, my divorce order identifies me as a managing conservator:

_____ yes or _____ no

_9-4-94_
Date

Figure 4.7 Parental Release Form.

PERMISSION FOR
CONSULTATION/TAPING/RESEARCH

In order to provide the best quality of services possible, it is sometimes helpful for the therapist to consult with other supervisory therapists regarding a particular client's difficulties. It is necessary to receive your permission in order to discuss your situation with other professional therapists. Video or audio taping of sessions is also helpful for the therapist to review in order to gain more insights regarding the clients. These tapes can also be helpful for clients to review themselves by making special arrangements with the therapist. Research efforts can improve the quality of services offered.

AGREEMENT:

We understand that our privacy will be treated with utmost professionalism and respect. We realize that permission for consultation and taping is extremely helpful to the therapist to constantly improve the quality of services, but refusal to give permission will not in any way interfere with receiving professional services. Permission for research is voluntary and means that information about our family will possibly be used anonymously and confidentially for research purposes only.

This agreement will remain in effect until 1 year following termination of services with J&L Human Systems Development.

I give permission for (initial each):

consultation   *MR   CR   JR*

taping   *MR   CR   JR*

research   *MR   CR   JR*

Client *Maria Rodriguez*   Date *8-27-95*

Client *José Rodriguez*   Date *8-27-95*

Therapist *Mary S. Dobby, PhD*

Figure 4.8   Permission for Consultation/Taping/Research Form.

willing to provide his records; therefore, José and Maria completed the Consent for the Release of Confidential Information form (Figure 4.9).

    After the above permission forms were signed, Mary began videotaping the remainder of the session. She interviewed the family and completed Section C of the Clinic Client Intake form (Figure 4.5). Mary observed that the parents were keeping the focus on Cecilia, who responded in a surly, withdrawn manner. She did not like being talked about, especially when they discussed her recent history of drug usage and gang involvement. The family indicated that there were few well-maintained routines and that communication was inadequate to solve family problems. Cecilia and Maria joined together to prevent José from participating. Emotionally, the family was in despair. The couple's interactions were

CONSENT FOR THE RELEASE OF CONFIDENTIAL INFORMATION

I understand that my records are protected under federal and state regulations and cannot be disclosed without my written consent unless otherwise provided for in the regulations. I also understand that I may revoke this authorization at any time except to the extent that action has been taken in reliance on it. I also understand that permission to release records must come from all members of the family participating in treatment. This authorization automatically expires 6 months following termination of treatment with _CHSD_ .

• •

I/we authorize therapist [_Mary S. Dobbs, PhD_] TO OBTAIN INFORMATION FROM:

name: _Plano ISD_ phone: _972-356-4110_ fax:_____

address:_____

Check all which apply:

Purpose: ✓ Treatment planning
___ Monitoring of treatment progress
___ Other (must specify):_____

Content: ✓ Information regarding attendance at scheduled apointments
✓ Status with program: admitted, discharged, etc.
___ Assessment of treatment needs
___ Treatment progress
✓ Other (must specify): _school records, including testing_

• •

I/we authorize therapist [_Mary S. Dobbs_] TO RELEASE INFORMATION TO:

name: _Plano ISD_ phone: _972-356-4110_ fax:_____

address:_____

Check all which apply:

Purpose: ___ Treatment planning
✓ Monitoring of treatment progress
___ Other (must specify):_____

Content: ✓ Information regarding attendance at scheduled apointments
✓ Status with program: admitted, discharged, etc.
___ Assessment of treatment needs
✓ Treatment progress
___ Other (must specify):_____

• •

Client name: _CECILIA RODRIQUEZ_ Signature: _Cecilia Rodriquez_ Date: _8-27-95_
MARIA RODRIQUEZ _Maria Rodriquez_
Client name: _JOSÉ RODRIQUEZ_ Signature: _Jose Rodriquez_ Date: _8-27-95_

Therapist name: _MARY S. DOBBS, PhD_ Signature: _Mary S. Dobbs_ Date: _8-27-95_

Figure 4.9 Consent for the Release of Confidential Information.

PROFILE CHART:

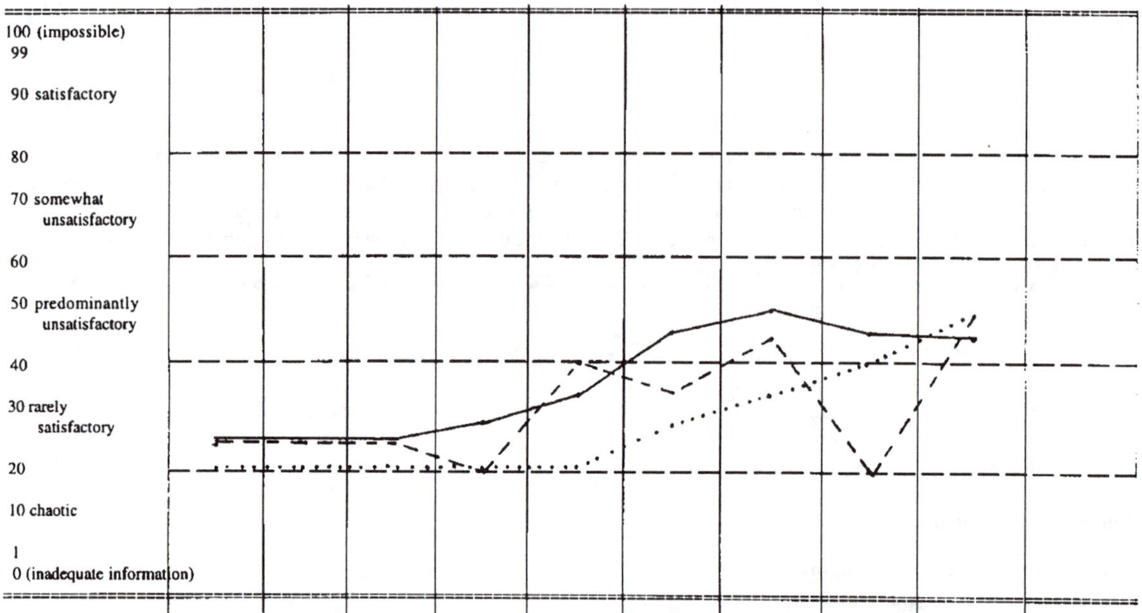

ASSIGNMENT OF SCORES SUMMARY TABLE:

SESSION NUMBER: [indicate termination session by circling session number]	1	2	3	4	5	6	7	8	⑨	10
DATE:	9-27-95	9-4-95	9-11-95	9-18-95	10-1-95	10-8-95	10-15-95	10-22-95	10-29-95	
INTERACTIONAL:	25	25	25	20	40	35	45	20	50	
ORGANIZATIONAL:	25	25	25	30	35	45	50	45	45	
EMOTIONAL CLIMATE:	20	20.	20	20	20	30	35	40	50	
GLOBAL: THERAPIST	23	20	22	30	22	37	43	35	47	
TEAM X NOTES	INTAKE	SUICIDAL NO MEDS	GENOGRAM	MOVE?	CONFRONT MOM	F-D COALITION	M DEPRESSED	GAS		
CLIENTS PRESENT:	M,F,D	D	M,F,D	M,F,D,S,S	M,F,D	F,D	M,F,D	M,F,D	M,F,D	

case file number/name: ___1206___   therapist: ___MSD___

Figure 4.10 GARF Profile Chart for Case Illustration.

openly hostile. No family member seemed to know how to support another. Mary gave the GARF Self-Report metaphor form and the SAFE to the family members, requesting that they complete it in her absence. She returned to the office to obtain a No Suicide Agreement form for Cecilia's completion. After the no suicide agreement was discussed and signed, the session was summarized, and planning for future sessions was introduced. The family agreed that Cecilia would come to the next session alone, to relate her personal concerns and that after that session they would all return on a weekly basis.

Mary rated the family on the GARF scales and plotted it on the graph (Figure 4.10). She scored the BDIs, scored and plotted the SAFE (Figure 4.11), looked at the GARF Metaphor Self-Report (Figure 4.12), and completed the Contact Summary Sheet (Figure 4.13), Case Notes (Figure 4.14), and Therapist Periodic Assessment (Figure 4.15). Mary rated the family a 23 on the GARF. Families who are marked in that range generally are viewed as obviously and seriously dysfunctional and have few periods of satisfactory relations.

SYSTEMIC ASSESSMENT OF THE FAMILY ENVIRONMENT [SAFE]

SCORING & GRAPHING INSTRUCTIONS

Using the assigned weights to each response, total the interactional scores under each A/B/C subsystem level [1st 6 questions] and plot that sum with the organizational score [last question under each level] as the coordinates on the graph; identify the plotted points as A-1, B-1, and C-1 [using the number to identify the family member]. To obtain a total family system mean score, sum the scores for all the subsystem levels used [T blank below] and divide by the number of levels used to obtain the M [mean] score; plot M-1 on the graph. Using different colors to mark each family member provides a visual family system comparison on one graph. For research purposes, obtain a SAFE score by adding together the interactional and organizational average scores; use the SAFE score to correlate with other assessment scores, such as the GARF.

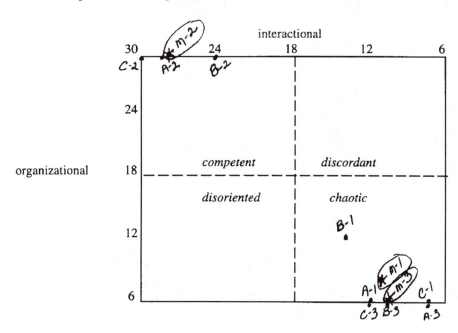

Client file number: *1206*

SAFE Scores Compiled:

Family member: 1 = mother/wife
2 = father/husband
3 = daughter
4 = son
5 = other:_____

	interactional					organizational				
	1	2	3	4	5	1	2	3	4	5
A	*12*	*28*	*8*	___	___	*6*	*30*	*6*	___	___
B	*14*	*24*	*10*	___	___	*12*	*30*	*6*	___	___
C	*8*	*30*	*12*	___	___	*6*	*30*	*6*	___	___
[T	*34*	*82*	*30*	___	___	*24*	*90*	*18*	___	___] (not plotted)
M	*11.3*	*27.3*	*10*	___	___	+ *8*	*30*	*6*	___	___

Date of completion *8-27-94*

GARF rating today *23*
[I = *25* ; O = *25* ; E = *20*]

divided by # of family members = SAFE score: *30.9*

Figure 4.11 SAFE scores plotted.

Case file no: _____ 1206

GARF Self-Report for Families

These stories were adapted from Goldilocks and the Three Bears by Robert Southey, Little Red Riding Hood by Charles Perrault, Cinderella by Charles Perrault, Hansel and Gretel by Grimm Brothers, and The Ugly Duckling by Hans Andersen. These stories, created by Alice McDonald, are used as metaphors to explain family functioning. June 1996.

Directions: Please read through each story below and decide which fairy tale is most like the family you live in right now. Put a check in the blank by your first choice.

_____ THE THREE BEARS

The three bears were normally a very happy family. When they had problems, they would have a round table discussion to work through new goals or rules. The parents were definitely in charge with baby bear following through with his chores and obeying the rules of the house. When baby bear wanted something special or wanted to go somewhere, his parents always discussed baby bear's requests and presented the decision to him. The parents always made baby bear feel secure and safe because he knew he could rely on his parents. The parent bears were affectionate toward one another and very loving to their young son. Baby bear said he wanted to be just like his daddy when he grew up. When the break-in by Goldilocks occurred, they had been out in the park playing together. When they discovered that their house had been broken into, they were very angry that their possessions had been tampered with. They called the police, changed the locks on the doors, and remembered always to close the windows before they left the house again.

Jose _____ LITTLE RED RIDING HOOD

Little Red Riding Hood's parents were generally happy with one another. Little Red's daddy went to work every day while her mother cleaned house, cooked, and sewed for the family. Little Red had some chores to do and she usually followed through with them. She knew she was loved by both parents and enjoyed playing board games with her parents and going places with them. Sometimes, however Little Red's dad would get upset with his wife because she would spend too much money or tell him some critical remark that her mother had made about their lifestyle. When they had these arguments, they would send Little Red off to grandma's so they could argue. They never seemed to be able to solve these problems. When Little Red crossed paths with the wolf in the woods, she realized that she had not really learned from her parents how to communicate well or solve problems. She felt a little uneasy facing such stressful encounters.

Maria _____ CINDERELLA

Cinderella lived in a family where, if you were to draw a circle, she would be standing outside the circle by herself. Her step-mother and step-sisters only communicated with Cinderella when they told her to do some chore or when they wanted to be sarcastic to her. Since Cinderella's daddy was not around very often, his wife and step-daughters were able to put on a friendly front to Cinderella in the presence of her dad. Cinderella's dad sensed some unidentified anxiety in himself when he was with his family, but could never quite put his finger on the problem. When Cinderella was 16 years old, she met the Prince of the Realm who asked her to marry him. It was after Cinderella had left home that her dad realized how his wife and step-daughters had emotionally and verbally abused Cinderella.

Cecilia _____ HANSEL AND GRETEL

Hansel and Gretel were two happy children until their mother died. They were still grieving over their mother's death when their father remarried. Their father was a wood cutter and they had never had enough money for luxuries. But now that the demand for wood was at an all-time low, they barely had enough to eat. The step-mother knew that Hansel and Gretel resented her, and she did everything she could to make them feel unwanted. The step-mother grabbed control of the family when she married the wood cutter. She demanded that her husband and step children do what she wanted without talking about it together. On two occasions, she had her husband take his two children to the woods and run off leaving them there. During the last trip to the woods, Hansel and Gretel found a gang to join and did not return home. They learned to steal, take illegal drugs, and drink alcohol. The step-mother lived to regret her actions because her husband left her over the grief that he experienced in losing his children.

_____ THE UGLY DUCKLING

The ugly duckling was born to a mother duck that did not want babies. Therefore, she ignored them as best she could. One of the ducks in the family felt especially isolated and detached. He was called the "ugly-one" by everyone in the pond. His desire was to be in a family like other families that ate their meals together, played together, cared for each other, and showed affection to one another. What the ugly duckling learned in his family was that everyone fended for himself with regard to food, clothing, fun, and affection. He learned to fight in order to survive. Ugly duckling tried to make a connection with the other ducks in the pond, but he was rebuffed at every turn. He spent more and more time by himself, until finally he had little desire to make a connection with others and went to live in a corner of the pond by himself.

PLEASE COMPLETE:

Today's date: 8-27-95

Family Member completing:
_____ mother _____ father _____ daughter _____ son
_____ grandmother _____ grandfather _____ other;

Figure 4.12 GARF Self-Report Family Summary.

CONTACT SUMMARY SHEET
[attached to front of folder]

Client no: *1206*

Family name: *RODRIQUEZ*

Therapist: *M S D*

Insurance carrier: *PRUDENTIAL*

Date	Interview #/ phone contact	family members present	client fee check #/cash	insurance fee: amount	authorization #	date billed	date received
8-25-95	?	Mother scheduled appt					
8-27-95	I #1	M, F, D	—	$50.00	18593-01	10-1-95	11-1-95
9-4-95	I #2	D	—	$50.00	" -02	10-1-95	11-1-95
9-11-95	I #3	M, F, D	—	$50.00	"	10-1-95	11-1-95
9-18-95	I #4	M, F, D, S, S	—	$50.00	"	10-1-95	11-1-95
10-1-95	I #5	M, F, D	—	$50.00	"	11-1-95	12-1-95
10-8-95	I #6	F, D	—	$50.00	"	11-1-95	12-1-95
10-9-95	?	Mother called to confirm would be in next week					
10-15-95	I #7	M, F, D	—	$50.00	"	11-1-95	12-1-95
10-22-95	I #8	M, F, D	—	$50.00	"	11-1-95	12-1-95
10-29-95	I #9	M, F, D	—	$50.00	"	11-1-95	12-1-95

Figure 4.13 Case Contact Summary Sheet.

CASE NOTES

Client Number __1206__   Clients present __Cecilia, Marie, Jose__

Session Number __1__   Therapist __Dobbs, M.__   Team __none__

Date __8/27/95__   Next apt. date __9/4/95__ , time __4pm__

GARF rating: therapist __23__   [I = __25__, O = __25__ , E = __20__];   team members average global __N/A__

[use attached code sheet for "interventions used" & "interventions planned" below; write in "other" as appropriate; check & explain "goals"]

INTERVENTIONS USED: __Joining - 1,3,4; Assessing - 7,8,11; Strategizing - 22,25__

SYSTEMIC HYPOTHESIS [including extended as well as nuclear family system]:

Organizational = Power issues predominate. Suicide threats and attempts serve as a power play to focus attention on Cecilia, who feels her older brothers are more special. Mother and daughter collude openly; Father and daughter covertly.

Interactional = The family is stressed by work routine and chronic depression. There is little energy for negotiation of solutions.

THERAPEUTIC GOAL [check focus goal/s for next session]:

organizational:
   ✓ marital: __strengthen dyad__
   ✓ parental: __discuss Cecilia's ability to manipulate__
   ✓ sibling: __strengthen Cecilia's place here__
   ___ former parent: _____

interactional:
   ✓ improve understanding needed to ___ solve problems / ✓ negotiate boundaries through speaking/listening skills
   ✓ increase supportedness outcome of communication through greater ✓ togetherness / ✓ autonomy

ASSIGNMENT:

NEXT SESSION INTERVENTIONS PLANNED: __Interactional autonomy work with Cecilia.__

SIGNIFICANT FAMILY EVENTS OF THE WEEK:

Figure 4.14   Research Case Notes Form.

The SAFE family self-assessment illustrated that the family members generally viewed their situation differently from one another, though Maria and Cecilia tended to agree. The "As it is now" scores indicated that both Maria and Cecilia viewed the family as chaotic. José, on the other hand, viewed the family as competent (see Figure 4.11). Apparently José either viewed their situation much more favorably or attempted to present their situation as less problematic than did the rest of the family. Discrepancies in perception/representation are helpful to note in planning treatment. In this case, the IPs in the family were able to reveal the system problem on paper.

Mary then recorded her case notes. Because she tracks her interventions for research purposes, she used a Research Case Note form (Figure 4.14). Planning for the second session was noted on this form. Mary planned to address autonomy issues with Cecilia, who appeared to be manipulative in order to control her ability to be included as an important member of the family. During the second session, Cecilia discussed the week's

THERAPIST PERIODIC ASSESSMENT

Therapist_____M SD_____   Date___8-27-95___

Family Name___RODRIQUEZ___   Client Number___1206___

1. Presenting problem/s of each family member:

   Cecilia (14) - I'm not treated equally. Mom is never home. Rape.
   Maria (47) - Cecilia's suicide attempts. Her obesity & diabetes.
   José (47) - Cecilia's suicide attempts

2. Family's attempted solution(s) & results:

   In patient therapy for mother & daughter - depression → limited results
   Brief family therapy at the hospital - they see limited results

3. Life cycle stage: ___Young Adult ___Married ___Young Children ___Adolescents ✓Launching ___Later Life

   Family Structure: ___Married ___Separated ___Divorced ✓Remarried ___Never Married

4. Therapist Conceptualizations:

   A. Organizational & interactional 3-level hypothesis:

   This family is "warring" for leadership. Interactionally, there are few effective communication skills in place and apparently few problem solving skills. The family structure includes few established routines. The daughter promotes coalitions with both parents, preventing strong parenting. Despair is evident in all.

   B. External stressor/s

   Father on night shift. Mother on days. He insists on driving her to work and gets little sleep. Poor maternal extended family relationships; paternal extended family in Mexico. Cultural differences between mother & father

   C. External & family strengths:

   The family has a strong work ethic and a strong desire to be a happy family

   D. Family typology (from SAFE/other assessment instrument):

   Mother & daughter - chaotic, Father = competent

   E. Family of origin influences: genogram in file

   F. GARF: Initial = __23__   Current = _____   GAF: Initial = __30__   Current = _____

   G. DSM IV Diagnosis: Axis I __294.32 · daughter__   Axis II __V 71.09__

   Axis III __250.00 Diabetes - II - mother__ Axis IV _family support, educational problems_

5. Therapeutic goal/s & intervention plan:

   Address power imbalances and coalitions
   Explore causes of depression that permeate this family.
   Facilitate the establishment of routines and rituals.

Figure 4.15   Periodic Assessment Form.

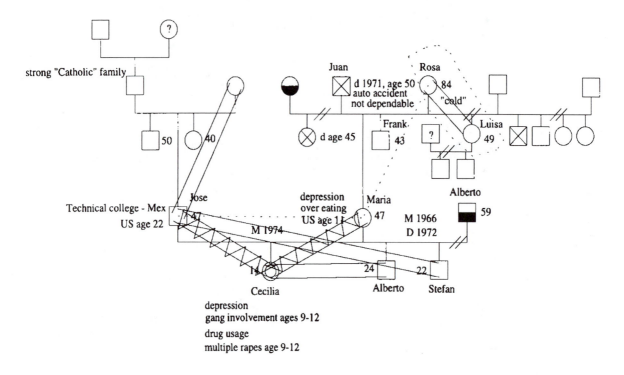

Case 1206 - Rodriquez 9-11-95

Figure 4.16 Case study family genogram.

events with the family. Nothing appeared to have changed, and the GARF notations remained relatively similar. She did respond with blame, calling her parents "neglectful" when confronted about her manipulative power stances around suicide. She calmed and agreed that this was her tactic and that it was time to look to more functional ways of relating to her family. She requested that her brothers be invited to a session by Mary, hoping that such an invitation would convey her need. She was encouraged to speak directly with her brothers about this.

Session 3 was attended by Maria, Cecilia, and José. A genogram (Figure 4.16) was done to explore family-of-origin concerns. It became apparent that Maria and her mother and sister did not have functional relationships. José perceived that he was close to his family of origin and believed this closeness was healthy. He discussed how he missed them. This session basically explored the emotional understructure of the family. Little movement was noted but, overall, the emotional tone seemed to improve.

Session 4 was attended by all family members. The financial stressors were the topic brought into the session by the family, who was considering moving because of limited funds. They had just recently purchased a home that was expensive for them and believed that they should return to their previous home, which they were currently renting to the second son. Maria took an active role in this session, becoming a sharer of overt power with José as they discussed this. They made little progress in problem-solving skills but did begin to shift organization through shared power. In the next family session, Cecilia chose to confront her mother, stating that Maria had no empathy for Cecilia's past suffering. Cecilia stated that Maria had intentionally neglected her. José "stayed in his corner" and let the women speak. He was distressed because of his cultural belief that mother and

GOAL ATTAINMENT SCALE

NAME/I.D. #: _____1206_____   Time Likely Needed to Achieve Goals: _____4_____ WEEKS

Date Developed: _10-22-95_ Date Evaluated: _____   Total # of Sessions Goals Worked on: _____   Total GAS Score: _____

LEVEL OF GOAL ACHIEVEMENT FOR FAMILY CHANGE:	FAMILY CHANGE NEEDED: To work together (José + Maria) regarding finances IMPORTANCE: ( )	FAMILY CHANGE NEEDED: IMPORTANCE: ( )	FAMILY CHANGE NEEDED: IMPORTANCE: ( )
MORE CHANGE THAN BELIEVE IS POSSIBLE	They follow a budget and plan together		
MORE CHANGE THAN REALLY EXPECT	They make a budget		
SATISFACTORY CHANGE	They talk about expenses		
SOME CHANGE BUT STILL ROOM TO GROW	José gives Maria extra money		
NO CHANGE FROM WHEN STARTED	José takes the money and no one else sees it		

REVISED 12-8-96: form developed by Lynelle C. Yingling, PhD, J&L Human Systems Development, 570 E. Quail Run Rd., Rockwall, TX 75087, 972/771-9985

Figure 4.17 Goal Attainment Scale.

daughter must get along. Cecilia appeared to be challenging Maria's attempt to align with José (previous session). Maria held her own and began to strengthen family rules. Communication skills and empathy were the focus.

Maria did not come to Session 6. José and Cecilia had formed a coalition during a family argument, and Maria chose not to participate, asserting her independence. Emotional empathy also improved as José and Cecilia discussed Maria and her depression. They began to regard her needs. However, during the following week, José became angered at Cecilia and punished her by hitting her with a broom. This became the focus of Session 7, when it is revealed that the family had experienced this kind of violence before. A nonviolence contract is negotiated. José had a difficult time, invoking his stance that his actions were culturally acceptable. A shift began to happen in interaction and structure, and Mary and he addressed this concern. Maria and Cecilia actively negotiated with José to resolve the conflict. By Session 8, Maria's depression had reached suicidal levels. She withdrew from the family, stating that no one listens to her needs. However, this time Cecilia and José listened and did not unite against her. There was some emotional support emerging for this family. By Session 9, the family was talking together. Many issues were unresolved. The GAS (Figure 4.17) was used to address negotiating skills. Maria and José were beginning to work as a team. Although there was still much pain present, they were beginning to support each other. This false sense of success caused the family to leave therapy (see Figure 4.18). They returned later, after Cecilia was again hospitalized.

TERMINATION FORM

client no: _____1206_____   therapist: _____MSD_____

date: _____11-1-95_____   family name: _____Rodriguez_____

1. Summary of case to date: [no. of sessions, issues addressed, family members participating in therapy, degree of progress made]

This family was seen for 9 sessions with all members in the home participating at least once.

Goals worked on:

1. more overt power balance + improved communication in marital dyad
2. stronger parental dyad
3. increased emotional connectedness among all members

Assessments indicated improved in all goal areas, though still functioning at a marginally satisfactory level.

2. Significant information regarding the last session, including date and reason/s for termination:

10-29-95

Family was beginning to negotiate and seemed to be more confident. Depression in mother and daughter had subsided. Family chose to leave therapy.

3. Recommendations for further treatment:

Address communication skills.
Address perceptions of cultural differences between family members
There is still a need for more boundary work.

Figure 4.18 Case Study Termination Form.

ETHICAL GUIDELINES FOR USE OF THE GARF

As illustrated above, the GARF can be a valuable, practical instrument for clinical assessment of family functioning. Ethical guidelines for use of the GARF are the same guidelines that would be appropriate for any other clinical assessment instrument: (a) the clinician performing the assessment must be competent, and (b) the scores are protected as private client information.

The AAMFT, American Counseling Association (ACA), and American Psychological Association ethical codes require that their members perform within the boundaries of their competence; however, the ethical code of the National Association of Social Workers (NASW) permits members to "accept responsibility or employment only on the basis of existing competence or the intention to acquire the necessary competence" (1996, Section I.B.1). The ACA and American Psychological Association ethical codes are the most stringent concerning assessment and require that assessments be performed only by persons (a) who have training in testing and assessment, (b) who are familiar with psychometric principles (e.g., reliability, validity, related standardization, and error of measurement), and (c) who protect against the misuse of results and include adequate interpretations when releasing the results. Once the GARF score has been assigned to a family, it becomes part of the private client information that must be protected under the ethical codes of the AAMFT, ACA, American Psychological Association, and NASW.

The clinician should review specific requirements for assessment contained within the various codes of ethics that are applicable to his or her setting. If a clinician is required to comply with several codes of ethics, then it is recommended the clinician adhere to the most stringent requirements. The following section briefly discusses the ethical use of the GARF in the contexts of clinical practice, supervision, education, and research.

Clinical Practice

In a clinical practice, the ethical use of the GARF includes many areas, such as the therapist's competency in family assessment, understanding of the GARF and definitions associated with the scale, and protection of client confidentiality. The GARF was intended to be a reliable, global scale of family functioning that would be useful to therapists and nonspecialists (Wynne, 1992). As with all clinical instruments, the therapist should use the GARF in conjunction with other sources of information and not as a substitute for comprehensive client assessment.

Family assessment is an ongoing process that may include, but is not limited to, an intake form completed by the client, a clinical interview by the therapist, a genogram jointly constructed by therapist and client, self-assessments by the clients, and the therapist's observations. W. C. Nichols (1988) recommends that assessment and alliance formation occur simultaneously; thus he defined *clinical assessment* as "a recursive, repetitive process by which the clinician secures adequate understanding of the clients for the purpose of making informed decisions and interventions" (p. 103). The GARF permits a therapist to incorporate assessment into an active system of evaluating the family's current functioning, forming/refining hypotheses, selecting interventions, evaluating therapeutic progress, and planning treatment.

In compliance with the ethical codes of the ACA (1995), AAMFT (1991), and American Psychological Association (1992), therapists may only use those assessment techniques with which they are competent. Competency in using the GARF for assessment requires both training and supervisory feedback. Training may include reading and becoming familiar with the descriptions associated with specific scores on the GARF, practicing by viewing and scoring standardized videotaped vignettes, and viewing client families and comparing assessed scores with those assigned by more experienced clinicians.

Supervision

The ethical use of the GARF in supervision, as discussed here, will focus on the supervisee's overall competency and the supervisee's competency in using the GARF to assess families. MFTs who comply with the AAMFT, ACA, and American Psychological Association codes of ethics are required to evaluate their supervisees. Specifically, "Marriage and family therapists do not permit students, employees, or supervisees to perform or to hold themselves to be competent to perform professional services beyond their training, level of experience, and competence" (AAMFT, 1991, Section 4.2). According to the ACA Code of Ethics (Section E.2.b), the counselor is required to "take reasonable measures to ensure the proper use" of assessment techniques used by supervisees. Thus, the supervisor is required to evaluate the supervisee's overall performance and the supervisee's proper use of assessment.

The supervisor may incorporate the GARF into supervision by allowing the supervisee to compare his or her assessment of the family with the assessment by a supervisor or team. Supervisees may also be required to present their work in a case presentation that includes the GARF assessment scores. If the GARF score assigned by the supervisee and by the supervisor or team are quite similar, this consensus can be helpful feedback to the supervisee. The supervisee may, on the other hand, assess a family much differently than the team or supervisor, and the assigned GARF scores can be useful in quantifying this assessment difference during supervision. In such a case, a supervisor might use the GARF scores to assist a supervisee in gaining more awareness of the family functioning as rated by other clinicians.

Furthermore, the supervisor can use the disparate GARF scores to assist the supervisee in becoming more aware of his or her own personal issues that possibly influence the supervisee's assessment and conceptualization of the family. Jordan and Quinn (1996) discuss three categories of marriage and family therapist impairment: unresolved family-of-origin issues; emotional instability; and false competency. These types of supervisee impairment may surface in various ways, including GARF scores assigned by the supervisee that are quite different from those assigned by other therapists. For example, a supervisee who is assessing a family and experiences transference might assign an unusually high or low GARF score based on the supervisee's unresolved family-of-origin issues or emotional instability. Similarly, a supervisee who is unable to adequately conceptualize a family and plan interventions may assign GARF scores that appear random or unrelated to the family's current functioning. When the supervisor faces decisions regarding remediation or retention of a supervisee, it may be helpful to examine the difference, if any, between GARF scores assigned by the supervisee and those assigned by other therapists. A supervisor also might question the appropriateness of a supervisee who consistently rates families much higher or much lower on the GARF than do experienced therapists.

Education

Ethical use of the GARF in an educational setting focuses on the trainee's competency in assessment. Because the GARF is a measure of relational functioning, we believe an adequate training in family systems is crucial to using the GARF appropriately in a clinical setting. The GARF concepts and classification levels may be useful to professionals and nonspecialists; however, a therapist who is knowledgeable about family systems has likely had the additional training and experience found valuable in using the GARF.

Training methods used in the MFCCC (Yingling et al., 1994a, 1994b) have been discussed earlier in this volume. It is recommended that the trainee complete an introductory course in systemic marriage and family theories before using the GARF. The trainee should also complete an introductory course in family assessment and become familiar with the major psychometric principles (e.g., reliability, validity, related standardization, and error of measurement). Furthermore, the trainee should understand the descriptions assigned to the three categories (interactional, organizational, emotional) and the levels of functioning used in the GARF. Next, the trainee should practice assigning GARF scores and compare those scores with the scores assigned by more experienced therapists who are assessing the same clients. Finally, the trainee should incorporate the GARF scores into cases presented in supervision so the trainee can receive feedback.

Research

Ethical use of the GARF in research includes protection of the clients' welfare, voluntary participation, informed consent, protection of clients' confidentiality, and the appropriate reporting and use of information collected. A researcher should become familiar with the relevant professional codes of ethics, institutional rules, and the federal and state laws and regulations regarding research with humans. The codes of ethics for the AAMFT, ACA, American Psychological Association, and NASW require that a member informs clients that (a) research participation is voluntary, the potential risks of participation, and that they will not be penalized if they decline to participate; (b) the clients' welfare will be protected; and (c) the information gathered about a client will be treated as confidential unless the client has previously signed a waiver. Because of the complex and evolving nature of federal and state laws and regulations, plus any institutional rules and requirements, a detailed discussion of ethical research is beyond the scope of this volume; however, the following presents some of the specific requirements of various codes of ethics and how these were addressed in the MFCCC research.

The AAMFT Code of Ethics (1991) requires, in part, that therapists "respect the participants' freedom to decline or withdraw from the research at any time" (Section 5.3), "be dedicated to high standards of scholarship and present accurate information" (Section 3.3), and "make efforts to prevent the distortion or misuse of their clinical research findings" (Section 3.7). Thus, a therapist using the GARF in research should include procedures that permit subjects to decline to participate and withdraw from the research. The therapist should include procedures to protect the study from internal and external threats to validity (Meara & Schmidt, 1991). After the research is completed, the therapist must accurately report the findings, including any limitations or caveats related to the findings. Participants in the MFCCC study gave their written consent on the Permission for Consultation/Taping/ Research form (Appendix F), usually during the initial therapy session. In Chapter 2 of this volume we attempted to present the MFCCC research findings clearly and in the context of other relevant research.

The Ethical Principles of the American Psychological Association (1992) further require that confidential information entered into databases "available to persons whose access has not been consented to by the recipient" (Section 5.07) be protected by use of coding or other techniques that replace personal identifiers. In the MFCCC study, the database contained a case number instead of the family name, and corresponding clinical information was coded (see Chapter 2).

The NASW Code of Ethics (Section I.E.) similarly requires that the research be "guided by the conventions of scholarly inquiry" and the social worker "consider carefully possible consequences to human beings." Furthermore, the social work clinician is required to "protect participants from unwarranted physical or mental discomfort, distress, harm, danger, or deprivation" (NASW, 1996, Section I.E.). A clinician using the GARF in research would likely plan the proposed study on the basis of a review of the literature, research hypotheses and questions, and a methodology that will likely answer the research questions. Furthermore, the research will incorporate procedures designed to protect participants (Meara & Schmidt, 1991). In the MFCCC study, a comprehensive review of the existing literature was completed, then research hypotheses and questions were developed. The participants in the MFCCC study were attending family therapy and had previously consented to participate in research. The MFCCC research was descriptive and correlational; therefore, the participants were not exposed to experimental treatments that might potentially cause unwarranted discomfort, distress, harm, danger, or deprivation.

SUMMARY

The GARF appears to be potentially useful in various clinical settings, both as a screening instrument and for treatment planning. Clinicians who want to ethically use the GARF should have a fundamental knowledge of family systems and assessment, become familiar with the GARF instrument, and read the applicable professional codes of ethics and the federal and state laws and regulations. We believe the GARF can be useful in clinical practice, trainee education, supervision, and research.

CHAPTER 5

Comparison with Other Family Assessment Tools

Foundations for the GARF
Model Highlights: Beavers System, Circumplex, and McMaster Models
Newly developed related assessment tools: SAFE and GAS
Clinical interview assessment tools: Impact on the GARF

This chapter puts the GARF in context by comparing it with other family assessment tools. The three models from which the GARF evolved are reviewed. Instruments that we have developed and used as adjuncts to the GARF are described. Last, the impacts of the rater's clinical interview assessment skills on the GARF rating are noted.

FOUNDATIONS FOR THE GARF

The GARF was not intended to be another new and different model, but rather an integration of already-known models. Three models provided the conceptual foundation: the Beavers Systems Model, the Olson Circumplex Model, and the McMaster Model of Family Functioning (GAP, 1996). All three models have been in existence and undergone extensive discussion and testing for over a decade. Tables 5.1, 5.2, 5.3, and 5.4 compare the variables, scoring groupings, and typologies of these three models with the GARF. Included in the comparison is the SAFE (Systemic Assessment of the Family Environment), developed by Yingling parallel to the introduction of the GARF. The SAFE is a self-report global functioning scale that uses a multigenerational perspective that we have found to be very helpful to use in combination with the GARF.

The Beavers (Beavers & Hampson, 1990), Olson (Kaslow, 1996; Walsh, 1993), and Mc-Master (Walsh, 1993) models described in Walsh (1993) each have procedures for scoring observational clinical ratings (outsider perspective) as well as self-report instruments (insider perspective). Our collective assessment experience draws heavily from the Beavers and Olson models, with no practical experience with the McMaster Model. Being familiar with these various models is a way of deepening one's understanding of the GARF.

Table 5.1
Foundational Family Assessment Model Comparison: Variables Measured

Model	Major Variables	Subscale Descriptors
Beavers Systems Model	Interactional competence	Overt power, parental coalition, closeness, mythology, goal-directed negotiation, clarity of expression, responsibility, permeability, range of feelings, mood and tone, unresolvable conflict, empathy, & global
	Interactional style	Dependency, adult conflict, proximity, social presentation, expressed closeness, aggressive/assertive behavior, expression of positive/negative feelings, and global
Circumplex Model	Cohesion (disengaged/ separated/connected/ enmeshed)	Emotional bonding, boundaries, coalitions, time, space, friends, decision making, interests and recreation
	Flexibility (rigid/ structured/flexible/ chaotic)	Leadership (control, discipline), negotiation styles, role relationships, and relationship rules
	Communication (low/ facilitating/high)	Listening skills, speaking skills, self-disclosure, clarity, continuity tracking, respect and regard
McMaster Model of Family Functioning	Problem solving	Level to maintain effective family functioning
	Communication	Clear verbal messages directed at person for whom message intended
	Roles	Established patterns for providing resources, nurturance, support; supporting personal development; maintaining and managing family systems; providing adult sexual gratification; tasks clearly and equitably assigned and carried out responsibly
	Affective responsiveness	Members able to experience appropriate affect over range of stimuli
	Affective involvement	Members interested in and value each other's activities and concerns
	Behavior control	Expresses and maintains standards for physical protection, psychobiological needs, and social situations

Variable Comparisons

If one compares the identified variables across the various models in Table 5.1, one will see that the GARF concepts of problem solving seem to weave through the other models. Beavers names both of his subscales *interactional* and uses descriptors such as *goal-directed negotiation, clarity of expression, unresolvable conflict, aggressive/assertive behavior*, and *expression of positive/negative feelings*. Olson's clinical rating scale includes a dimension specifically on communication, including descriptors such as *listening skills, speaking skills, self-disclosure, clarity, continuity tracking*, and *respect and regard*. He also includes negotiation styles in his description of flexibility and *decision making* under cohesion. The McMaster model includes two related variables: *problem solving* and *communication*, meaning clear verbal messages directed at the correct person. Descriptions of the SAFE (Table 5.2) interactional processes variable include *self-disclosure, listening*, and *understanding*. These various model descriptors seem compatible with the GARF description of problem solving as "skills in negotiating goals, rules, and routines; adabtability to stress; communication skills; ability to resolve conflict" (American Psychiatric Association, 1994, p. 758).

The GARF organization variable seems to be described in the Beavers model with such terms as *overt power, parental coalition, responsibility*, and *proximity*. Olson uses such terms

Table 5.2
New Family Assessment Model Comparison: Variables Measured

Model	Major Variables	Subscale Descriptors
GARF	Problem solving/interactional	Skills in negotiating goals, rules, and routines; adaptability to stress; communication skills; ability to resolve conflict
	Organization	Maintenance of interpersonal roles and subsystem boundaries; hierarchical functioning, coalitions and distribution of power, control and responsibility
	Emotional climate	Tone and range of feelings; quality of caring, empathy, involvement and attachment/commitment; sharing of values; mutual affective responsiveness, respect and regard; and quality of sexual functioning
SAFE	Organizational structure	Egalitarian marital/executive subsystem, parental hierarchy in nuclear family, egalitarian power structure in adult extended family
	Interactional processes	Self-disclosure, listening, understanding; joining, allowing change and individuality, and providing appropriate supportiveness in each of the three subsystem levels: marital, parent–child, and adult–former parent

as *boundaries, coalitions, leadership, role relationships,* and *relationship rules.* The McMaster model variables of roles and behavior control seem to be compatible with GARF organization, using such phrases as *maintaining and managing family systems, tasks clearly and equitably assigned and carried out responsibly,* and *maintains standards.* The SAFE variable of organizational structure identifies appropriate role definitions in terms of decision-making power in the marital, parental, and adult extended family subsystems. Again, all these descriptors seem compatible with the GARF description of organization: "maintenance of interpersonal roles and subsystem boundaries; hierarchical functioning, coalitions and distribution of power, control and responsibility" (American Psychiatric Association, 1994, p. 758).

The emotional climate is described in the *DSM–IV* as "tone and range of feelings; quality of caring, empathy, involvement and attachment/commitment; sharing of values; mutual affective responsiveness, respect and regard; and quality of sexual functioning" (American Psychiatric Association, 1994, p. 758). Beavers uses the terms *closeness, mythology, empathy, dependency,* and *expressed closeness.* Olson describes *emotional bonding, interests and recreation,* and *respect and regard.* The McMaster model seems to emphasize this dimension heavily, with such descriptors as *patterns for providing resources, nurturance, support; supporting personal development; providing adult sexual gratification; affective responsiveness; affective involvement;* and *physical protection, psychobiological needs, and social situations.* Related SAFE comments are described under such interactional processes as *joining, allowing change and individuality,* and *providing appropriate supportiveness* in each of the three subsystem levels.

Typologies Comparison

The family functioning typologies used with each model are charted in Table 5.3. The GARF and the Beavers Systems Model each use five levels of functioning, whereas the Circumplex Model and McMaster Family Model restrict the delineation to three. The SAFE has four categories, though the two categories in the middle are grouped together as one or the other weakness; therefore, the SAFE also has three discrete levels of functioning.

All the delineations follow a linear path of extremely low to extremely high functioning. People in the the high-functioning range are not likely to come in for therapy, and the low-

Table 5.3
Family Assessment Model Comparisons: Linear Typologies Used

GARF	Beavers Systems Model	Circumplex Model	McMaster Model	SAFE
Satisfactory	Optimal	Balanced	Superior	Competent
Somewhat unsatisfactory	Adequate			
Predominantly unsatisfactory	Midrange (CP/CF)	Mid-Range	Nonclinical	Discordant/disoriented
Rarely satisfactory	Borderline (CP/CF)			
Chaotic	Severely dysfunctional (CP/CF)	Unbalanced	Severely disturbed	Chaotic

functioning end describes families often needing extreme interventions such as hospitalization or legal constraints. The middle range of functioning may indicate a family that functions well until life stressors escalate their desire to seek therapy. Though each model uses distinct labels, they all appear parallel in concept.

Scoring Procedures Comparisons

Table 5.4 compares the raw score groupings of the five models. The GARF uses a 1–100-point range, with five interval divisions at 20, 40, 60, and 80 points. Use of this extensive scaling allows for very discrete distinguishing of functioning. If less discrete assignment of scores is necessary because of insufficient data, using midpoints of the five descriptive sections (90, 70, 50, 30, or 10) is recommended. Scoring of the GARF is parallel to that of the *DSM* GAF.

The Beavers Systems Model Health/Competence dimension uses a 10-point scale that is reversed, with 1 indicating the highest level of functioning and 10 indicating the lowest. Scaling for this model can also be collapsed into five levels of functioning similar to the GARF. The five scoring groupings of the GARF and the Beavers Systems Model parallel the five distinct typologies. Scoring of the Beavers Stylistic dimension of functioning is based on a 1–5 scale. Similar to the Circumplex Model, the orthogonal mapping of the two dimensions provides a delineation of typologies useful in treatment but not combined for achieving a global rating of functioning. Beavers and Hampson (1990) use the Health/Competence dimension as the primary global rating of functioning. The Self-Report Family Inventory (SRI) uses a scoring sheet to track each question into subscale groupings, identify reversed-scoring items, and calculate a subscale mean for each of the five subscales: Health/Competence, Conflict, Cohesion, Leadership, and Expressiveness. A matrix is provided to profile the family rating using the SFI global and subscale ratings with the clinical rating scale results for the Competence scale (Beavers & Hampson, 1990).

The Circumplex Model and the McMaster Family Model use a less parallel scoring format, based on the number of subscales included in the model. The Circumplex Model (Olson, 1996) uses a linear scoring range of 1–8 for the Family Cohesion and Family Flexibility subscales; both scales are included in the clinical rating scale model and the self-report FACES instrument. The 1–8 range parallels the four typologies included in those two subscales, leading to an orthogonal plotting of 1 of 16 typologies. The rating for the Communication subscale included only in the clinical rating scale uses a 1–6 linear range. No scoring instructions are provided for combining the various subscales into one global rating.

Table 5.4
Family Assessment Model Comparisons: Raw Score Groupings

GARF	Beavers Systems Model	Circumplex Model[a]	McMaster Model	SAFE
100	1	8	7	60
90				
	2	7		
-80-	—		6	
	3			48
70		6		
	4		5	
-60-	—			
	5	5		
50			4	36
	6	4		
-40-	—			
	7		3	
30		3		
				24
-20-	8			
	—	2	2	
10	9			
1	10	1	1	12

Note. High functioning = top of chart.
[a]Linear scoring

Scoring of the McMaster Clinician's Rating Scale (McCRS) is a 1–7 range for each of the seven subscales: General Functioning, Problem Solving, Communication, Roles, Affective Responsiveness, Affective Involvement, and Behavior Control (Fristad, 1989). The General Functioning score is used as the global assessment comparable to the GARF score. Scoring of the self-report Family Assessment Device (FAD) uses a scoring sheet that separates the questions for each of the seven subscale scores, identifies reverse scores, records item and sum values for each subscale, and calculates a mean scale score for each subscale. The mean scale score for each subscale ranges from 1.00 (healthy) to 4.00 (unhealthy).

The self-report SAFE total score also is broken into five levels of scoring, from 12 to 60, based on the numbering assignment given the self-report responses.

MODEL HIGHLIGHTS: BEAVERS SYSTEM, CIRCUMPLEX, AND MCMASTER MODELS

Though all the models overlap substantially with the variables in the GARF, each is more complex in structure and has been developed using a more specific interpretation of family functioning. Identifying the particular characteristics of each model will help the clinician select a model for refining family assessment skills.

Beavers Systems Model Overview

The Beavers Systems Model has evolved over several decades of clinical observation and research, with the first study of communication patterns in families of hospitalized adolescents published in 1965. In 1976, the Timberlawn study was published, detailing "well-functioning families using an interactional, systemic viewpoint" (Walsh, 1993, p. 73). The Beavers Systems Model emphasizes the assessment of family functioning on a continuum of strengths and weaknesses rather than a focus on symptom-based diagnostic categories. Understanding family functioning requires assessment both from the observer/therapist and the family members' self-report; hence, the model includes two clinical rating scales and a self-report instrument (the SFI). A detailed explanation and copy of the clinical rating scales and the self-report instrument are found in Beavers and Hampson's *Successful Families: Assessment and Intervention* (1990).

The original observational scale developed in 1972 (Beavers & Hampson, 1990) entitled Beavers-Timberlawn Family Evaluation Scales has been revised and renamed the Beavers Interactional Competence Scale (Walsh, 1993). The observational scales for Competence and Style use a brief 10-min taped interactional task of the family without the therapist present to allow the researcher/therapist to make neutral ratings. The task generally used is to ask family members what they would like to see changed in the family. This procedure is based on the belief that patterns of system functioning are maintained even in small tasks (Walsh, 1993). The Family Competence scale contains 12 subscale ratings identified in Table 5.1, along with a Global Health-Pathology Scale. Each of the subscale ratings uses a 5-point Likert scale plus half-steps for each point, whereas the Global Scale is a 10-point distribution. The Global Scale is not intended to be an arithmetic mean of the 12 subscales, though it will likely be close. Measurement of Competence is a linear measure, with 10 being the lowest level and 1 being the highest. The companion Family Style scale contains 7 subscale ratings as well as a Global Centripetal (CP)/Centrifugal (CF) Style rating. Each of the stylistic ratings use a 5-point Likert scale. Unlike the linear measurement of the Competence scale, the healthiest Style ratings are generally the middle 3, with 1 indicating an extremely CP style and 5 indicating an extremely CF style (Beavers & Hampson, 1990).

Following observational experience of families, the 36-item SFI was developed as a basic screening tool and a collaborative perspective of family functioning assessment (Beavers & Hampson, 1990). The principal scale measured by the SFI is the Health/Competence score, parallel to the Global Scale in the clinical rating scale model. Four additional subscales are measured for scoring: Conflict, Cohesion, Leadership, and Emotional Expressiveness. All four of these subscales relate to the construct of competence rather than style. However, the Cohesion subscale has been used as a general estimate of style (Walsh, 1993). Measuring the concept of style seems to be problematic in self-report inventories, though a 15-item inventory has been developed specifically for measuring style (Hampson, Beavers, & Hulgus, 1989). A scoring grid is available in *Successful Families* (Beavers & Hampson, 1990) that indicates which items are reversed in scoring and which items are included in each subscale. Three items in the SFI have been identified as indicators of style with a complex mathematical formula for converting those raw scores into a parallel rating with the observational rating. A separate profiling grid is provided in Appendix D of *Successful Families* that combines the subscale results of the SFI with the observational results of the Global Competence scale and the Style scale onto one profiling chart.

Perhaps the most well-known charting method for the Beavers Systems Model, whether using the observational or the self-report scales, is the "pair of pants" (Figure 5.1) familiar to all students of this model. This graph (Beavers & Hampson, 1990; Hampson & Beavers, 1996; Walsh, 1993) plots the health/competence dimension horizontally with the stylistic dimension vertically. The health/competence dimension continuum is divided into the Optimal Healthy, Adequate Healthy, Midrange, Borderline, and Se-

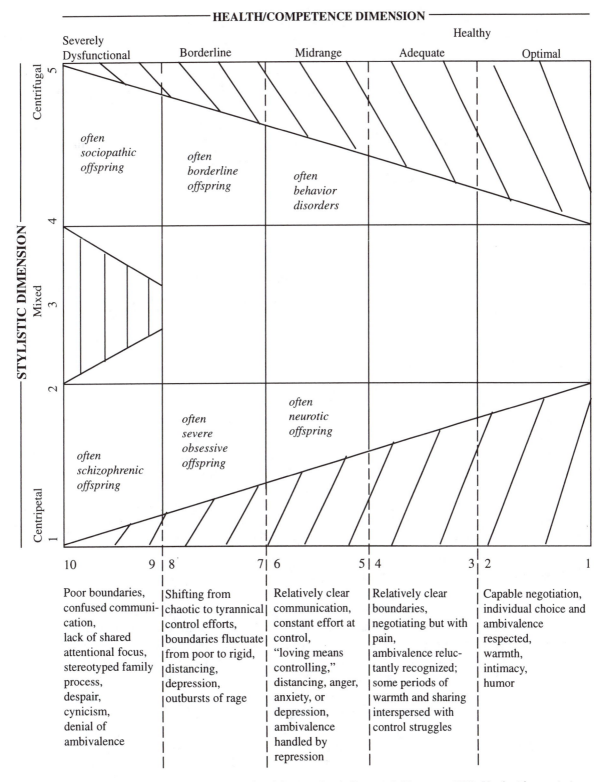

HEALTH/COMPETENCE DIMENSION

Severely Dysfunctional — *Borderline* — *Midrange* — *Adequate* — *Healthy* — *Optimal*

STYLISTIC DIMENSION

Centrifugal 5

often sociopathic offspring

often borderline offspring

often behavior disorders

Mixed 3

Centripetal 1

often neurotic offspring

often severe obsessive offspring

often schizophrenic offspring

10 | 9 | 8 | 7 | 6 | 5 | 4 | 3 | 2 | 1

| Poor boundaries, confused communication, lack of shared attentional focus, stereotyped family process, despair, cynicism, denial of ambivalence | Shifting from chaotic to tyrannical control efforts, boundaries fluctuate from poor to rigid, distancing, depression, outbursts of rage | Relatively clear communication, constant effort at control, "loving means controlling," distancing, anger, anxiety, or depression, ambivalence handled by repression | Relatively clear boundaries, negotiating but with pain, ambivalence reluctantly recognized; some periods of warmth and sharing interspersed with control struggles | Capable negotiation, individual choice and ambivalence respected, warmth, intimacy, humor |

Figure 5.1 The Beavers Systems Model Theoretical and Scoring Graph (Beavers & Hampson, 1990). Used with permission.

verely Dysfunctional categories, with identified scores and interactional characteristics at the bottom of the graph. The Stylistic Dimension is divided into Centripetal, Mixed, and Centrifugal categories. *DSM* diagnostic symptoms associated with different categorical system assessments are included on the chart. The stylistic dimension becomes more influential in identifying discrete symptoms when the system functioning is Midrange or below. Severely Dysfunctional families generally have a rigid stylistic pattern of either CP or CF. The "pair of pants" metaphor is derived from the rotated viewing of the graph to resemble a diminished waist and separated legs created by the stylistic correlation with competence.

The two constructs that frame the clinical rating scales and the self-report instrument are competence and style. Table 5.1 delineates the specific descriptors of competence and style. *Competence* defines how well the family system interacts to nurture development of its members. Organizational structure is a major component of this construct. Leadership in the family should be egalitarian and effective, maintaining generational boundaries. Effective communication processes lead to the development of trust, which allows for autonomy of family members to emerge in a healthy way. The safety in the system promotes spontaneous expression of diverse feelings and a general mood of optimism. All three of the GARF variables seem to be included in the competence construct.

Style defines the focus family members use to obtain nurturance and developmental support. CP families turn inward to gain support from within the family, whereas CF families turn outside the family. CP families rely on the family strengths and tend to overemphasize the positive, thus keeping the family tightly connected. CF families have not found their needs met within the family, thus they are distrustful of caring and more comfortable with negative or angry feelings in the family, which encourage them to move outward. Stylistic adaptability is important over the family life cycle. Young families need an inward focus in order to provide nurturance for young children. They need an outward focus when it is time for the adolescent to leave home. The stylistic dimension of family functioning is especially useful clinically. It is not surprising that CP family members may exhibit internalizing symptoms such as anxiety and depression when the level of togetherness is not developmentally appropriate. CF family members correspondingly exhibit externalizing symptoms such as socially aggressive conduct. Perhaps the style construct captures the essence of the emotional climate variable in the GARF.

A recent focus of research in the Beavers Systems Model is the second-order cybernetics interface between the style of family functioning and the style of therapeutic intervention (Hampson & Beavers, 1996). This study used the observational Competence and Style scales along with the SFI to assess family functioning. Measures completed by the therapist included the Therapist Perceived Relationship Scale and the Therapist Evaluation of Treatment. The Therapist Perceived Relationship Scale measured the degree of openness in disclosing strategy with the family, the degree of partnership in joining the family, and the degree of power differential in directing and conducting versus developing more egalitarian relationships with family members. This conceptualization of the therapeutic relationship attempts to capture distinctions recognizable in the major schools of family therapy. The third primary variable, treatment outcome based on goal attainment, seems particularly relevant to the managed-care demand for efficiency. Results of Hampson and Beavers' study indicate that adapting the therapeutic style to the family functioning style will produce better outcome. Highly functioning families seemed to do better with a more disclosing, partnering, collaborating therapeutic style, whereas severely dysfunctional families responded better to a lower level of openness and partnership with a higher level of power differential. This area of research offers much promise for the future development of continuously improving clinical services.

Circumplex Model Overview

The Circumplex Model of marital and family systems was introduced through the dissertation works of Sprenkle and Russell under the supervision of Olson in the late 1970s (Olson, Sprenkle, & Russell, 1979) as a model to bridge theory, research, and clinical practice. It has been refined and evaluated since then as a major model in family assessment. Though it includes both a clinical rating scale and a self-report instrument, the self-report FACES has been used to generate a massive volume of research on the Circumplex Model. The original Family Adaptability and Cohesion Scales (FACES), developed in 1978 through the dissertation work of Portner and Bell, has evolved into FACES III (Olson, Portner, & Lavee, 1985; Olson & Tiesel, 1991), with a FACES IV being developed. FACES III measures the flexibility and cohesion of a family system. The model includes a 16-type map of family typologies based on the orthogonal plotting of the cohesion and flexibility measurements. FACES IV is intended to capture the distinction between first-order change (a curvilinear static assessment concept based on the 16 types depicted in Figure 5.2) and a slow therapeutic linear movement from one of the three system types to another (Unbalanced, Mid-Range, Balanced). The clinical rating scale adds the variable of communication as a skill to facilitate change in flexibility and cohesion (Olson et al., 1985; Olson et al., 1989). Table 5.1 describes these three variables. Figure 5.2 graphically depicts the orthogonal curvilinear concepts of the model, with less problematic families being balanced in the center of the axis and more problematic families being in the extreme corners beyond the circle.

One author, Alice McDonald, has found the Circumplex Model particularly useful in clinical practice. The treatment goal could be to guide the family toward change from enmeshed or disengaged to separated or connected on the cohesion scale, and from chaotic or rigid to structured or flexible on the flexibility scale. A realistic objective would be to try to move the family from the extremes on both dimensions to the adjacent pattern of functioning. The change needs to be gradual, and care must be taken that the family does not rush to the other extreme of the scale.

To facilitate this change process, McDonald asks each member of the family to complete FACES III. The scores are then plotted on the Circumplex Model graph (see Figure 5.2), and a copy of the plotted scores is given to the family. A posterboard with the Circumplex Model printed on the board is shown to the clients. The family is then able to find their spot(s) on the board while the therapist explains the cohesion scale in metaphorical terms, using animals as examples. The *enmeshed* variable is explained by looking at the pig family. The piglets all hang on the mother pig for sustenance. There are no boundaries, and the piglets do not want to be released. The family's ideal is to roll around in the mud together. If the pigs lived in houses, there would be no doors separating rooms and no bathroom door. There is no time or space to be alone. Family loyalty is at an all-time high. Piglets are not allowed to spend time at a friend's house, and friends are not welcome at the pig's home. The exclusion of friends into the home concerns the importance of secrets. Daddy may be drunk, or brother and sister pig may be having an incestuous relationship. One pig received a scholarship to a distant college and could not go because it was too far from home. This family is so close to each other that there is never a breath of fresh air. The fatality rate among the piglets is sometimes high. The *connected* family is similar to the fox family. The baby fox depends on its mother for food and protection for about 6 months.

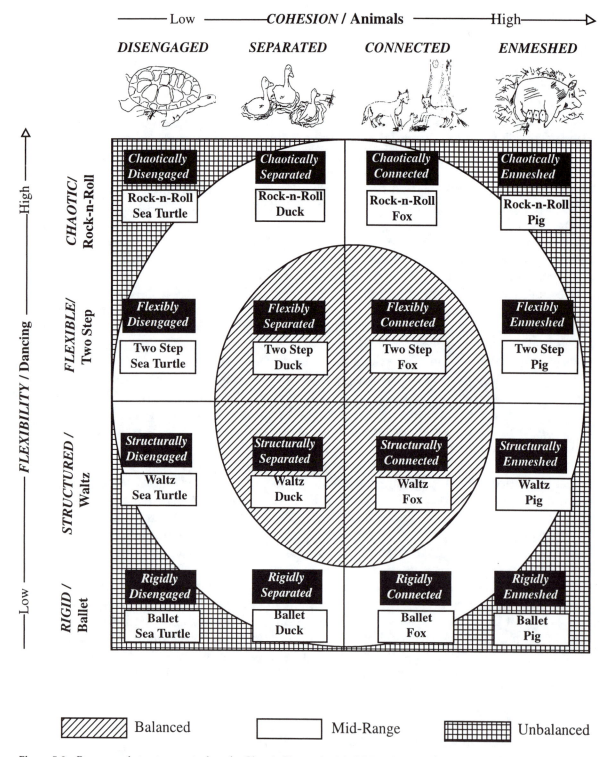

Figure 5.2   Process and structure metaphors for Olson's Circumplex Model Typologies. Based on D. H. Olson, "Circumplex model of marital and family systems: Assessing family functioning." In F. Walsh (Ed.). (1993), *Normal family processes* (pp. 104–137). New York: Guilford Press. Drawings by Isaac Fuller and Susan Vaughn.

Father fox stays around to protect his mate and offspring for about 2 months. The fox family members are very close to one another, but they do allow the baby fox some freedom so that he or she can learn the territory of their domain. Mother and father are very affectionate toward their baby and like to lick his or her fur and bring the baby food. When the young wander off to explore, they always return. When the male adolescent fox is old enough, he is permitted to leave home and look for a female fox, providing she comes from a family with the same standards and value system as theirs. The *separated* family is represented by the duck family. The mother duck builds her nest near the water and sits on the nest for 3 or 4 weeks. She feeds and shelters her young for about 6 weeks. The mother duck leads her ducklings to the water as soon as they can travel. The ducks join flocks so that they experience a great deal of independence. They may see members of their family again, or they may not. If ducks lived in houses, they would each have their own room, perhaps eat supper together, and have their own friends. They would learn at an early age that they are individuals who have a family but that it is important to have connections with others in society. The sea turtle is an example of a *disengaged* family. The sea turtle swims to land, runs to a spot in the sand, digs a hole, lays her eggs in the hole, covers the eggs with sand, and departs. She swims out to sea and never sees her babies. When the turtles hatch, they make a mad dash to the ocean and may be picked off by birds or other predators. The ones who survive never know who their father or mother are. They are on their own to make their own decisions concerning eating, making friends, mating, and pursuing their interests. Because they have no parents to model themselves after, they live by instincts and have to learn by trial and error. They do not have the experience of being cared for by another or even making a connection with another turtle except for mating purposes.

The flexibility scale is explained by using different dance steps. The *chaotic* family is portrayed in the rock-n-roll dance. Each participant in this dance is autonomous. There is no set routine and no one person leading in the dance. If a dancer decides to do something spontaneous, he or she is free to perform. Because there is no structure to the dance, the rules can change constantly. The participants in this type of family feel little stability in their lives and have very weak rules and routines. The *flexible* family is portrayed in the two-step country-and-western dance. This dance is more organized than rock-n-roll and requires coordination with a partner. Couples are flexible, but there is a certain amount of congruence in the movement. In the dance, as in marriage, couples may agree to switch leadership. In this dance, couples feel comfortable in their roles because there are no hard-and-fast rules that cannot be changed. The *structured* family is portrayed in the waltz, because there is one simple step in which the dancers move all around the room together. In this structured dance, there is one person in the lead, with the other following. To make a parallel with a family, we find the parents in a leadership capacity with children following the rules. The children feel safe and secure, and they know if they break the rules there are consequences. Because the parents are in charge and make the decisions, they are the ones who may change the rules or routines. The *rigid* family is exemplified in the ballet. There is one way to perform each step, and instructions do not change. The arabesque has certain guidelines that must be followed. There is no freedom for negotiation. There is one way to perform, and the dancer is under the strict supervision of the choreographer. Children in this type of family are fully controlled by the parents; they obey or are punished.

By observing their location on the model and hearing the explanation, the client family is then able to discuss with the therapist the direction they need to move in order to become a more balanced family. This metaphorical interpretation of the Circumplex Model parallels the construct of cohesion with organizational structure providing identity (animal species with identifiable behavioral patterns) and the construct of flexibility with interactional processes that maintain the structure while responding effectively to stressors (dance steps). The Circumplex Assessment Package (CAP) includes a series of self-report assessment tools based on the Circumplex Model. It is available from Dr. David Olson at the Family Social Science Department of the University of Minnesota, 290 McNeal Hall, St. Paul, Minnesota 55108. Guides for the clinical rating scale are printed in the *Handbook of Relational Diagnosis and Dysfunctional Family Patterns* (Kaslow, 1996) and *Normal Family Processes* (Walsh, 1993).

McMaster Model of Family Functioning

Like the Beavers Systems Model, the McMaster Model has roots dating back to the late 1950s. Developmental work on the model continued at McGill University for a decade. The first published work on the model was in 1969 with Westley and Epstein's *The Silent Majority*. In the late 1970s, work on the model moved to McMaster University and continued there until the 1980s. Epstein, Bishop, and Levin published the current model description in 1978. In the 1980s, work on the model moved to the current Brown University Family Research Program. A description of the model is published in Walsh's *Normal Family Processes* (1993). Detailed information about the continued work on psychometric instruments is available from Drs. Christine Ryan or Ivan Miller in the Mood Disorders Program, Rhode Island Hospital, 593 Eddy St., Providence, Rhode Island 02903; fax: (401) 444-3298; phone: (401) 444-3534. Materials available for purchase include

- The Family Assessment Device (FAD) packet, available in English, French, Hungarian, Swedish, Portuguese, Spanish, and Chinese;
- FAD computerized scoring program in Macintosh or IBM-PC/PC compatible format;
- McMaster Clinician's Rating Scale (McCRS) manual;
- Structured Interview of Family Functioning (McSIFF) manual for intact families, single parent families, or couples; and
- Manual of Problem Centered Systems Therapy treatment.

The McMaster Model of Family Functioning (MMFF) was developed from a review of the family literature, teaching, research, and clinical application. A more pragmatic than theoretical stance was taken in deciding what to include. If a concept did not work, it was eliminated or changed. On the basis of a concept of identifying factors that contribute to family health, the language of "most effective" and "most ineffective" is prominent. Assumptions about family systems that are crucial to this model are summarized below (Walsh, 1993, p. 140):

1 The parts of the family are interrelated.
2 One part of the family cannot be understood in isolation from the rest of the system.
3 Family functioning cannot be fully understood by simply understanding each of the parts.
4 A family's structure and organization are important factors in determining the behavior of family members.
5 Transactional patterns of the family system are among the most important variables that shape the behavior of family members.

Organization and problem-solving characteristics of the GARF are evident in Items 4 and 5.

Table 5.5
Conceptual Overview of McMaster Model of Family Functioning

I. **Problem Solving**
   Two types of problems: instrumental and affective
   Seven stages to the process:
   1. Identification of the problem
   2. Communication of the problem to the appropriate person(s)
   3. Development of action alternatives
   4. Decision on one alternative
   5. Action
   6. Monitoring the action
   7. Evaluation of success
   Postulated:
   • *Most effective when all seven stages are carried out*
   • *Least effective when families cannot identify problem (stop before Step 1)*

II. **Communication**
   Instrumental and affective areas
   Two independent dimensions:
   1. Clear and direct
   2. Clear and indirect
   3. Masked and direct
   4. Masked and indirect
   Postulated:
   • *Most effective: clear and direct*
   • *Least effective: masked and indirect*

(table continued on next page)

Another important dimension of the MMFF is a developmental perspective. Perhaps our identification of the GARF emotional climate variable being associated with developmental nurturance is influenced by the MMFF emphasis on developmental tasks more than the other two models. In order to nurture the development of family members on the social, psychological, and biological system levels, the family system must fulfill tasks in three areas (Walsh, 1993):

1 The basic task area, which includes basic instrumental needs such as food, clothing, and shelter.
2 The developmental task area, which incorporates tasks of the individual and family life cycle stages from family studies literature.
3 The hazardous task area, which is the response pattern to unpredicted external shock crises in the family, drawing from the family crises literature.

The six dimensions of family functioning the developers have selected as most critical are outlined in Table 5.5. The developers take responsibility for making value judgments in selecting and directionally describing postulated effective and ineffective patterns under each dimension. They emphasize that these value judgments must be modified according to cultural norms (Walsh, 1993).

The MMFF has been operationalized in three different psychometric instruments (Novack & Gage, 1995; Walsh, 1993): the McMaster FAD, the MCRS, and the McSIFF. The FAD is a 60-item self-report inventory covering the six dimensions in Table 5.5 plus the General Functioning Index. Responses range from *strongly agree* to *strongly disagree* on a 4-point scale. All family members age 12 and over complete the inventory in approximately 15–20 min (Epstein, Baldwin, & Bishop, 1983). Continued testing (Kabacoff, Miller, Bishop, Ep-

Table 5.5
Conceptual Overview of McMaster Model of Family Functioning (*Continued*)

III. **Roles**
Two family function types: necessary and other
Two areas of family functions: instrumental and affective
Necessary family function groupings:
1. Instrumental
   a) Provision of resources
2. Affective
   a) Nurturance and support
   b) Adult sexual gratification
3. Mixed
   a) Life skills development
   b) Systems maintenance and management
Other family functions: adaptive and maladaptive
Role functioning is assessed by considering how the family allocates responsibilities and handles accountability for them
Postulated:
- *Most effective when all necessary family functions have clear allocation to reasonable individual(s) and accountability is built in*
- *Least effective when necessary family functions are not addressed and/or allocation and accountability are not maintained*

IV. **Affective Responsiveness**
Two groupings: welfare emotions and emergency emotions
Postulated:
- *Most effective when a full range of responses is appropriate in amount and quality to stimulus*
- *Least effective when range is very narrow (one or two affects only) and/or amount and quality is distorted, given the context*

V. **Affective Involvement**
A range of involvement with six styles identified:
1. Absence of involvement
2. Involvement devoid of feelings
3. Narcissistic involvement
4. Empathic involvement
5. Overinvolvement
6. Symbiotic involvement
Postulated:
- *Most effective: empathic involvement*
- *Least effective: symbiotic involvement and absence of involvement*

VI. **Behavior Control**
Applies to three situations:
1. Dangerous situations
2. Meeting and expressing psychobiological needs and drives (eating, drinking, sleeping, eliminating, sex, and aggression)
3. Interpersonal socializing behavior inside and outside the family
Standard and latitude of acceptable behavior determined by four styles:
1. Rigid
2. Flexible
3. Laissez-faire
4. Chaotic
To maintain the style, various techniques are used and implemented under "role" functions (systems maintenance and management)
Postulated:
- *Most effective: flexible behavior control*
- *Least effective: chaotic behavior control*

Note. Walsh, 1993, pp. 142–143. Used with permission.

stein, & Keitner, 1990; Walsh, 1993) attempts to address the psychometric criticisms of the FAD (L'Abate & Bagarozzi, 1993; Novack & Gage, 1995).

The MCRS uses a 7-point Likert scale to assess each of the six dimensions in Table 5.5, with a score of 1 representing the lowest level and 7 representing the highest. Scores of 5–7 are considered nonpathological functioning levels. One possible method of obtaining information for the MCRS is to complete an extensive McSIFF semistructured interview with the family. The interview covers the six dimensions in greater detail than does the FAD. The comprehensiveness of the McSIFF may be offset by considerable administrative time and training. The McSIFF and the MCRS still need further psychometric verification (Novack & Gage, 1995). However, a review of the GARF variable descriptions indicates the strong influence of the MMFF in the GARF development.

NEWLY DEVELOPED RELATED ASSESSMENT TOOLS: SAFE AND GAS

Systemic Assessment of the Family Environment (SAFE)

The SAFE self-report instrument was developed by Yingling in 1991, concurrently with our initial work with the GARF. However, the contents were not intentionally modeled after the GARF. The instrument had been evolving over the previous 2 years, based originally on dissertation research using the FACES III. After using the SAFE and GARF together, we began identifying parallel constructs that were useful in clinical work. Both are designed to be global assessments that are very user friendly and yet provide a clear immediate intervention direction, considering both the outsider and insider perspectives. Copies of the instrument versions with scoring sheets are included in Appendix D for duplication and use.

Description

The SAFE is designed to measure three relational subsystem levels of the family system functioning using two system functioning factors for each subsystem level. Scores can be graphed to indicate the family's organizational and interactional strengths by placing each pair of scores in one of four categories: competent, discordant, disoriented, or chaotic. The SAFE can be used if one, two, or three subsystem levels are completed by calculating a mean score for whichever levels are appropriately used by family members. Marking with an "X" for how the family member thinks the family is functioning now and with an "O" for how the family member would like it to be gives clear family goal directedness for the therapist to explore. This difference in perspective score could be considered a satisfaction score, or perhaps an assessment of the emotional climate of the system for meeting needs.

The three subsystem levels of family system functioning assessed are the:
A. dyadic marital/executive subsystem (spouses or former spouses or spousal substitutes with each other),
B. parent–child subsystem (parents or parent substitutes with children), and
C. the extended family subsystem (each spouse with that spouse's respective "former parents").

The two factors assessed under each subsystem level are the:

I. **Organizational structure** (the last question under each subsystem level on the instrument)
- A. egalitarian marital/executive subsystem
- B. parental hierarchy in the nuclear family system
- C. egalitarian power structure in the adult extended family system (parent firing or personal authority or differentiation of self status)

II. **Interactional processes** (the first six questions under each subsystem level on the instrument)
- A. *process* of how family members
  1. talk—self-disclose
  2. listen—hear others' disclosure
  3. understand—get through to each other
- B. *product* of communication process resulting in the appropriate ability to
  1. connect—join together
  2. release—allow change and individuality
  3. support—provide appropriate level of supportiveness without suffocation

The categories of functioning identified on the plotted graph are: (a) competent: strong organizational structure + strong interactional processes; (b) discordant: strong organizational structure + weak interactional processes; (c) disoriented: weak organizational structure + strong interactional processes; and (d) chaotic: weak organizational structure + weak interactional processes.

If a scoring for a family results in a *competent* rating, perhaps the family has many strengths within the family system but is experiencing an overwhelming level of stress at the moment. They may benefit from brief solution-focused therapy. Or this high self-report rating could indicate a need to create a false impression of the family functioning by "therapy-sophisticated" clients. Discrepant ratings by different family members can be very helpful in providing clues about reality. Families with *discordant* ratings may respond well to behavioral communication skill-building interventions because their organizational structures seem to be appropriate. Some families (*disoriented* ratings) may have effective interactional processes that unfortunately perpetuate ineffective organizational structures. Structural family therapy interventions may be helpful to their reorganization of the family hierarchy in the needed subsystems. Families in the *chaotic* category may have significant weaknesses in the family's organizational structure as well as ineffective interactional processes that are necessary to negotiate a change in the structure. Strategic interventions may be necessary before extended/nuclear family structural or dyadic behavioral interventions will be helpful.

Markings on the X + O version of the instrument indicate two time perspectives: (1) how the respondent perceives the family to be functioning currently when stress occurs and (2) how the respondent would like to have the family functioning. Current functioning is marked with an X, and desired functioning is marked with an O. The difference between these markings can be used to measure satisfaction scores (S) and help establish goals for treatment/change. If using the two perspectives seems to be confusing to clients, use only the "X = as it is now" version of the instrument and scoring graph.

Instrument Formats

The SAFE is a one-page instrument for each family member to complete with 21 semantic differential pairings to mark both with an X and with an O. Three different versions are designed to be answered by members of the three different generations in the family system. The family member identification at the bottom of the page indicates which family member is completing the form. The wordings on the A, B, and C headings also indicate which generation that particular version fits. Be sure to hand the correct version to each family member to avoid confusion.

The version with the black background around the title with directions only for marking the system as it is now (X) is used for research to predict outcome of therapy or mediation intervention. With high-stress families or families with lowered conceptualization skills, using the version with only one perspective ("X = as it is now") may provide more reliable results.

A Spanish translation is included for all three versions from each of the two perspectives. The cartoon version can be used with children under the age of 10 to select which picture looks most like their family now. Results can be globally compared with scored results of other family members. The cartoon assessment also provides a very effective discussion tool with children to begin exploring the child's perception of family functioning.

Scoring

The fully completed instrument results in 42 numbers to use in analyzing results. The enclosed graph with instructions guides the therapist/researcher in calculating the scores for each of the three subsystem levels (A/B/C) on the two factors (organizational and interactional) from the two time perspectives (as it is now and how they would like it to become). Blanks in the bottom left of the page provide a work space for recording the numbers to be plotted on the graph above. The attached Assigned Weights form can be put on a transparency to facilitate quick calculations of scores. The combined first six items under each level (the interactional score) have been assigned numbers to equal the weight of the seventh item (organizational score). A total family SAFE score can be calculated by averaging the level scores of each member first and then by averaging the combined interactional and organizational scores for the family (dividing the total combined score by the number of family members completing the form). The bottom right corner of the scoring sheet includes a place for GARF scores to be recorded for correlational studies of the SAFE and GARF. Data are also readily available from the scoring sheet for correlating the GARF subscores on interactional processes, organizational structure, and emotional climate with the interactional, organizational, and satisfaction scores on the SAFE. Further research may reveal that questions 4, 5, and 6 combined under each level represent a closer correlation with the emotional climate score of the GARF rather than being a part of the interactional score. The SAFE is in an experimental stage for research purposes. However, the straightforward profile scoring provides an instantly usable tool for clinical intervention planning, as the clinician can glance at the results and immediately identify areas of concern for the family member who is completing it. These concerns can be assessed further during the initial session interview.

GAS

Another instrument the authors developed to be parallel with the GARF is the GAS form and structured procedures specifically designed for family change according to GARF variables. See Appendix C for a copy of the form, family instruction sheet, and therapist/researcher instructions for use. This tool is intended to be collaborative in nature, combining the self-report of the family's discussions with the therapist's assessment interview to jointly define manageable change goals for family functioning. Lambert and Hill (1994) describe many uses of the goal-attainment scaling process for evaluating treatment outcome, along with its many research weaknesses. However, from a family systems perspective, assessment is continuous and reciprocal with treatment. In that sense, the GAS can be a useful tool for influencing family perception as a method of initiating change in the system. At the same time, it provides a basis for quantifying change and does it in a collaborative manner with the family. Periodic progress checks can be made and dates of level achievement identified on the form, reinforcing the concept of gradual change so as to keep the system in balance.

The unique feature of our procedure is to delineate the variables of the GARF on a separate selection sheet for family review. We hope that this structuring of the process will help reframe the presenting problem from an individual to a systemic one. Language on the forms has been carefully selected to promote growth-oriented systemic thinking of the family, the therapist, and/or the researcher. We hope that delineating the GARF variables as goal options will promote further research correlating system change with intervention approaches as well as identifying system functioning assessments correlating with specific presenting problems.

CLINICAL INTERVIEW ASSESSMENT TOOLS: IMPACT ON THE GARF

From a systemic perspective, assessment is intervention, and intervention is assessment. As a clinical rating scale, the GARF output is only as good as the GARF input. How does a clinician gather data to conceptualize into the GARF model?

From a modernist perspective, the choice of data gathering procedures creates a relatively complete or incomplete picture. How can one define the organizational structure of the family without constructing a genogram and mapping the relationships? If the therapist does not pay attention to the seating arrangement of family members, what critical information is overlooked? Perhaps the therapist has roots in individual therapy and does not even see the necessity of including the entire family in therapy sessions. How often does the entire picture change when key members of the system appear? Can a valid system assessment be made without the complete system, including the extended family? If the therapist does not recognize the stuckness of the family being associated with structural developmental delays from the family of origin, will important information about the rigidity of family rules be missed? If the therapist is not familiar with the techniques of sculpting, will the input data on structure be distorted?

From a postmodernist perspective, how does the assessment process the therapist chooses to use influence the output? Circular questioning is a critically important skill for understanding and perturbing family functioning. But how does the asking of circular questions dynamically change the assessment output during the assessment process? If the therapist assessor is personally struggling with the same or similar issues as the family, how might the therapist's blind spots skew the family functioning assessment?

All these challenges to valid family functioning assessment seem overwhelmingly complex. But as we grow in our understanding of systems, including the therapeutic system and the broader cultural system, we will begin to look at these factors as they influence the family functioning and the assessment process. The GARF seems to mark a milestone in integrating basic concepts woven throughout the various models and techniques of assessment developed in our field. Perhaps we are ready for a second-order change into exploration of the process of assessment.

CHAPTER 6

GARF in Multi-Systems Partnering

Meeting the needs of stakeholders
Applying business principles to clinical practice
Establishing a record system for outcome data: Agency/solo practice
Future challenges for GARF users: Clinicians, business managers, and educators

Our final chapter in the journey of the *Sourcebook* returns us to the first paragraph of Chapter 1. We have attempted to introduce the reader to the GARF as a resource for integrating assessment into clinical practice in a clear, measurable way. In this chapter we emphasize again the importance of partnering with all the stakeholders in the mental health system and of benefiting from that partnering by applying effective systemic business practices. A clear guide for how to establish a research-based record system precedes our final challenges for continuous improvement of our work with the GARF.

MEETING THE NEEDS OF STAKEHOLDERS

Systemic thinking requires inclusiveness, partnering, and collaboration. If we are to use information about family functioning assessment to its fullest value, who should be included in the training process? With whom will family therapists partner in order to solve critical problems in our society? How can we establish an effective collaborative communication system with the critical stakeholders?

   If we begin with a definition of the family-related problems we are trying to solve, the list might include the following:

* drug use among youth and adults, influencing work productivity, health care costs, and crime prevalence;
* depression, affecting all family members internally as well as their functioning in society;

- dropouts from school, creating a large segment of nonproductive members of future society who burden taxpayers and increase crime rates; and
- divorce complications, leading to school difficulties for children and work/health interference for parents.

These problems seem to be unmanageable in our society, and yet their resolution is critical to our future quality of life.

Who are the stakeholders most invested in finding solutions? Possible answers include the symptomatic individual, the "pinched" family system of that individual, the clinician, the managed care staff, and the business company payer. In a less direct definition, friends, neighbors, schools/agencies, governmental bodies, and all taxpayers who are affected by symptomatic members of society could be identified as stakeholders.

The primary stakeholder in the outcome of therapy is the member of the pinched family system who is exhibiting the symptoms. Relieving that person's or persons' pain is a primary goal of therapeutic intervention, along with improved problem-solving skills and coping mechanisms that improve the client's quality of life. But a quick fix is not enough—we must bring more long-lasting relief. To bring long-lasting relief, we must view our client as the system causing the symptom. Therefore, another critical stakeholder is the entire family system. Because the family system is a primary stakeholder, members' evaluations of change are critical to the clinician's definition of success. Collaborative goal setting for system change and objective evaluation of attainment are necessary.

Another key stakeholder is the therapist. If one's clinical work is not producing successful quality outcomes, the clinician loses motivation to continue to improve. Thus, assessment of outcome is also critical to the provider's well-being and continued productivity. The ineffective clinician may also be affected by ethics charges for incompetence, lost clients, lost income, lost future referrals, and lost license to practice.

Assessing outcome is becoming increasingly important to the managed care stakeholder. As the liaison between the provider and the payer (for-profit or nonprofit business organization or governmental agency contractor), managed care staff are responsible for obtaining the best results possible for the clients with the least expenditure possible to the payer. With the development of NCQA standards for outpatient behavioral mental health care (NCQA, 1996), managed care staff are searching for innovative ways to meet the standards. A report by Dr. Bruce Roberts, the Regional Medical Director for Merit Behavioral Care Corporation, (June 1996) identified three critical issues affecting quality: (1) assessment of imminent risk, (2) understanding what factors escalate the need for therapy at this time (perhaps lack of a family support system), and (3) identifying factors that keep the client stuck in a problem state (perhaps dysfunctional relationships). Are managed care staff aware and supportive of moving toward family systems work in order to eliminate individual member symptoms with long-lasting relief? We have investigated this question, with encouraging results. A recent survey of managed care companies by a committee of a local professional organization chapter (Dallas Association for Marriage and Family Therapy Managed Care Committee, 1995), along with results of interviews conducted by two of the present authors, suggested a generally positive attitude toward using family therapy in a managed care environment. The majority of companies said they did authorize reimbursement for family therapy (*Physician's Current Procedural Terminology* code 90847), and most did include licensed MFTs as providers. The business contracting for services, the other critical stakeholder, often sets limits on the managed care company; hence, specific answers were difficult to obtain.

The business emphasis on quality assurance is based on systemic thinking, a natural partner with family systems therapists. Perhaps the real challenge is for clinicians to use effective communication processes to inform corporate decision makers of the common styles and processes they share with systemic mental health providers. The other challenge is to produce the outcome data that verify the effectiveness of systemic assessment and intervention.

APPLYING BUSINESS PRINCIPLES TO CLINICAL PRACTICE

To help clinicians improve partnering skills, principles from Deming's (1993) TQM philosophy have been translated into systemic clinical practice. This delineation parallels TQM and MFT styles and processes, forming the natural partner for the managed care link. A summarization of principles for establishing a healthy system structure includes the following (Chewning & Yingling, 1995): transformation intent, cooperative leadership, profound knowledge, clear methods and principles, and future focus.

What does the principle of *transformation intent* mean for clinicians? It means that the owner/manager must commit to empower all staff to meet the client needs without fear of criticism or losing a job. The top decision maker must also invest in time for strategic planning at all levels of system functioning, maintaining a vision while creating a mission statement that responds to targeted customer needs. *Cooperative leadership* implies a collaborative mentorship role versus an authoritarian evaluative role of management, including clinical supervisors. What is the *profound knowledge* holding the key? Deming suggests profound knowledge is a valuing of human resources above all else and applying human relations principles to the business staff. Using human relations principles requires assessing human systems functioning at multiple levels:

- How effective is the client referral source contact with office staff?
- How customer-focused is the client's first contact with the staff (receptionist, therapist, business manager, practice owner/agency director)?
- How does the physical environment of the office affect the client?
- What emotional climate is created by staff members' interactions with each other?
- What impact do board/owner rules have on staff organization and interactional processes?
- How does the view of MFT usefulness held by managed care or the general public influence the stock value of your clinical service?

In the operation of the clinical practice, having a clear predictive theory base from which to operate, while continuously testing the conceptualized hypotheses, will promote success. Profound knowledge of systemic functioning means reducing variation of family functioning outcomes within the specifications of managed care by constantly improving the system that supports the therapy process.

Establishing a clear policy manual based on a stable structure with interactional guidelines for implementing and adapting the structure to needed change exemplifies effective *methods and principles*. These methods and principles will lead to effective implementation of the strategic plan to meet the needs of the customer. Success will take the practice into the *future*, where the clinician will continue to deliver quality services that meet and exceed the customer needs and consequently keep the practice alive.

Deming's interactional principles of how to maintain a functional system include the following (Chewning & Yingling, 1995): stable process, process improvement, human effort, future focus, and customer feedback. Maintaining a *stable process* in a therapeutic practice leads to producing predictable client outcomes. Defining the client population that consistently leaves therapy with predictable changes and setting this population as the core of the practice is a key—specialize the practice. *Process improvement* involves strategically planning to periodically reevaluate the mission and goals of the practice and how all staff can work together more effectively to achieve higher order goals with less outcome variation for the identified core population of clients. *Human effort* focuses on supporting each staffperson's efforts to meet his or her personal human needs. These needs may include job achievement, collegiality, intellectual stimulation, recognition for importance to the process, and so on. Being *future focused* means anticipating market demands and training staff to respond with quality services. *Customer feedback* is a critical part of the effective functioning of a clinical practice system. Customer feedback includes soliciting non-fear-driven feedback from the internal customers through regular staff meetings, suggestion boxes, open door policies, and team functioning outcomes. Soliciting external customer feedback can be achieved through client satisfaction surveys, outcome research for publication to the professional community and for managed care companies, and problem-solving communication with referral sources that include managed care staff.

Using the above principles for establishing and maintaining a functional therapeutic system will produce outputs. To measure the quality of outputs, we must develop and use objective assessment tools to identify changes in the family system as the family progresses through therapeutic interventions. Our challenge is to quantify those measurements appropriately with accurate data collection tools and procedures, along with statistical interpretations that fit a dynamic systemic perspective. Analytical techniques used in TQM statistical process control (SPC), such as the control chart, would be worth exploring for systemic evaluation of output (Chewning, 1996; Wheeler, 1995). The statistical process control approach is designed to understand the functioning of the system first before determining whether the symptoms are a result of a system malfunctioning internally or a result of a special outside stressor/s affecting the system. Changing the system when the cause of the symptoms is truly external will result in a chaotically dysfunctional system producing more symptoms in the future when the external stressor has dissipated. Treating the symptom without a true system assessment may be comparable on the individual system level to prescribing medication for depression when the client is experiencing early menopause.

This SPC approach can be useful in predicting outputs of the therapist–client system as well as of the family system. Being able to predict future results of a process allows the team of client–therapist–managed care staff–business contractor to work together to reduce variation in the therapeutic system, identify whether to intervene in system functioning or to reduce outside stressors, and reduce/eliminate symptoms of client systems in an efficient manner. Though reaching this level of systemic functioning is truly a futuristic challenge, we offer the following information as a first step for improving the research component of the therapeutic system in order to evaluate systemic intervention process and outcome.

ESTABLISHING A RECORD SYSTEM FOR OUTCOME DATA: AGENCY/SOLO PRACTICE

The following section offers practical suggestions for incorporating forms and procedures to establish a record system for outcome data. It is expected that most MFTs will be members of one or more of the following national professional organizations: AAMFT, ACA, American Psychological Association, and NASW. Each therapist or clinical agency will likely have specifications of the client/patient records that are necessary for compliance

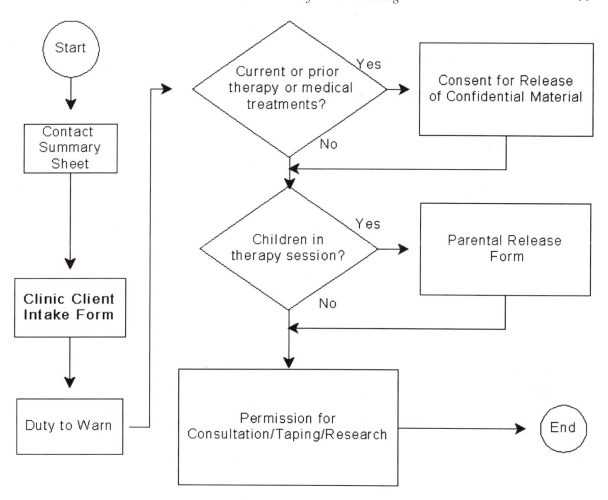

Figure 6.1 Flow Chart for Clinical Intake Forms.

with relevant professional ethical standards (AAMFT, 1991; ACA, 1995; American Psychological Association, 1992; NASW, 1996) and legal requirements. Professional ethics, federal and state legislation and/or regulation, and case law further require the therapist and agency to take sufficient steps to protect the client/patient records. Because of the rapid and continuing changes in this complex area of therapeutic practice, detailed discussion is outside the scope of this volume; therefore, the practitioner is well advised to consult an attorney who is familiar with all applicable ethical standards and laws.

This section includes descriptions of forms that we found helpful but focuses on the forms and procedures especially helpful in recording outcome data in a clinical setting. The therapist may find it helpful to complete the initial forms in the sequence shown in Figure 6.1 during the intake portion of the first session. This section also includes descriptions of forms (e.g., SAFE, GAS, etc.) and contracts (e.g., Contract for Non-Violence, No Suicide Contract, etc.) that may be used after the initial forms are finished.

Instruments and Forms

Contact Summary Sheet

A therapist will probably find it helpful to document each and every contact with the client. The Contact Summary Sheet (see Appendix F) should be attached to the inside front of the client folder so that it is readily accessible. This form offers a central place for the clerical staff and therapist to record client phone calls, session attendance, payments, and billings. Although the therapist will likely want to document more details in the clinical case notes, the advantage of this form is that it consolidates pertinent information. During clinical supervision or case management, the Contact Summary Sheet can be reviewed for patterns of communication with the client, session attendance, billing, and payments.

Clinic Client Intake Form and Intake Form

The record system continues during the first contacts with the client family because of the opportunity to collect basic important information. The Clinic Client Intake Form (see Appendix F) provides a format on which to organize the intake information collected by the office staff (Sections A and B) and the therapist (Sections C and D). Families initially request therapy to address a specific presenting problem, then frequently reveal additional and often more severe problems in later sessions. Please note that in Section C one can record in which session each problem becomes known to the therapist. Therapists who want a less comprehensive format may prefer the Intake Form (see Appendix F).

Duty to Warn

The Duty to Warn (see Appendix F) addresses the important clinical, ethical, and legal concerns of confidentiality and clearly specifies the circumstances under which the therapist's *duty to warn* supersedes the client's right to confidentiality. The form is a written waiver within the definition of Subprinciple 2.1 (d) of the AAMFT's Code of Ethics (AAMFT, 1992) that explicitly spells out to the client what is included in the therapist's duty to warn. The reader may note that the second paragraph of the Duty to Warn informs the family that the therapist has a duty to warn not only in cases of threatened homicide and suicide (ACA, 1995; AAMFT, 1991) but also in cases of threatened exposure of a spouse to AIDS (ACA, 1995, Section B.1.d). The therapist is encouraged to explain this form, allow the family members sufficient time to read it, and answer any client questions about the form before requesting the clients' signatures on this waiver.

Consent for the Release of Confidential Material

A therapist can use the upper section of the Consent for the Release of Confidential Material (Appendix F) to document the client's written permission for a previous or concurrent therapist, physician, hospital, and so on to release confidential information to the therapist. Similarly, the lower section can be used when the client requests the therapist to release confidential information to others.

Parental Release Form

Many states require parental consent before a minor child can receive health care, including mental health care (Corey, Corey, & Callanan, 1993). The American Psychological Association Ethical Standard 4.02 (b) requires parental consent when persons are incapable of giving informed consent to treatment and when such consent is permitted by law (American Psychological Association, 1992). Similarly, Section B.3 of the ACA Code of Ethics permits the parents of minor children to be included in the counseling process as appropriate. A family therapist may find the Parental Release Form (Appendix F) useful in documenting parental consent. If the child's parents have divorced, the parent named *managing conservator* (custodial parent) in the divorce decree is usually the only parent authorized to give parental consent; accordingly, the form provides for this situation.

Permission for Consultation/Taping/Research

Several purposes are served by the Permission for Consultation/Taping/Research form (Appendix F). First, a therapist in compliance with the AAMFT or NASW ethical codes must obtain a family's written permission before the therapist permits third-party observation, audiotaping, or videotaping (AAMFT, 1992; NASW, 1996). Sections 5 and 6 of the American Psychological Association Code of Ethics (1992) require the therapist to obtain the clients' permission before taping. The AAMFT ethical code also requires that families who are asked to participate in research must be (a) adequately informed about aspects of the research that might influence their decision whether to participate and (b) given freedom to decline to participate in research. Section I.E.2 of the NASW ethical code, in part, requires the therapist to "ascertain that the consent of the participants in the research is voluntary and informed, without any implied deprivation or penalty for refusal to participate" (NASW, 1996).

Case Notes

This form was used to standardize the clinical case notes maintained by therapists at the MFCCC. The therapist was expected to record all pertinent information about the completed session and therapeutic goal for the next session on the Case Notes form (Appendix E). The GARF ratings assigned by the therapist were recorded first. Ratings by the observing team were recorded on the Case Notes form from the back of the team message. GARF ratings were then copied onto the Profile Chart (Appendix B). One feature of the Case Notes is the therapist's use of numbers to code the interventions used and planned. Also, the form provides a convenient format for recording the therapist's systemic hypotheses. We found the Case Notes provided a concise format for recording session information. Therapists could and frequently did use the back of the form to further expand on the session. An alternative Case Notes form (Appendix E) is offered for therapists who prefer a less comprehensive format.

GARF Profile Chart

The GARF scores that were recorded on the Case Notes were then transferred and plotted on the GARF Profile Chart (Appendix B), which was attached to the inside front of the client's folder. By reviewing the plotted GARF scores for a given family, the therapist and supervisor could gain a quick overview of the family's functioning. Anomalies on the plotted GARF scores for a given therapy session could be further investigated by referring to the session Case Notes. We recommend this form be affixed beneath the Contact Summary Sheet (Appendix F), on the inside front of the client folder so that both are readily available.

GAS (GARF Version)

The outcome goals of therapy may be negotiated between the therapist and family members, then entered onto the GAS (Appendix C). The reader is encouraged to refer to an earlier discussion in Chapter 5 that presented this form in greater detail. The GAS may be useful to therapists who comply with the ethical code of the ACA and are required to "work jointly" (ACA, 1995, Section A.1.c) with their clients to establish and periodically review counseling plans.

SAFE

The SAFE (Appendix D) has been discussed extensively in a prior section of this volume (see Chapter 5). The family members are asked to mark the SAFE assessment form, then the therapist scores the forms and plots the results. We recommend that therapists provide family members with sufficient uninterrupted time to complete the SAFE, perhaps asking the family to arrive early and complete the SAFE in the waiting room prior to the initial therapy session.

Contract for Non-Violence

This form may be helpful to a therapist working with families in which the presenting problems include violence. The Contract for Non-Violence (see Appendix F) provides a convenient form for spouses to (a) document their mutual agreement to refrain from violence toward one another and (b) agree that if one spouse is violent, then the second spouse will immediately file for divorce. The form can be easily modified to address violence between nonspouses or among many family members. Section 1 of the AAMFT Code of Ethics (AAMFT, 1991) states that "Marriage and family therapists advance the welfare of families and individuals." Accordingly, we believe that this non-violence contract advances the clients' welfare. The Contract for Non-Violence may also be viewed as a structural and interactional intervention that specifies legal consequences if the couple's or family's level of functioning deteriorates into violence. As earlier discussed in this volume, the MFCCC research indicated that such families tended to have several months of low GARF scores indicating seriously low levels of family functioning.

No Suicide Contract

After assessing a client's potential lethality, a therapist may decide the client's risk of suicide is high enough to warrant requesting a written contract from the client. The reader may note that the No Suicide Contract (Appendix F) includes a sequence of steps for the client to follow if a crisis develops. The clinician's request for a client to sign such a contract may be viewed as an interactional intervention; therefore, the client's response is significant. The client declining to sign the No Suicide Contract may indicate a higher risk of client lethality. Even if the client does sign a No Suicide Contract, there may still be significant risk. Although the therapist may feel somewhat reassured that a client has agreed to sign the No Suicide Contract, the therapist is urged to exercise clinical judgment and evaluate the client for referral to more intensive treatments such as medication or hospitalization.

Therapist Periodic Assessment

We suggest the therapist use this form (Appendix E) to consolidate information about the client family, the therapist's conceptualizations of the family, and treatment goals with intervention plan. This form incorporates the GARF assessment along with individual DSM–IV axes diagnoses. When the therapist completes this assessment on a regular interval, such as every six sessions, he or she may gain an overall clinical perspective from which to evaluate therapy progress. This form meets and exceeds many managed care assessment requirements when additional sessions are being requested. MFT supervisees might be required to present and discuss this form during supervision. A great deal of information is collected on this single page to plan intervention strategies and to facilitate process and outcome research.

Supervision Case Presentation Guidelines

This form (see Appendix E) specifies the format and documents that a supervisee should prepare for supervision. We believe that the guidelines can assist the supervisor and supervisee by establishing an explicit agenda and clear expectations for the supervision. Assessment information, including the GARF, is prominent on the form. A supervisor may customize this form to meet the developmental needs of specific supervisees. For example, supervisees may be required to analyze and discuss videotapes of their therapy sessions.

Termination Form

When treatment is terminated, a clinician can document concluding therapeutic information on the Termination Form (Appendix F). Termination is part of the therapeutic process (Delaney & Eisenberg, 1972; Egan, 1994; W. C. Nichols, 1988) and may be attributed to successful therapy or other factors (Kottler & Blau, 1989). Therapists may briefly summarize such information as the family's presenting problem, issues addressed, payment and attendance patterns (who attended and when), therapeutic interventions used, and the clients' progress. Pertinent information about the final session can be recorded on this form plus the reason(s) for termination. The therapist may also document recommendations and referrals for further treatment.

Computer Requirements

In today's technological world, computer skills and equipment are almost a necessity for providers. The computer should be purchased on the basis of the software that will be used. More commonly available today are computers that are designated "Pentium" or "486," 133 MHz (or faster), and contain 16 or more megabytes of random access memory (RAM). The reader is encouraged to buy a high-quality computer monitor that is at least SVGA in order to reduce eyestrain. If the computer will be used extensively with a variety of complex software (e.g., word processing, spreadsheet, statistical analysis, and desktop publishing, etc.), then the reader may well consider a Pentium computer, 200 MHz (or faster), with 32 (or more) megabytes of RAM. Newer software tends to require large amounts of disk space and, accordingly, newer computers are sold with 2 gigabyte or larger hard drives. As of this writing (January 1997), the Windows 95 operating system continues to become a requirement for new software on the market.

Spreadsheet and database software

A variety of spreadsheet and database software is available and should be chosen on the basis of the needs of the user. Spreadsheet and database software are designed for different purposes, thus the reader is encouraged to select the software that best meets his or her specific needs.

Spreadsheet software was originally developed to emulate the multiple-column worksheets often used by accountants. People who want to type one number into the computer, type mathematical formulas that use the first number, then quickly calculate other numbers will probably prefer a spreadsheet program. By using a spreadsheet program, a user can easily change the first number and see the effects on the calculated numbers. Among the more popular spreadsheet programs currently available are Lotus 1-2-3, Microsoft Excel, and Corel Quattro Pro.

Database software was originally designed to conveniently store, sort, and retrieve data that the user had entered. A database program would serve the needs of people wanting to type data (e.g., client name, address, phone number, insurance policy, diagnosis, session attendance, etc.) into the computer, then later retrieve all or part of the data. The more popular database programs include Borland Dbase, Borland Paradox, Claris FileMaker Pro, Microsoft Access, and Symantec Q & A.

Session data and GARF scores may be entered into these spreadsheet or database programs, then conveniently analyzed or plotted to observe trends. Some word-processing programs, such as Microsoft Word or Corel WordPerfect offer limited ability to summarize and/or chart data; however, the user will probably be more satisfied with the added flexibility found in a spreadsheet or database program. Those who use Microsoft Office products may find that Microsoft Excel will serve their needs and more easily exchange data or graphs with other Microsoft products such as Word. Corel Quattro Pro also offers a spreadsheet program with powerful graphing features and may be preferred by people who use other Corel products. Purchasing statistical analysis software such as SPSS would provide a more versatile and powerful, yet considerably more expensive, alternative to using a spreadsheet/database. Software such as SamplePower (Borenstein, Rothstein, Cohen, & SPSS Inc., 1997) may help researchers as they seek a practical balance among sample size, effect size, and criterion for significance.

Scanners and optical character recognition (OCR) and optical mark recognition (OMR) software

Scanners are available in a variety of sizes (hand-held or desktop), shapes (scanner only or scanner with fax and/or answering machine), and capabilities (black and white, color, photo negatives, and transparencies). Scanners convert printed information on a sheet of paper or document into a digitized input for the computer. Some scanners can use an automated document feeder that permits the unattended processing of several documents. The printed information may include text, numbers, or pictures. A combination of text and numbers is commonly referred to as *alphanumeric*. OCR software translates the digitized text into an exportable alphanumeric format that can then be exported to other programs, such as word processing, desktop publishing, or statistical analysis programs. An example of versatile and powerful OCR software is OmniPage Pro for Windows 95 (Caere Corporation, 1996), which converts pictures and text into a variety of exportable formats. Another approach promises to let the therapist use a scanner to scan an answer sheet or bubble sheet, then use OMR software to convert the scanned image into an exportable format. As of this writing, SPSS (1996) is beginning to offer Remark Office OMR software designed to translate digitized images of bubble sheets, check boxes, and bar codes into a variety of exportable alphanumeric formats.

Staff Training Necessities

Each therapist or clinical setting will establish a process to record and protect information required by clients, clinicians, researchers, administrators, governmental regulatory and financial bodies, and third-party payers. Figure 6.2 illustrates several of the many possible documents containing information that could be entered into the record system. It is suggested that the record system be designed to collect and protect pertinent information, summarize the information into meaningful reports, and require minimal changes once established.

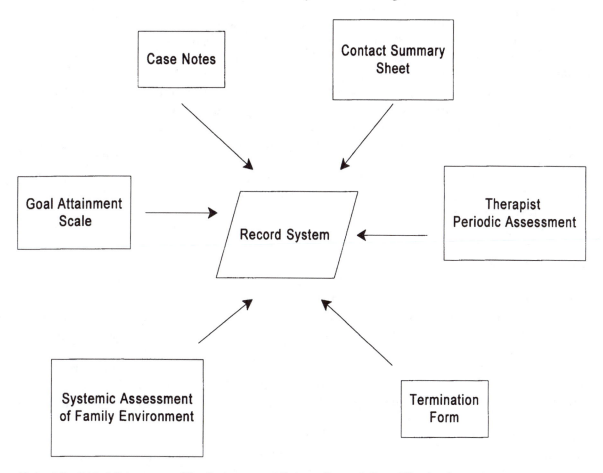

Figure 6.2 Critical Components of Family Assessment Outcome Research Record Keeping System.

The staff should be informed of the necessity of accurate and timely data collection, the criticalness of client record confidentiality and client data security, and the value of the research. If a computer is used for data storage, all users must be aware of the necessary steps to protect client data (e.g., only authorized persons have access to client data, store all data on floppy disks that are secured in a locked cabinet, etc.).

It is recommended that the therapist be responsible for initially recording and collecting the GARF data as part of daily routine charting duties. The therapist then copies the GARF data onto an input form for later input by the therapist or clerical staff. After the data are typed into the database from the input form, the data are printed out and checked against the data on the input form. All staff should be professional and diligent in protecting the private and confidential information that may appear on printouts; therefore, the printouts should be either stored in a locked cabinet or shredded before being discarded.

Practical Research Designs

It is important to determine the purpose or intent of the proposed research before establishing data collection procedures. In other words, what questions does the researcher want to answer? Exploratory research seeks to find and define new conceptual relationships and usually uses qualitative designs and methods. Confirmatory research usually uses quantitative designs and methods to expand on prior research, further describe a given group or population, or test a hypothesis about a given group or population. The researcher will likely need to conduct a review of the existing literature in order to clarify his or her research hypotheses and questions (Lambert, Masters, & Ogles, 1991). At this point, operational definitions will probably be needed to specify exactly what is meant by each variable in the proposed research.

Next, the clinician must determine whether the proposed research is significant. In other words, are the results likely to be worth the effort, expense, and potential risks to clients? Remember that participants in research are considered to be "human subjects" that are protected under federal and state laws and regulations. Furthermore, professional ethics (AAMFT, 1991; ACA, 1995; American Psychological Association, 1992; NASW, 1996) require informed client permission, voluntary participation, protected data, and protected client identity when the results are presented or published.

If the research questions have been clearly defined, and the proposed research appears to be justifiable, then the research design should be established. A *research design* has been defined as "a set of plans or procedures that reduce error and simultaneously help the researcher obtain empirical evidence (data) about the isolated variables of interest" (Heppner, Kivlighan, & Wampold, 1992, p. 44). The research design will specify the variables of interest, the method of collecting data, and data analysis with respect to the research hypotheses and questions. During this planning stage, the researcher is encouraged to consider how the sample size and the criterion for significance (alpha) both affect the power of a statistical test (Cohen, 1988). Research design has been extensively examined by several authors (e.g., Alexander, Holtzworth-Munroe, & Jameson, 1994; Campbell & Stanley, 1963; Denzin & Lincoln, 1994; Heppner et al., 1992; Pedhazur & Schmelkin, 1991; Schumacher & McMillan, 1993; Sprenkle & Moon, 1996.). The reader is referred to these comprehensive resources.

As described earlier, the MFCCC research project (Yingling et al., 1994a, 1994b) was exploratory (e.g., what services are sought by clients in family therapy? can such diverse client information be somehow organized for further research?). The MFCCC research project was also descriptive in attempting to better describe the clients served by a regional family therapy clinic and to verify the utility of the GARF in a clinical setting. We believe the findings of the MFCCC project were important and intriguing; however, many of the initial research questions remain unanswered, and the findings themselves have generated additional questions, such as the following:

- If a research study included a much larger, more diverse sample of families and raters, (a) will the GARF interrater reliability remain sufficiently high? and (b) which of the three GARF subscales would most reliably and accurately predict the overall GARF rating assigned to the client family?
- If a research study included a much larger, more diverse sample of families and raters and then compared the GARF with existing clinical measurements, (a) would the GARF as a global rating and by subscales correlate significantly with various family assessment clinical rating scale and self-report instruments already in use? and (b) if so, what could be learned by examining measured variables and the indicated treatment recommendations from each?
- If a research study included a much larger, more diverse sample of families and raters and then compared the GARF with existing clinical measurements, (a) would there be a correlational relationship between the GARF changes and the level of DSM–IV symptomology?; (b) would the length of treatment required to make a substantial change in the GARF and reduce DSM–IV symptoms be different for different presenting problems?; (c) what DSM–IV diagnoses and GARF ratings would most likely be associated with particularly disturbing presenting problems, such as incest, do-

mestic violence, and gang involvement?; and (d) what intervention strategies would seem to predict quicker GARF changes and with what issues?

These and many other questions remain unanswered. We hope that this volume will provide a practical foundation for future researchers who will examine the above questions.

FUTURE CHALLENGES FOR GARF USERS: CLINICIANS, BUSINESS MANAGERS, AND EDUCATORS

We address this book to a wide audience of readers and believe that this volume will be particularly helpful to therapists in clinical practice and also useful to managed care staff and therapist educators/researchers. We have presented initial findings that indicate the GARF is a promising instrument for screening client families to plan efficient therapeutic interventions and for evaluating therapeutic outcome. Furthermore, we have offered some practical suggestions for incorporating the GARF into the therapy system. We recognize that the GARF is a new instrument and much more research is needed to explore and confirm its psychometric properties, as well as practical use in family therapy. The following briefly discusses the areas that we encourage future investigators to examine.

Therapists in Clinical Practice

The primary focus of GARF research for therapists in clinical practice might be whether the GARF is useful in measuring therapy outcome. If the GARF is found to be a sufficiently reliable and valid measure of therapy outcome, then therapists may begin to compare the effectiveness of various treatment modalities and theories for specific family problems. The therapist may want to examine which GARF subscales (Interactional, Organization, and Emotional) best predict future changes in the family's overall functioning in order to target interventions at the most appropriate subscale. The clinician may also want to examine what combinations of GARF subscale scores are associated with DSM–IV diagnostic criteria and presenting problems. Being able to clearly plan which shifts in the family system most efficiently eliminate DSM–IV diagnosed symptoms will mark a real breakthrough in mental health treatment.

Business Managers

Managed care quality assurance staff may want to examine whether the GARF is useful in evaluating the effectiveness of therapists and their interventions. Learning what works best will allow managed care staff to train their providers to do more of what works. Managed care staff may also want to explore whether the GARF can be useful in evaluating requests for additional therapy. Additional authorizations may be contingent on effective GARF-based systemic treatment plans. Finally, managed care staff may want to examine the GARF as a measure of family functioning correlated with the DSM–IV's traditional measure of individual pathology. A first step would be to include GARF ratings on the provider's required assessment forms. This initiation of systemic thinking in the management of mental health services will add a very compatible systemic model to the payer business company's TQM philosophy.

Therapist Educators/Researchers

Normative GARF data need to be established by clinical researchers for diverse families judged to be at various levels of symptom-associated functioning, including families who are functioning sufficiently well that therapy is not warranted. These data can then be shared with managed care staff for utilization review purposes. The therapist educator/ researcher may want to pursue research focused on the specific teaching/supervision interventions that increase the trainees' competence in using the GARF as an assessment instrument. The educator may also want to conduct studies that delineate the specific constructs measured by the SAFE and the GARF (including the GARF subscales). A therapist educator may want to examine whether the GARF is appropriate in assessing families from various ethnic and cultural backgrounds. Further research comparing the GARF with other family assessment models currently in use will lead to a more clear understanding of how families best function in order to solve their problems effectively and self-reliantly.

All settings can benefit from improved system assessment skills. Our use of GARF as a foundational clinical assessment tool has been rewarding. We hope the *GARF Assessment Sourcebook* will be helpful to your growth plans for assessment of relational functioning.

References

Alexander, J. F., Holtzworth-Munroe, A., & Jameson, P. J. (1994). The process and outcome of marital and family therapy: Research review and evaluation. In A. E. Bergin & S. L. Garfield (Eds.), *Handbook of psychotherapy and behavior change* (4th ed., pp. 595–630). New York: Wiley.

American Association for Marriage and Family Therapy. (1991). *AAMFT code of ethics*. Washington, DC: Author.

American Association for Marriage and Family Therapy. (1993). *Approved supervisor designation: Standards and responsibilities*. Washington, DC: Author.

American Counseling Association. (1995). *Code of ethics and standards of practice*. Alexandria, VA: Author.

American Psychiatric Association. (1994). *Diagnostic and statistical manual of mental disorders* (4th ed.). Washington, DC: Author.

American Psychiatric Association. (1994–1996). *DSM–IV Sourcebook* (Vols. 1–3). Washington, DC: Author.

American Psychological Association. (1992). *Ethical principles of psychologists and code of conduct*. Washington, DC: Author.

Anastasi, A. (1988). *Psychological testing* (6th ed.). New York: Macmillan.

Anderson, H. (1997). *Conversation, language, and possibilities*. New York: Basic Books.

Aponte, H. (1981). Structural family therapy. In A. Gurman & D. Kniskern (Eds.), *Handbook of family therapy* (pp. 310–360). New York: Brunner/Mazel.

Bateson, G., Jackson, D. D., Haley, J., & Weakland, J. (1956). Toward a theory of schizophrenia. *Behavioral Science, 1,* 251–264.

Beavers, W. R., & Hampson, R. B. (1990). *Successful families: Assessment and intervention*. New York: W.W. Norton.

Beck, A. T., & Beck, R. W. (1972). Screening depressed patients in family practice: A rapid technique. *Postgraduate Medicine, 52,* 81–85.

Becvar, D. S., & Becvar, R. J. (1996). *Family therapy: A systemic integration* (3rd ed.). Boston: Allyn & Bacon.

Borenstein, M., Rothstein, H., Cohen, J., & SPSS Inc. (1997). SamplePower (Version 1.0) [Computer software]. Chicago, IL: SPSS Inc.

Boscolo, L., Cecchin, G., Hoffman, L, & Penn, P. (1987). *Milan systemic family therapy: Conversations in theory and practice*. New York: Basic Books.

Brown, M., Hitchcock, D., & Willard, M. (1994). *Why TQM fails and what to do about it*. Burr Ridge, IL: Irwin Professional Publishing.

Bussell, D., Matsey, K., Reiss, D., & Hetherington, M. (1995). Debriefing the family: Is research an intervention? *Family Process, 34,* 145–160.

Campbell, D. T., & Stanley, J. C. (1963). *Experimental and quasi-experimental designs for research*. Chicago: Rand McNally.

Chewning, D. (1996). *Improving therapy with analytical statistics*. Manuscript submitted for publication.

Chewning, D., & Yingling, L. (January, 1995). *Will TQM improve your practice?* Paper presented at the meeting of the Texas Association for Marriage and Family Therapy, Austin.

Child Well-Being Scales [Computer software]. (1996). Rochester, MN: Oakwood Behavioral Systems.

Cohen, J. (1988). *Statistical power analysis for the behavioral analysis* (2nd ed.). Hillsdale, NJ: Lawrence Erlbaum Associates.

Corey, G., Corey, M. S., & Callanan, P. (1993). *Issues and ethics in the helping professions* (4th ed.). Pacific Grove, CA: Brooks/Cole.

Dallas Association for Marriage and Family Therapy Managed Care Committee. (1995). *Survey of the leading managed care companies.* Unpublished report.

Dausch, B. M., Miklowitz, D. J., & Richards, J. A. (1996). Global Assessment of Relational Functioning Scale: II. Reliability and validity in a sample of families of bipolar patients. *Family Process, 35,* 175–189.

Delaney, D.J., & Eisenberg, S. (1972). *The counseling process.* Chicago: Rand McNally.

Deming, W. E. (1986). *Out of the crisis.* Cambridge, MA: Massachusetts Institute of Technology Center for Advanced Engineering Study.

Deming, W. E. (1993). *The new economics for industry, government, education.* Cambridge, MA: Massachusetts Institute of Technology Center for Advanced Engineering Study.

Denzin, N. K., & Lincoln, Y. S. (Eds.). (1994). *Handbook of qualitative research.* Thousand Oaks, CA: Sage.

Dickey, M. (1996). Quantitative design in family therapy: Insider hints on getting started. In D. H. Sprenkle & S. M. Moon (Eds.), *Research methods in family therapy* (pp. 191–215). New York: Guilford Press.

Dyche, L., & Zayas, L. (1995). The value of curiosity and naiveté for the cross-cultural psychotherapist. *Family Process, 34,* 389–400.

Egan, G. (1994). *The skilled helper* (5th ed.). Pacific Grove, CA: Brooks/Cole.

Epstein, N. B., Baldwin, L. M., & Bishop, D. S. (1983). The McMaster Family Assessment Device. *Journal of Marital and Family Therapy, 9*(2), 171–180.

Epstein, N. B., Bishop, D. S., & Levin, S. (1978). The McMaster Model of Family Functioning. *Journal of Marriage and Family Counseling, 4,* 19–31.

Falicov, C. (1995). Training to think culturally: A multidimensional comparative framework. *Family Process, 34,* 373–388.

Framo, J. (1992). *Family-of-origin therapy: An intergenerational approach.* New York: Brunner/Mazel.

Framo, J. (1996). A personal retrospective of the family therapy field: Then and now. *Journal of Marital and Family Therapy, 22*(3), 289–316.

Fristad, M. (1989). A comparison of the McMaster and Circumplex family assessment instruments. *Journal of Marital and Family Therapy, 15*(3), 259–269.

Gordon, E. (1997). *The Global Assessment of Relational Functioning (GARF): Reliability and validity.* Unpublished master's thesis, Southern Methodist University, Dallas, TX.

Group for the Advancement of Psychiatry Committee on the Family. (1989). The challenge of relational diagnoses: Applying the biopsychosocial model in DSM–IV. *American Journal of Psychiatry, 146,* 1492–1494.

Group for the Advancement of Psychiatry Committee on the Family. (1996). Global assessment of relational functioning scale (GARF): I. Background and rationale. *Family Process, 35,* 155–172.

Hampson, R. B., & Beavers, W. R. (1996). Family therapy and outcome: Relationships between therapist and family styles. *Contemporary Family Therapy, 18,* 345–370.

Hampson, R. B., Beavers, W. R., & Hulgus, Y. F. (1989). Insiders' and outsiders' views of family: The assessment of family competence and style. *Journal of Family Psychology, 3,* 118–136.

Hampson, R. B., Henney, S. M., & Beavers, W. R. (1996). *Relational diagnosis and assessment in family therapy.* Manuscript submitted for publication.

Hawking, S. (1988). *A brief history of time: From the big bang to black holes.* New York: Bantam Books.

Heppner, P. P., Kivlighan, D. M., Jr., & Wampold, B. E. (1992). *Research design in counseling.* Pacific Grove, CA: Brooks/Cole.

Howard, K. I., Kopta, S. M., Krauss, M. S., & Orlinsky, D. E. (1986). The dose–effect relationship in psychotherapy. *American Psychologist, 41,* 159–164.

Howard, K. I., Orlinsky, D. E., & Lueger, R. J. (1994). Clinically relevant outcome research in individual psychotherapy. *British Journal of Psychiatry, 165,* 4–8.

Imber-Black, E. (1988). *Families and larger systems: A family therapist's guide through the labyrinth.* New York: Guilford Press.

Jacob, T. (1995). The role of time frame in the assessment of family functioning. *Journal of Marital and Family Therapy, 21*(3), 281–288.

Jacobsen, N. (1981). Behavioral marital therapy. In A. Gurman & D. Kniskern (Eds.), *Handbook of family therapy* (pp. 556–591). New York: Brunner/Mazel.

Jacobson, N. S., & Truax, P. (1991). Clinical significance: A statistical approach to defining meaningful change in psychotherapy research. *Journal of Consulting and Clinical Psychology, 59,* 12–19.

Jennings, C., & Towers, J. (1996). Interview: Cary Sennett, MD, PhD, Vice President for Performance Measurement, National Committee for Quality Assurance (NCQA). *Journal of the American Academy of Nurse Practitioners, 8*(6), 265–267.

Johnston, K., (1992). *Interrater reliability of the Global Assessment of Relational Functioning.* Unpublished master's thesis, Florida Institute of Technology, Melbourne, Florida.

Jongsma, A. E., Jr., Peterson, L. M., & McInnis, W. P. (1997). Therascribe (Version 3.0) [computer software]. Somerset, NJ: John Wiley & Sons, Inc.

Jordan, K., & Quinn, W. (1996). Ethical concerns for supervising the impaired marriage and family therapist. *Family Therapy, 23,* 51–57.

Kabacoff, R. I., Miller, I. W., Bishop, D. S., Epstein, N. B., & Keitner, G. I. (1990). A psychometric study of the McMaster Family Assessment Device in psychiatric, medical, and nonclinical samples. *Journal of Family Psychology, 3,* 431–439.

Kadera, S. W., Lambert, M. J., & Andrews, A. A. (1996). How much therapy is really enough? A session-by-session analysis of the psychotherapy dose effect relationship. *Journal of Psychotherapy and Research, 5(2),* 132–151.

Kaslow, F.W. (Ed.). (1996). *Handbook of relational diagnosis and dysfunctional family patterns.* New York: Wiley.

Kerr, M., & Bowen, M. (1988). *Family evaluation: An approach based on Bowen theory.* New York: W.W. Norton.

Kottler, J. A., & Blau, D. S. (1989). *The imperfect therapist.* San Francisco: Jossey-Bass.

L'Abate, L., & Bagarozzi, D. A. (1993). *Sourcebook of marriage and family evaluation.* New York: Brunner/Mazel.

Lambert, M. J., & Cattani-Thompson, K. (1996). Current findings regarding the effectiveness of counseling: Implications for practice. *Journal of Counseling and Development, 74,* 601–608.

Lambert, M. J., & Hill, C. E. (1994). Assessing psychotherapy outcomes and progress. In A. E. Bergin & S. L. Garfield (Eds.), *Handbook of psychotherapy and behavior change* (4th ed., pp. 72–113). New York: Wiley.

Lambert, M. J., Masters, K. S., & Ogles, B. M. (1991). Outcome research in counseling. In C. E. Watkins, Jr. & L. J. Schneider (Eds.), *Research in counseling* (pp. 51–83). Hillsdale, NJ: Erlbaum.

Licensed Marriage and Family Therapist Act, Texas Civil Statutes, Article 4512c-1, §2(5), (1991, amended 1993).

McGoldrick, M., & Gerson, R. (1985). *Genograms in family assessment.* New York: W.W. Norton.

Meara, N. M., & Schmidt, L. D. (1991). The ethics of researching counseling/therapy processes. In C. E. Watkins, Jr. & L. J. Schneider (Eds.), *Research in counseling* (pp. 237–259). Hillsdale, NJ: Erlbaum.

Microsoft Excel 97 [Computer software]. (1997). Redmond, WA: Microsoft Corporation.

Microsoft Word 97 [Computer software]. (1997). Redmond, WA: Microsoft Corporation.

Mills, S., & Sprenkle, D. (1995). Family therapy in the postmodern era. *Family Relations, 44*(4), 368–376.

Minuchin, S., Baker, L., Rosman, B., Liebman, R., Milman, L., & Todd, T. (1975). A conceptual model of psychosomatic illness in children. *Archives of General Psychiatry, 32,* 1031–1038.

Minuchin, S., Montalvo, B., Guerney, B., Rosman, B., & Schumer, F. (1967). *Families of the slums.* New York: Basic Books.

Minuchin, S., Rosman, B., & Baker, L. (1978). *Psychosomatic families: Anorexia nervosa in context.* Cambridge, MA: Harvard University Press.

Mohr, D. C., Beutler, L. E., Engle, E., Shoham-Salomon, V., Bergan, J., Kaszniak, A. W., & Yost, E. B. (1990). Identification of patients at risk for nonresponse and negative outcome in psychotherapy. *Journal of Consulting and Clinical Psychology, 58,* 622–628.

National Association of Social Workers. (1996, November). *Code of ethics.* [Online]. Available: http://www.naswca.org/ethics/html.

National Committee for Quality Assurance. (April 1, 1996). *Draft accreditation standards for managed behavioral healthcare organizations.* Unpublished document. Available from: National Committee for Quality Assurance, 2000 L St., NW, Ste. 500, Washington, DC 20036. Phone: (202) 955-3500 fax: (202) 955-3599, http://www.ncqa.org.

NCQA develops standards for behavioral healthcare organizations. (1996, June). *Spectrum: The quarterly provider newsletter of Merit Behavioral Care Corporation, II*(2), 2.

NCQA releases accreditation summary reports on health plans. (1996). *American Family Physician, 54*(2), 434.

Nichols, W. C. (1988). *Marital therapy: An integrative approach.* New York: Guilford Press.

Nichols, M., & Schwartz, R. (1995). *Family therapy: Concepts and methods.* (3rd ed.). Boston: Allyn & Bacon.

Novack, T. A., & Gage, R. J. (1995). Assessment of family functioning. In L. A. Cushman & M. J. Scherer (Eds.), *Psychological assessment in medical rehabilitation* (pp. 275–297). Washington, DC: American Psychological Association.

O'Hanlon, W., & Weiner-Davis, M. (1989). *In search of solutions: A new direction in psychotherapy.* New York: W. W. Norton.

Olson, D. H. (1996). Clinical assessment and treatment interventions using the family Circumplex Model. In F. W. Kaslow (Ed.). *Handbook of relational diagnosis and dysfunctional family patterns* (pp. 59–80). New York: Wiley.

Olson, D. H., Portner, J, & Lavee, Y. (1985). *FACES III.* St. Paul: University of Minnesota Press.

Olson, D. H., Sprenkle, D. H., & Russell, C. S. (1979). Circumplex Model of marital and family systems I: Cohesion and adaptability dimensions, family types, and clinical applications. *Family Process, 18,* 3–28.

Olson, D. H., Sprenkle, D. H., & Russell, C. S. (1989). *Circumplex Model: Systemic assessment and treatment of families.* New York: Haworth Press.

Olson, D., & Tiesel, J. (1991). *FACES III: Linear scoring & interpretation.* St. Paul: University of Minnesota Press.

OmniPage Pro for Windows 95 (Version 7.0) [Computer software]. (1996). Los Gatos, CA: Caere Corporation.

Pare, D. (1995). Of families and other cultures: The shifting paradigm of family therapy. *Family Process, 34,* 1–19.

Pare, D. (1996). Culture and meaning: Expanding the metaphorical repertoire of family therapy. *Family Process, 35,* 21–42.

Pederson, P. B. (1991). Multiculturalism as a generic approach to counseling. *Journal of Counseling and Development, 70,* 6–12.

Pedhazur, E. J., & Schmelkin, L. P. (1991). *Measurement, design, and analysis: An integrated approach.* Hillsdale, NJ: Erlbaum.

Pierce, J. L. (1993). *Cross-method congruence and clinical validity of the assessment instruments of the Beavers Family Systems Model.* Unpublished doctoral dissertation, Southern Methodist University, Dallas, TX.

Pike-Urlacher, C. L., Mackinnon, D. P., & Piercy, F. P. (1996). Cost-effectiveness research in family therapy. In D. H. Sprenkle & S. M. Moon (Eds.), *Research methods in family therapy* (pp. 365–387). New York: Guilford Press.

Pinsof, W. (1988). Strategies for the study of family therapy research. In L. Wynne (Ed.), *The state of the art in family therapy research: Controversies and recommendations* (pp. 159–174). New York: Family Process Press.

Ratliff, D., & Yingling, L. (Eds.) (1996). *Reviewing our common body of knowledge: MFT license exam preparation manual.* Austin: Texas Association for Marriage and Family Therapy.

Remark Office OMR [Computer software]. (1996). Chicago: SPSS, Inc.

Roberts, B. (1996, June). The provider and the care manager: A partnership for quality and effectiveness in behavioral healthcare. *Spectrum: The quarterly provider newsletter of Merit Behavioral Care Corporation, II(2),* 1–2.

Satir, V. (1983). *Conjoint family therapy* (3rd ed.). Palo Alto, CA: Science and Behavior Books.

Satir, V., & Baldwin, M. (1983). *Satir step by step: A guide to creating change in families.* Palo Alto, CA: Science and Behavior Books.

Schumacher, S., & McMillan, J. H. (1993). *Research in education: A conceptual introduction* (3rd ed.). New York: HarperCollins.

Snyder, D. K., & Rice, J. L. (1996). Methodological issues and strategies in scale development. In. D. H. Sprenkle & S. M. Moon (Eds.), *Research methods in family therapy* (pp. 216–237). New York: Guilford Press.

Speight, S. L., Myers, L. J., Cox, C. I., & Highlen, P. S. (1991). A redefinition of multicultural counseling. *Journal of Counseling and Development, 70,* 29–36.

Sprenkle, D. H., & Moon, S. M. (Eds.). (1996). *Research methods in family therapy.* New York: Guilford Press.

SPSS (Version 7.0) [Computer software]. (1996). Chicago: SPSS, Inc.

Walsh, F. (1993). *Normal family processes* (2nd ed.). New York: Guilford Press.

Wesley, S., & Waring, E. M. (1996). A critical review of marital therapy outcome research. *Canadian Journal of Psychiatry, 41,* 421–428.

Westley, W. A., & Epstein, N. B. (1969). *The silent majority.* San Francisco: Jossey-Bass.

Wheeler, D. J. (1995). *Advanced topics in statistical process control.* Knoxville, TN: SPC Press.

Williamson, D. (1991). *The intimacy paradox: Personal authority in the family system.* New York: Guilford Press.

Wylie, M. S. (1990). Brief therapy on the couch. *Family Therapy Networker, 14,* 34–35.

Wynne, L. C. (1992). *Field trial of a proposed additional axis for DSM–IV: Global Assessment of Relational Functioning (GARF).* Unpublished manuscript, University of Rochester, Rochester, NY.

Wynne, L. (Ed.). (1988). *The state of the art of family therapy research: Controversies and recommendations.* New York: Family Process Press.

Yingling, J.R. (1994). *TQM training manual.* Unpublished manuscript.

Yingling, L. (1996a). *Systemic family therapy: Resource for the '90's. Tape 1: Overview.* Richardson, TX: Video Classifieds.

Yingling, L. (1996b). [Video family assessment exercise]. Unpublished raw data.

Yingling, L. C. (1996c). *A manual for the use of the Systemic Assessment of the Family Environment (SAFE): A self-report instrument for assessing multi-level family system functioning.* Rockwall, TX: J&L Human Systems Development.

Yingling, L. C., Miller, W. E., Jr., McDonald, A. L., & Galewaler, S. T. (1994a, January). *Verifying outcome: Paradigm for the therapist–researcher.* Paper presented at the meeting of the Texas Association for Marriage and Family Therapy, San Antonio.

Yingling, L. C., Miller, W. E., Jr., McDonald, A. L., & Galewaler, S. T. (1994b, November). *Verifying outcome: Paradigm for the therapist–researcher.* Paper presented at the meeting of the American Association of Marriage and Family Therapy, Chicago.

Appendixes

With the purchase of a single copy of this book, the authors grant permission to the purchaser to duplicate all forms in the appendixes (excluding the description of the GARF taken from the DSM–IV) to be used in a clinical practice/research setting. The Center for Human Systems Development will serve as a clearinghouse for information on the GARF, sharing information with Dr. Lyman Wynne and others interested in ongoing research. To compile GARF research results, please submit a summary of your results (research data or clinical utility impressions) to:

Dr. Lynelle C. Yingling, Director
Center for Human Systems Development
Texas A&M University System
570 E. Quail Run Road
Rockwall, Texas 75087-7321
Fax: (972) 772-3669
E-mail: LynelleYingling@compuserve.com

Appendixes:
A. Systemic MFT Skill Development Scale
B. GARF Training and Record Keeping Charts:
- DSM–IV Description
- Levels of Functioning by Sub-Scales
- GARF Profile Chart
C. Developed GARF Tools:
- GARF Self-Report for Families
- Goals Attainment Scale (GARF Version)
D. Systemic Assessment of the Family Environment (SAFE)
E. Record Keeping Forms Including GARF Ratings:
- Coded Research Case Notes
- Clinical Case Notes
- Therapist Periodic Assessment
- Supervision Case Presentation Guidelines

F. Clinic Research/Clinical Forms Not Including GARF Ratings:
- Clinic Client Intake Form
- Intake Form
- Contact Summary Sheet
- Duty to Warn
- Permission for Consultation/Taping/Research
- Consent for the Release of Confidential Information
- Parental Release Form
- No Suicide Contract
- Contract for Non-Violence
- Termination Form
- Family's Evaluation of Services

Appendix A

Systemic MFT Skill Development Scale

Evaluation of _____ on _____ by _____

Directions: Evaluate current skill development level. First rate the level of achievement by placing a number [1 = lowest level; 10 = highest level] on each blank line. Circle selected skill numbers to focus on. Use assessment to develop a few realistic change goals for the near future.

A. ADMINISTRATIVE FUNCTIONS:
_____ 1. keeping up with paper work
_____ 2. keeping on schedule in sessions
_____ 3. organizing any special materials needed for sessions
_____ 4. taping sessions routinely & reviewing as needed
_____ 5. working effectively with office staff

B. TEAM FUNCTIONING:
_____ 1. paying full attention to the case in progress
_____ 2. developing messages based on current assessment
_____ 3. sharing ideas during consultation & supervision
_____ 4. processing conflicts appropriately with team members
_____ 5. providing support for team members which facilitates their growth

C. PERSON OF THE THERAPIST ATTRIBUTES:
_____ 1. aware of own issues which could impact relationship with clients
_____ 2. sufficient resolution of own issues or appropriate use of referral, team, or supervision to protect clients
_____ 3. appropriate sensitivity to gender & ethnic issues in self which could interfere with effective client services
_____ 4. monitors all interactions with clients to set appropriate sexual boundaries

D. JOINING SKILLS:
_____ 1. confirm family members with empathic responses
_____ 2. absolve individuals from personal responsibility for the problem
_____ 3. track information as a neutral listener
_____ 4. understand and use the family's language
_____ 5. emphasize the expert position to create a therapeutic context and engender hope

E. ASSESSMENT SKILLS:
Strategic [macro lens] = tracking interactional patterns around the symptom/presenting problem which are a result of the family's attempts to get fundamental needs met by responding to the stress of the necessary change
_____ 1. problem solving enactment/reenactment
_____ 2. circular questioning
_____ 3. clinical rating scale family assessment models (GARF/Circumplex Model/Beavers Systems Model)
Structural [50 mm lens] = defining how the family structure maintains the ineffective patterns by identifying the family rules about boundaries which define power bases/decision-making authority and consequently inhibit the system's ability to use more effective interactional patterns for meeting their needs
_____ 4. sculpting/choreographing
_____ 5. listing family rules
_____ 6. self-report family assessment written instruments (FACES/SFI/SAFE)
Family-of-Origin [wide-angle lens] = identifying loyalties which inconspicuously lock in the ineffective family structure which supports the interactional patterns which perpetuate the symptom and rigidify the patterns
_____ 7. genogram construction
_____ 8. listing family-of-origin rules
_____ 9. tracking reactions to "parent firing" assignments

F. HYPOTHESIS FORMULATION SKILLS: *[conceptualizing/writing based on 1 key dimension or an integration of dimensions]*
_____ 1. interactional = identifying interactional patterns around the symptom until a structural identification begins to emerge
_____ 2. organizational = identifying ineffective dyadic, nuclear, and extended family rules which establish boundaries around subsystems and designate power bases

G. STRATEGIZING SKILLS: *[formulating, executing, & evaluating interventions based on the hypothesis]*
Strategic
_____ 1. focus on solution of the presenting problem in a way which will provide a systemic change that will strengthen future problem solving capabilities
_____ 2. reframe the motives of the interactional patterns as an attempt to make the structure more functional
_____ 3. reframe the stuckness into hopefulness through metaphor
_____ 4. use paradoxical/straightforward directives to help the family experience new interactional patterns
_____ 5. reduce anxiety about behavioral change by giving "go slow" directives
_____ 6. coach the family on improving problem-solving skills
Structural
_____ 7. join effectively before beginning stroke-kick approach to facilitate restructuring
_____ 8. interrupt & redirect communication interchanges to redirect power bases/alliances
_____ 9. use rearranging of family member seatings to imply alliance shifts
_____ 10. affirm all efforts at positive structural changes
_____ 11. facilitate family bringing about positive structural changes:
      _____ -strengthened egalitarian marital subsystem
      _____ -strengthened parental hierarchy
      _____ -strengthened sibling support subsystem
      _____ -strengthened adult relationship with former parents
Family-of-Origin
_____ 12. use genogram construction to help family identify FOO patterns consciously
_____ 13. refer to FOO members by given names vs. role names in session
_____ 14. use practice exercises (unmailed letters, etc.) to help client identify desired changes in relationship with FOO member/s
_____ 15. give assignments to begin changing the interaction patterns with FOO to adult-adult interaction, using the nuclear family as the support resource to help protect from regression to child-adult interactions
_____ 16. invite FOO members into session & coach a renegotiation of interactional rules for an adult-adult relationship; include the spouse as co-therapist if possible

116

Appendix B

GARF Training and Record Keeping Charts:

DSM–IV Description
Levels of Functioning by Sub-Scales
GARF Profile Chart

GLOBAL ASSESSMENT OF RELATIONAL FUNCTIONING (GARF) INSTRUCTIONS

Analogous to Axis V (Global Assessment of Individual Functioning) in DSM-III-R, the GARF Scale permits the clinician to rate the degree to which a family or other ongoing relational unit meets the affective and/or instrumental needs of its members. Consider the affective and instrumental functioning of the relational unit in the following areas:

A. *Problem Solving* (skills in negotiating goals, rules, and routines; adaptability to stress; communication skills; ability to resolve conflict).

B. *Organization* (maintenance of interpersonal roles and subsystem boundaries; hierarchical functioning, coalitions and distribution of power, control and responsibility).

C. *Emotional climate* (tone and range of feelings; quality of caring, empathy, involvement and attachment/commitment; sharing of values; mutual affective responsiveness, respect and regard; quality of sexual functioning).

GARF RATING SCALE

Note: Use specific, intermediate codes when possible, e.g., 45,68,72. If detailed information is not adequate to make specific ratings, use midpoints of the five descriptive sections, that is, 90,70,50,30, or 10.

5. (81-99)

OVERALL: **Relational unit is functioning satisfactorily from self-report of participants and from perspectives of observers.**

Agreed-upon patterns or routines exist that help meet the usual needs of each family/couple member; there is flexibility for change in response to unusual demands or events; occasional conflicts and stressful transitions are resolved through problem-solving communication and negotiation.

There is a shared understanding and agreement about roles and appropriate tasks; decision making is established for each functional area; there is recognition of the unique characteristics and merit of each subsystem (e.g., parents/spouses, siblings, and individuals).

There is a situationally appropriate, optimistic atmosphere in the family; a wide range of feelings is freely expressed and managed within the family; there is a general atmosphere of warmth, caring, and sharing of values among all family members. Sexual relations of adult members are satisfactory.

4. (61-80)

OVERALL: **Functioning of relational unit is somewhat unsatisfactory. Over a period of time, many but not all difficulties are resolved without complaints.**

Daily routines are present but there is some pain and difficulty in responding to the unusual. Some conflicts remain unresolved, but do not disrupt family functioning.

Decision making is usually competent, but efforts at control of one another quite often are greater than necessary and/or are ineffective. Individuals and relationships are clearly demarcated but sometimes a specific subsystem is depreciated or scapegoated.

A range of feeling is expressed, but instances of emotional blocking and/or tension are evident. Warmth and caring are present but are marred by a family member's irritability and frustrations. Sexual activity of adult members may be reduced or problematic.

3. (41-60)

OVERALL: **Relational unit has occasional times of satisfying and competent functioning together but clearly dysfunctional, unsatisfying relationships tend to predominate.**

Communication is frequently inhibited by unresolved conflicts that often interfere with daily routines; there is significant difficulty in adapting to family stress and transitional change.

Decision making is only intermittently competent and effective; either excessive rigidity or significant lack of structure is evident at these times. Individual needs are quite often submerged by a partner or coalition.

Pain and/or ineffective anger or emotional deadness interfere with family enjoyment. Though there is some warmth and support for members, it is unusually unequally distributed. Troublesome sexual difficulties between adults are often present.

2. (21-40)

OVERALL: **Relational unit is obviously and seriously dysfunctional; forms and time periods of satisfactory relating are rare.**

Family/couple routines do not meet the needs of members; they are grimly adhered to or blithely ignored. Life cycle changes, such as departures or entries into the relational unit, generate painful conflict and obviously frustrating failures of problem solving.

Decision making is tyrannical or quite ineffective. The unique characteristics of individuals are unappreciated or ignored by either rigid or confusingly fluid coalitions.

There are infrequent periods of enjoyment of life together; frequent distancing or open hostility reflect significant conflicts that remain unresolved and quite painful. Sexual dysfunction among adult members is commonplace.

1. (1-20)

OVERALL: **Relational unit has become too dysfunctional to retain continuity of contact and attachment.**

Family/couple routines are negligible (e.g., no mealtime, sleeping, or waking schedule); family members often do not know where others are or when they will be in or out; there is little effective communication among family members.

Family/couple members are not organized in such a way that personal or generational responsibilities are recognized. Boundaries of relational unit as a whole and subsystems cannot be identified or agreed upon. Family members are physically endangered or injured or sexually attacked.

Despair and cynicism are pervasive; there is little attention to the emotional needs of others; there is almost no sense of attachment, commitment, or concern about one another's welfare.

GARF: LEVELS OF FUNCTIONING BY SUB-SCALES

ADAPTED FROM THE GARF SCALE IN DSM IV, pp. 758-9

INTERACTIONAL/PROBLEM SOLVING: *Skills in negotiating goals, rules, and routines; adaptability to stress; communication skills; ability to resolve conflict*

ORGANIZATION: *Maintenance of interpersonal roles and subsystem boundaries; hierarchical functioning; coalitions and distribution of power, control, and responsibility*

EMOTIONAL CLIMATE: *Tone and range of feelings; quality of caring, empathy, involvement, and attachment/ commitment; sharing of values; mutual affective responsiveness, respect, and regard; quality of sexual functioning.*

81-100: Agreed-on patterns or routines exist that help meet the usual needs of each family/couple member; there is flexibility for change in response to unusual demands or events; and occasional conflicts and stressful transitions are resolved through problem-solving communication and negotiation.

81-100: There is a shared understanding and agreement about roles and appropriate tasks, decision making is established for each functional area, and there is recognition of the unique characteristics and merit of each subsystem (e.g., parents/ spouses, siblings, and individuals).

81-100: There is a situationally appropriate, optimistic atmosphere in the family; a wide range of feelings is freely expressed and managed within the family; and there is a general atmosphere of warmth, caring, and sharing of values among all family membeers. Sexual relations of adult members are satisfactory.

61-80: Daily routines are present but there is some pain and difficulty in responding to the unusual. Some conflicts remain unresolved, but do not disrupt family functioning.

61-80: Decision making is usually competent, but efforts at control of one another quite often are greater than necessary or are ineffective. Individuals and relationships are clearly demarcated but sometimes a specific subsystem is depreciated or scapegoated.

61-80: A range of feeling is expressed, but instances of emotional blocking or tension are evident. Warmth and caring are present but are marred by a family member's irritability and frustrations. Sexual activity of adult members may be reduced or problematic.

41-60: Communication is frequently inhibited by unresolved conflicts that often interfere with daily routines; there is significant difficulty in adapting to family stress and transitional change.

41-60: Decision making is only intermittently competent and effective; either excessive rigidity or significant lack of structure is evident at these times. Individual needs are quite often submerged by a partner or coalition.

41-60: Pain or ineffective anger or emotional deadness interfere with family enjoyment. Although there is some warmth and support for members, it is usually unequally distributed. Troublesome sexual difficulties between adults are often present.

21-40: Family/couple routines do not meet the needs of members; they are grimly adhered to or blithely ignored. Life cycle changes, such as departures or entries into the relational unit, generate painful conflict and obviously frustrating failures of problem solving.

21-40: Decision making is tyrannical or quite ineffective. The unique characteristics of individuals are unappreciated or ignored by either rigid or confusingly fluid coalitions.

21-40: There are infrequent periods of enjoyment of life together; frequent distancing or open hostility reflect significant conflicts that remain unresolved and quite painful. Sexual dysfunction among adult members is commonplace.

1-20: Family/couple routines are negligible (e.g., no mealtime, sleeping, or waking schedule); family members often do not know where others are or when they will be in or out; there is a little effective communication among family members.

1-20: Family/couple members are not organized in such a way that personal or generational responsibilities are recognized. Boundaries of relational unit as a whole and subsystems cannot be identified or agreed on. Family members are physically endangered or injured or sexually attacked.

1-20: Despair and cynicism are pervasive; there is little attention to the emotional needs of others; there is almost no sense of attachment, commitment, or concern about one another's welfare.

GARF PROFILE CHART

form developed by Lynelle C. Yingling, PhD

DIRECTIONS: Locate the functioning level [1-99] in each of the 3 functioning factors [interactional, organizational, and emotional climate]; assign a precise assessment score for each factor and record in the session summary table below. Also plot the 3 factors on the profile chart using the abbreviation of I, O, or E for each session on the profile chart; the three factor initials will be lined up on the profile chart above the session number in the summary table below. Compile an overall functioning score for each session by averaging the scores in the 3 areas and recording the score in the summary table below. The three factors are defined as follows:

INTERACTIONAL [I] = *skills in negotiating goals, rules, & routines; adaptability to stress; communication skills; ability to resolve conflict.*

ORGANIZATIONAL [O] = *maintenance of interpersonal roles & subsystem boundaries; hierarchial functioning, coalitions, & distribution of power, control, & responsibility.*

EMOTIONAL CLIMATE [E] = *tone & range of feelings; quality of caring, empathy, involvement, & attachment/commitment; sharing of values; mutual affective responsiveness, respect & regard; quality of sexual functioning.*

PROFILE CHART:

```
100 (impossible)
99

90 satisfactory

80

70 somewhat
   unsatisfactory

60

50 predominantly
   unsatisfactory

40

30 rarely
   satisfactory

20

10 chaotic

1
0 (inadequate information)
```

ASSIGNMENT OF SCORES SUMMARY TABLE:

SESSION NUMBER: [indicate termination session by circling session number]	1	2	3	4	5	6	7	8	9	10
DATE:										
INTERACTIONAL:										
ORGANIZATIONAL:										
EMOTIONAL CLIMATE:										
GLOBAL: THERAPIST										
TEAM X										
CLIENTS PRESENT:										

case file number/name:_____   therapist:_____

Appendix C

Developed GARF Tools:

GARF Self-Report for Families
Goal Attainment Scale (GARF Version)

GARF Self-Report for Families

These stories were adapted from <u>Goldilocks and the Three Bears</u> *by Robert Southey,* <u>Little Red Riding Hood</u> *by Charles Perrault,* <u>Cinderella</u> *by Charles Perrault,* <u>Hansel and Gretel</u> *by Grimm Brothers, and* <u>The Ugly Duckling</u> *by Hans Andersen. These stories, created by Alice McDonald, are used as metaphors to explain family functioning. Drawings by Janet & Isaac Fuller. June 1996.*

Directions: Please read through each story below and decide which fairy tale is most like the family you live in right now. Put a check in the blank by your first choice.

_____ THE THREE BEARS

The three bears were normally a very happy family. When they had problems, they would have a round table discussion to work through new goals or rules. The parents were definitely in charge with baby bear following through with his chores and obeying the rules of the house. When baby bear wanted something special or wanted to go somewhere, his parents always discussed baby bear's requests and presented the decision to him. The parents always made baby bear feel secure and safe because he knew he could rely on his parents. The parent bears were affectionate toward one another and very loving to their young son. Baby bear said he wanted to be just like his daddy when he grew up. When the break-in by Goldilocks occurred, they had been out in the park playing together. When they discovered that their house had been broken into, they were very angry that their possessions had been tampered with. They called the police, changed the locks on the doors, and remembered always to close the windows before they left the house again.

_____ LITTLE RED RIDING HOOD

Little Red Riding Hood's parents were generally happy with one another. Little Red's daddy went to work every day while her mother cleaned house, cooked, and sewed for the family. Little Red had some chores to do and she usually followed through with them. She knew she was loved by both parents and enjoyed playing board games with her parents and going places with them. Sometimes, however Little Red's dad would get upset with his wife because she would spend too much money or tell him some critical remark that her mother had made about their lifestyle. When they had these arguments, they would send Little Red off to grandma's so they could argue. They never seemed to be able to solve these problems. When Little Red crossed paths with the wolf in the woods, she realized that she had not really learned from her parents how to communicate well or solve problems. She felt a little uneasy facing such stressful encounters.

_____ CINDERELLA

Cinderella lived in a family where, if you were to draw a circle, she would be standing outside the circle by herself. Her step-mother and step-sisters only communicated with Cinderella when they told her to do some chore or when they wanted to be sarcastic to her. Since Cinderella's daddy was not around very often, his wife and step-daughters were able to put on a friendly front to Cinderella in the presence of her dad. Cinderella's dad sensed some unidentified anxiety in himself when he was with his family, but could never quite put his finger on the problem. When Cinderella was 16 years old, she met the Prince of the Realm who asked her to marry him. It was after Cinderella had left home that her dad realized how his wife and step-daughters had emotionally and verbally abused Cinderella.

_____ HANSEL AND GRETEL

Hansel and Gretel were two happy children until their mother died. They were still grieving over their mother's death when their father remarried. Their father was a wood cutter and they had never had enough money for luxuries. But now that the demand for wood was at an all-time low, they barely had enough to eat. The step-mother knew that Hansel and Gretel resented her, and she did everything she could to make them feel unwanted. The step-mother grabbed control of the family when she married the wood cutter. She demanded that her husband and step children do what she wanted without talking about it together. On two occasions, she had her husband take his two children to the woods and run off leaving them there. During the last trip to the woods, Hansel and Gretel found a gang to join and did not return home. They learned to steal, take illegal drugs, and drink alcohol. The step-mother lived to regret her actions because her husband left her over the grief that he experienced in losing his children.

_____ THE UGLY DUCKLING

The ugly duckling was born to a mother duck that did not want babies. Therefore, she ignored them as best she could. One of the ducks in the family felt especially isolated and detached. He was called the "ugly-one" by everyone in the pond. His desire was to be in a family like other families that ate their meals together, played together, cared for each other, and showed affection to one another. What the ugly duckling learned in his family was that everyone fended for himself with regard to food, clothing, fun, and affection. He learned to fight in order to survive. Ugly duckling tried to make a connection with the other ducks in the pond, but he was rebuffed at every turn. He spent more and more time by himself, until finally he had little desire to make a connection with others and went to live in a corner of the pond by himself.

PLEASE COMPLETE:

Today's date:_____

Family Member completing:
___mother ___father ___daughter ___son ___grandmother ___grandfather ___other:_____

123

GOAL ATTAINMENT SCALE

NAME/I.D. #: _____

Date Developed: _____   Date Evaluated: _____   Time Likely Needed to Achieve Goals: _____ WEEKS

Total # of Sessions Goals Worked on: _____   Total GAS Score: _____

LEVEL OF GOAL ACHIEVEMENT FOR FAMILY CHANGE:	FAMILY CHANGE NEEDED : IMPORTANCE: ( )	FAMILY CHANGE NEEDED: IMPORTANCE: ( )	FAMILY CHANGE NEEDED: IMPORTANCE: ( )
MORE CHANGE THAN BELIEVE IS POSSIBLE			
MORE CHANGE THAN REALLY EXPECT			
SATISFACTORY CHANGE			
SOME CHANGE BUT STILL ROOM TO GROW			
NO CHANGE FROM WHEN STARTED			

REVISED 12-8-96: form developed by Lynelle C. Yingling, PhD, J&L Human Systems Development, 570 E. Quail Run Rd., Rockwall, TX 75087, 972/771-9985

124

"GOAL ATTAINMENT SCALE" INSTRUCTIONS

When to administer:

Use the instrument as a pre- and post-test to determine the level of goal achievement. Complete the written description of goal levels the first assessment session and the family's conjoint discussions for the pre-test. Mark the level of attainment at the end of the final therapy session for the post-test. Progress checks can be made periodically throughout therapy and dates recorded on the different levels of attainment.

Who completes:

The "GOAL ATTAINMENT SCALE" form can be completed one of two ways:

1. The therapist can explain how to complete the form and ask the family to work together to write in responses themselves, using the enclosed guides.
2. The therapist can ask for responses to the items during the session with the family and write the information in the blanks for the family; this method may be necessary if the family reading level is quite low or the stress level in the family is extremely high.

How to complete:

1. Identify up to 3 changes the family wants to work on through therapy. These changes would be ways the family needs to change in order to solve their problem/s which brought them into therapy. Write this information below "Family Change Needed:" on the top row of the chart.
2. Rank order the importance of each change needed by putting a "1", "2", and "3" in the appropriate "( )" below the "Family Change Needed."
3. Identify the behaviors which would let them know if change had occurred for each area of change needed by the time they complete therapy. Complete the different levels of identifiable change under each "Family Change Needed" column before working on the other two areas. First, write down the way they are behaving now in the "No Change From When Started" row. Then write down what they would be doing if the change occurred in the number of weeks they contract for [generally 6-10] in the "Satisfactory Change" row [a realistic goal to achieve]. Now ask them to pretend they were able to achieve the impossible [the miracle question] and write down the behaviors showing that result in the "More Change Than Believe Is Possible" row. Now ask them to fill in the two levels of achievement which are blank: "More Change Than Really Expect" and "Some Change But Still Room To Grow."
4. Fill in the client name or ID number at the top of the page and the date the goals were developed.
5. At the conclusion of therapy, ask the family to mark an "X" across the space which describes the present level of achievement for each of the three change areas. Fill in the date of goal evaluation and the total number of therapy sessions attended at the top of the page.

How to score:

1. Mark a score for each achievement level [where the "X" is] by using the following scale:

   0 = "No Change From When Started"
   1 = "Some Change But Still Room To Grow"
   2 = "Satisfactory Change"
   3 = "More Change Than Really Expect"
   4 = "More Change Than Believe Is Possible"

2. Average the three change scores to achieve a total goal achievement score which can be used in data analysis.

FAMILY CHANGE GOAL OPTIONS FOR GOAL ATTAINMENT SCALE

Directions: *Review the possible areas for change listed below and identify three goals you would like to work on in therapy. If none of the descriptions seem to quite fit, write your own goal definition in the "Other" blank. Check the choices your family decides on together. You may decide to combine more than one numbered item into a single goal. This activity may take several minutes for the family to discuss together. After discussing your family choices with your therapist, write your chosen goals in the GOAL ATTAINMENT SCALE top row under "**Family Change Needed.**" After deciding and marking which goal is #1, #2, & #3 in **importance**, talk together about how you would know when you had made progress in achieving each goal. First, write down the way you are behaving now in the "**No Change From When Started**" row for the first goal. Then write down what you would be doing if the desired change occurred in the **number of weeks** [note in the upper right-hand corner blank] you agree to work on in therapy in the "**Satisfactory Change**" row. This is a realistic goal to expect to meet in a reasonable amount of time. Now pretend you were able to achieve the impossible and write down how that would look in the "**More Change Than Believe Is Possible**" row. If you like, fill in the two levels of achievement which are blank. Do the same for each of the other two goals. Goals will be evaluated periodically to determine your progress.*

A. Problem solving/interactional skills for making this family work well

1 _____ Negotiating family goals, rules, & routines
2 _____ Adapting to stress
3 _____ Communicating
4 _____ Resolving conflict
5 _____ Other:_____

B. The way this family is organized and structured

1 _____ Maintaining boundaries so that each individual has some personal "space"
2 _____ Keeping "space" for parents separate from kids
3 _____ Parents working together to lead this family effectively
4 _____ Distributing the power, control, & responsibility appropriately
5 _____ Other:_____

C. How members of this family feel about being a part of this family

1 _____ Feeling free to experience a wide range of feelings
2 _____ Showing a high quality of caring, empathy, involvement & attachment/commitment to each other
3 _____ Sharing of values
4 _____ Showing affection, respect, & regard
5 _____ Experiencing a high quality of appropriate sexual functioning
6 _____ Other:_____

126

Appendix D

Systemic Assessment of the Family Environment
(SAFE)

Systemic Assessment of the Family Environment [SAFE]

by Lynelle C. Yingling, PhD

Directions: For each of the descriptions below, mark a response describing relationships in your family now: place an X anywhere along the line showing whether you think the relationship is more like the description on the left or the description on the right.   Think of your family and how you all relate to each other when problems come up. Secondly, place an O on the line where you would really like your family to be.

X = as it is now when we are under stress
O = as I would really like my family to be

A. Me and My Spouse/Ex-Spouse

share openly with each other ____/____/____/____/____ keep many secrets from each other

listen to each other ____/____/____/____/____ never listen to each other

understand each other well ____/____/____/____/____ always misunderstand each other

work together with each other ____/____/____/____/____ work against each other

try new ways when one doesn't work ____/____/____/____/____ never change the way to solve problems

support each other ____/____/____/____/____ abandon each other

both work together equally ____/____/____/____/____ one controls & the other submits

B. Me and My Kids

free to tell anyone anything ____/____/____/____/____ keep a lot of secrets from each other

when I talk, someone listens ____/____/____/____/____ no one seems to listen to me

everyone understands when we talk about things ____/____/____/____/____ no one understands what to do after we've talked

family members work together as a team ____/____/____/____/____ we seem to be playing on different teams

when one way doesn't work, we try another ____/____/____/____/____ we never try new ways to solve problems

everyone feels extra support when they need it ____/____/____/____/____ everyone feels abandoned when they really need support

parents are ultimately in charge in this family ____/____/____/____/____ kids seem to have more control than parents

C. Me and My Own Parents

tell each other important things ____/____/____/____/____ keep many important secrets from one another

listen to each other respectfully ____/____/____/____/____ always butt in or ignore each other

get across well to each other ____/____/____/____/____ never seem to understand each other

work together when necessary ____/____/____/____/____ fight when cooperation is needed

try new ways to solve problems ____/____/____/____/____ do it the way it was always done

there for each other when really needed ____/____/____/____/____ always in the way or never there when needed

treat each other as adults ____/____/____/____/____ act like parents and children

Please circle which family member you are:

*mother /wife   father /husband   other:*_____   Date of completion:_____

Systemic Assessment of the Family Environment [SAFE]
by Lynelle C. Yingling, PhD

Directions: For each of the descriptions below, mark a response describing relationships in your family now: place an X anywhere along the line showing whether you think the relationship is more like the description on the left or the description on the right. Think of your family and how you all relate to each other when problems come up. Secondly, place an O on the line where you would really like your family to be.

X = as it is now when we are under stress
O = as I would really like my family to be

A. My Parents/Stepparents

share openly with each other _____/_____/_____/_____/_____ keep many secrets from each other

listen to each other _____/_____/_____/_____/_____ never listen to each other

understand each other well _____/_____/_____/_____/_____ always misunderstand each other

work together with each other _____/_____/_____/_____/_____ work against each other

try new ways when one doesn't work _____/_____/_____/_____/_____ never change the way to solve problems

support each other _____/_____/_____/_____/_____ abandon each other

both work together equally _____/_____/_____/_____/_____ one controls & the other submits

B. Me and My Parents/Stepparents

free to tell anyone anything _____/_____/_____/_____/_____ keep a lot of secrets from each other

when I talk, someone listens _____/_____/_____/_____/_____ no one seems to listen to me

everyone understands when we talk about things _____/_____/_____/_____/_____ no one understands what to do after we've talked

family members work together as a team _____/_____/_____/_____/_____ we seem to be playing on different teams

when one way doesn't work, we try another _____/_____/_____/_____/_____ we never try new ways to solve problems

everyone feels extra support when they need it _____/_____/_____/_____/_____ everyone feels abandoned when they really need support

parents are ultimately in charge in this family _____/_____/_____/_____/_____ kids seem to have more control than parents

C. My Parents & Grandparents

tell each other important things _____/_____/_____/_____/_____ keep many important secrets from one another

listen to each other respectfully _____/_____/_____/_____/_____ always butt in or ignore each other

get across well to each other _____/_____/_____/_____/_____ never seem to understand each other

work together when necessary _____/_____/_____/_____/_____ fight when cooperation is needed

try new ways to solve problems _____/_____/_____/_____/_____ do it the way it was always done

there for each other when really needed _____/_____/_____/_____/_____ always in the way or never there when needed

treat each other as adults _____/_____/_____/_____/_____ act like parents and children

Please circle which family member you are:

daughter   son   other:_____   Date of completion:_____

129

Systemic Assessment of the Family Environment [SAFE]

by Lynelle C. Yingling, PhD

Directions: For each of the descriptions below, mark a response describing relationships in your family now: place an X anywhere along the line showing whether you think the relationship is more like the description on the left or the description on the right. Think of your family and how you all relate to each other when problems come up. Secondly, place an O on the line where you would really like your family to be.

X = as it is now when we are under stress
O = as I would really like my family to be

A. My Grown Child & His/Her Spouse/Ex-Spouse

share openly with each other ____/____/____/____/____ keep many secrets from each other

listen to each other ____/____/____/____/____ never listen to each other

understand each other well ____/____/____/____/____ always misunderstand each other

work together with each other ____/____/____/____/____ work against each other

try new ways when one doesn't work ____/____/____/____/____ never change the way to solve problems

support each other ____/____/____/____/____ abandon each other

both work together equally ____/____/____/____/____ one controls & the other submits

B. My Grandchild/ren & Their Parent/s

free to tell anyone anything ____/____/____/____/____ keep a lot of secrets from each other

when I talk, someone listens ____/____/____/____/____ no one seems to listen to me

everyone understands when we talk about things ____/____/____/____/____ no one understands what to do after we've talked

family members work together as a team ____/____/____/____/____ we seem to be playing on different teams

when one way doesn't work, we try another ____/____/____/____/____ we never try new ways to solve problems

everyone feels extra support when they need it ____/____/____/____/____ everyone feels abandoned when they really need support

parents are ultimately in charge in this family ____/____/____/____/____ kids seem to have more control than parents

C. Me & My Grown Child

tell each other important things ____/____/____/____/____ keep many important secrets from one another

listen to each other respectfully ____/____/____/____/____ always butt in or ignore each other

get across well to each other ____/____/____/____/____ never seem to understand each other

work together when necessary ____/____/____/____/____ fight when cooperation is needed

try new ways to solve problems ____/____/____/____/____ do it the way it was always done

there for each other when really needed ____/____/____/____/____ always in the way or never there when needed

treat each other as adults ____/____/____/____/____ act like parents and children

Please circle which family member you are:

grandfather   *grandmother*   *other:*_____   *Date of completion:*_____

SYSTEMIC ASSESSMENT OF THE FAMILY ENVIRONMENT [SAFE]
SCORING & GRAPHING INSTRUCTIONS

Using the assigned weights to each response, total the interactional scores under each A/B/C subsystem level [1st 6 questions] and plot that sum with the organizational score [last question under each level] as the coordinates on the graph; identify the plotted points as A-X, A-O; B-X, B-O; C-X, C-O. Draw a line with an arrow pointing from the X to the O of each subsystem level [A/B/C]on the graph to visually show the area, direction, and extent of change desired. Results can be used to help set goals, realistically limiting the length of line to set as an initial goal. To obtain a total family system mean score, sum the scores for all the subsystem levels used [T blank below] and divide by the number of levels used to obtain the M [mean] score; plot M-X, M-O on the graph. Subtract the X score from the O score to determine the satisfaction score [S] for each level of family functioning, with lower numbers being higher satisfaction.

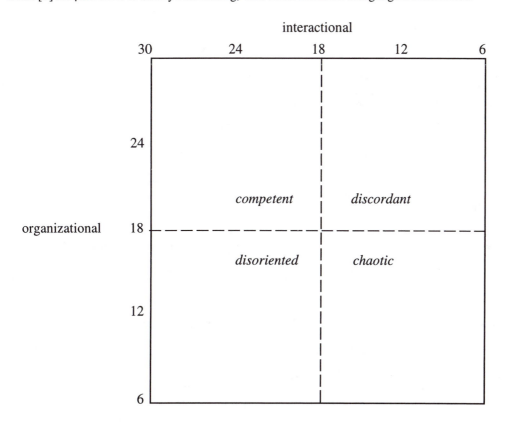

SAFE Scores Compiled:

         X   O   S [O-X=S]   X   O   S

A int = _____ _____ _____; org = _____ _____ _____

B int = _____ _____ _____; org = _____ _____ _____

C int = _____ _____ _____; org = _____ _____ _____

[T int = _____ _____ _____; org = _____ _____ _____] (not plotted)

M int = _____ _____ _____; org = _____ _____ _____

Client file number:_____

Family member:_____

Date of completion_____

GARF rating today_____

[I = _____; O = _____; E = _____]

131

Systemic Assessment of the Family Environment [SAFE]

by Lynelle C. Yingling, PhD

ASSIGNED WEIGHTS FOR EACH ITEM RESPONSE TO BE USED IN CALCULATING GRAPH

A. _____

interactional

share openly with each other __5__/__4__/__3__/__2__/__1__ keep many secrets from each other

listen to each other __5__/__4__/__3__/__2__/__1__ never listen to each other

understand each other well __5__/__4__/__3__/__2__/__1__ always misunderstand each other

work together with each other __5__/__4__/__3__/__2__/__1__ work against each other

try new ways when one doesn't work __5__/__4__/__3__/__2__/__1__ never change the way to solve problems

support each other __5__/__4__/__3__/__2__/__1__ abandon each other

organizational

both work together equally _30__/_24__/_18__/_12__/__6_ one controls & the other submits

B. _____

int

free to tell anyone anything __5__/__4__/__3__/__2__/__1__ keep a lot of secrets from each other

when I talk, someone listens __5__/__4__/__3__/__2__/__1__ no one seems to listen to me

everyone understands when we talk about things __5__/__4__/__3__/__2__/__1__ no one understands what to do after we've talked

family members work together as a team __5__/__4__/__3__/__2__/__1__ we seem to be playing on different teams

when one way doesn't work, we try another __5__/__4__/__3__/__2__/__1__ we never try new ways to solve problems

everyone feels extra support when they need it __5__/__4__/__3__/__2__/__1__ everyone feels abandoned when they really need support

org

parents are ultimately in charge in this family _30__/_24__/_18__/_12__/__6_ kids seem to have more control than parents

C. _____

int

tell each other important things __5__/__4__/__3__/__2__/__1__ keep many important secrets from one another

listen to each other respectfully __5__/__4__/__3__/__2__/__1__ always butt in or ignore each other

get across well to each other __5__/__4__/__3__/__2__/__1__ never seem to understand each other

work together when necessary __5__/__4__/__3__/__2__/__1__ fight when cooperation is needed

try new ways to solve problems __5__/__4__/__3__/__2__/__1__ do it the way it was always done

there for each other when really needed __5__/__4__/__3__/__2__/__1__ always in the way or never there when needed

org

treat each other as adults _30__/_24__/_18__/_12__/__6_ act like parents and children

132

Systemic Assessment of the Family Environment [SAFE]

by Lynelle C. Yingling, PhD

Directions: For each of the descriptions below, mark a response describing relationships in your family now: place an X anywhere along the line showing whether you think the relationship is more like the description on the left or the description on the right. Think of your family and how you all relate to each other when problems come up.

X = as it is now when we are under stress

A. Me and My Spouse/Ex-Spouse/Partner

share openly with each other _____/_____/_____/_____/_____ keep many secrets from each other

listen to each other _____/_____/_____/_____/_____ never listen to each other

understand each other well _____/_____/_____/_____/_____ always misunderstand each other

work together with each other _____/_____/_____/_____/_____ work against each other

try new ways when one doesn't work _____/_____/_____/_____/_____ never change the way to solve problems

support each other _____/_____/_____/_____/_____ abandon each other

both work together equally _____/_____/_____/_____/_____ one controls & the other submits

B. Me and My Kids

free to tell anyone anything _____/_____/_____/_____/_____ keep a lot of secrets from each other

when I talk, someone listens _____/_____/_____/_____/_____ no one seems to listen to me

everyone understands when we talk about things _____/_____/_____/_____/_____ no one understands what to do after we've talked

family members work together as a team _____/_____/_____/_____/_____ we seem to be playing on different teams

when one way doesn't work, we try another _____/_____/_____/_____/_____ we never try new ways to solve problems

everyone feels extra support when they need it _____/_____/_____/_____/_____ everyone feels abandoned when they really need support

parents are ultimately in charge in this family _____/_____/_____/_____/_____ kids seem to have more control than parents

C. Me and My Own Parents

tell each other important things _____/_____/_____/_____/_____ keep many important secrets from one another

listen to each other respectfully _____/_____/_____/_____/_____ always butt in or ignore each other

get across well to each other _____/_____/_____/_____/_____ never seem to understand each other

work together when necessary _____/_____/_____/_____/_____ fight when cooperation is needed

try new ways to solve problems _____/_____/_____/_____/_____ do it the way it was always done

there for each other when really needed _____/_____/_____/_____/_____ always in the way or never there when needed

treat each other as adults _____/_____/_____/_____/_____ act like parents and children

Please circle which family member you are:

mother /wife   father /husband   other:_____   Date of completion:_____

133

case file no.:_____

Systemic Assessment of the Family Environment [SAFE]
by Lynelle C. Yingling, PhD

Directions: For each of the descriptions below, mark a response describing relationships in your family now: place an X anywhere along the line showing whether you think the relationship is more like the description on the left or the description on the right. Think of your family and how you all relate to each other when problems come up.

X = as it is now when we are under stress

A. My Parents/Stepparents

share openly with each other _____/_____/_____/_____/_____ keep many secrets from each other

listen to each other _____/_____/_____/_____/_____ never listen to each other

understand each other well _____/_____/_____/_____/_____ always misunderstand each other

work together with each other _____/_____/_____/_____/_____ work against each other

try new ways when one doesn't work _____/_____/_____/_____/_____ never change the way to solve problems

support each other _____/_____/_____/_____/_____ abandon each other

both work together equally _____/_____/_____/_____/_____ one controls & the other submits

B. Me and My Parents/Stepparents

free to tell anyone anything _____/_____/_____/_____/_____ keep a lot of secrets from each other

when I talk, someone listens _____/_____/_____/_____/_____ no one seems to listen to me

everyone understands when we talk about things _____/_____/_____/_____/_____ no one understands what to do after we've talked

family members work together as a team _____/_____/_____/_____/_____ we seem to be playing on different teams

when one way doesn't work, we try another _____/_____/_____/_____/_____ we never try new ways to solve problems

everyone feels extra support when they need it _____/_____/_____/_____/_____ everyone feels abandoned when they really need support

parents are ultimately in charge in this family _____/_____/_____/_____/_____ kids seem to have more control than parents

C. My Parents & Grandparents

tell each other important things _____/_____/_____/_____/_____ keep many important secrets from one another

listen to each other respectfully _____/_____/_____/_____/_____ always butt in or ignore each other

get across well to each other _____/_____/_____/_____/_____ never seem to understand each other

work together when necessary _____/_____/_____/_____/_____ fight when cooperation is needed

try new ways to solve problems _____/_____/_____/_____/_____ do it the way it was always done

there for each other when really needed _____/_____/_____/_____/_____ always in the way or never there when needed

treat each other as adults _____/_____/_____/_____/_____ act like parents and children

Please circle which family member you are:

daughter   son   other:_____   Date of completion:_____

134

Systemic Assessment of the Family Environment [SAFE]

by Lynelle C. Yingling, PhD

Directions: For each of the descriptions below, mark a response describing relationships in your family now: place an X anywhere along the line showing whether you think the relationship is more like the description on the left or the description on the right.   Think of your family and how you all relate to each other when problems come up.

X = as it is now when we are under stress

A. My Grown Child & His/Her Spouse/Ex-Spouse/Partner

share openly with each other ____/____/____/____/____	keep many secrets from each other
listen to each other ____/____/____/____/____	never listen to each other
understand each other well ____/____/____/____/____	always misunderstand each other
work together with each other ____/____/____/____/____	work against each other
try new ways when one doesn't work ____/____/____/____/____	never change the way to solve problems
support each other ____/____/____/____/____	abandon each other
both work together equally ____/____/____/____/____	one controls & the other submits

B. My Grandchild/ren & Their Parent/s

free to tell anyone anything ____/____/____/____/____	keep a lot of secrets from each other
when I talk, someone listens ____/____/____/____/____	no one seems to listen to me
everyone understands when we talk about things ____/____/____/____/____	no one understands what to do after we've talked
family members work together as a team ____/____/____/____/____	we seem to be playing on different teams
when one way doesn't work, we try another ____/____/____/____/____	we never try new ways to solve problems
everyone feels extra support when they need it ____/____/____/____/____	everyone feels abandoned when they really need support
parents are ultimately in charge in this family ____/____/____/____/____	kids seem to have more control than parents

C. Me & My Grown Child

tell each other important things ____/____/____/____/____	keep many important secrets from one another
listen to each other respectfully ____/____/____/____/____	always butt in or ignore each other
get across well to each other ____/____/____/____/____	never seem to understand each other
work together when necessary ____/____/____/____/____	fight when cooperation is needed
try new ways to solve problems ____/____/____/____/____	do it the way it was always done
there for each other when really needed ____/____/____/____/____	always in the way or never there when needed
treat each other as adults ____/____/____/____/____	act like parents and children

Please circle which family member you are:
    *grandmother   grandfather   other:*_____   *Date of Completion:*_____

135

SYSTEMIC ASSESSMENT OF THE FAMILY ENVIRONMENT [SAFE]

SCORING & GRAPHING INSTRUCTIONS

Using the assigned weights to each response, total the interactional scores under each A/B/C subsystem level [1st 6 questions] and plot that sum with the organizational score [last question under each level] as the coordinates on the graph; identify the plotted points as A-1, B-1, and C-1 [using the number to identify the family member]. To obtain a total family system mean score, sum the scores for all the subsystem levels used [T blank below] and divide by the number of levels used to obtain the M [mean] score; plot M-1 on the graph. Using different colors to mark each family member provides a visual family system comparison on one graph. For research purposes, obtain a SAFE score by adding together the interactional and organizational average scores; use the SAFE score to correlate with other assessment scores, such as the GARF.

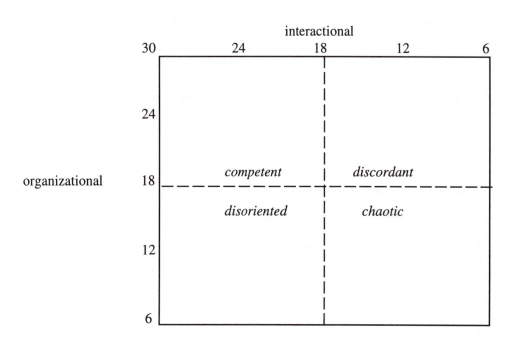

SAFE Scores Compiled:

Client file number:_____

Family member: 1 = mother/wife
                2 = father/husband
                3 = daughter
                4 = son
                5 = other:_____

Date of completion_____

GARF rating today_____
   [I = _____; O = _____; E = _____]

	interactional					organizational				
	1	2	3	4	5	1	2	3	4	5
A	___,	___,	___,	___,	___	___,	___,	___,	___,	___
B	___,	___,	___,	___,	___	___,	___,	___,	___,	___
C	___,	___,	___,	___,	___	___,	___,	___,	___,	___

[T ___, ___, ___, ___, ___   ___, ___, ___, ___, ___] (not plotted)

M ___, ___, ___, ___, ___ + ___, ___, ___, ___, ___ divided by # of family members = SAFE score:_____

136

Valoración Sistémica del Ambiente Familial

por Lynelle C. Yingling, PhD; traducido por Todd C. Smith

Instrucciones: Para cada una de las descripciones abajo, indique la respuesta que describe las relaciones en su familia en el momento presente: Ponga una "X" en la línea donde piensa la descripción coresponda a su familia (a la izquierda o a la derecha). Ud. tiene que pensar en su familia y como se relacionan los otros miembros los unos con los otros si hay un problema. También, ponga una "O" el la línea donde le qustaría ver su familia.

X = como es ahora cuando hay tensión
O = como me gustaría que fuera mi familia

A. Yo y mi Esposo/a o mi Esposo/a Pasado/a

nos compartimos uno a otro	—/____/____/____/____	mantenemos muchos secretos el uno del otro
nos escuchamos bien	—/____/____/____/____	nunca nos escuchamos bien
nos comprendemos bien	—/____/____/____/____	nos malentendemos siempre
trabajamos juntos bien	—/____/____/____/____	trabajamos en contra del uno a otro
tratamos de encontrar otras opciones si la primera no functiona bien	—/____/____/____/____	nunca cambiamos la manera que tratamos de resolver algo
nos apoyamos el uno al otro	—/____/____/____/____	no nos apoyamos el uno al otro/a
trabajamos juntos igualmente	—/____/____/____/____	el uno/a controla y el/la otra/a es sumiso

B. Yo y mis Niños

soy libre de decir lo que yo quiera	____/____/____/____/____	nos guardamos muchos secretos
cuando yo hablo, alguién escucha	____/____/____/____/____	me parece que nadie escucha
todos entienden cuando hablamos sobre asuntos	____/____/____/____/____	nadie entiende lo que tenemos que hacer después de hablar
los miembros de mi familia trabajan juntos como un equipo	____/____/____/____/____	me parece que estamos jugando en equipos diferentes
si algo no functiona bien tratamos de hacer algo diferente	____/____/____/____/____	nunca cambiamos la manera que tratamos de resolver algo
todos se sienten apoyo adicional cuando lo necesitan	____/____/____/____/____	no tenemos bastante apoyo cuando lo necesitamos
ultimamente, los padres controlan a la familia	____/____/____/____/____	me parece que los niños tienen más control que los padres

C. Yo y mis Padres

nos hablamos de asuntos importantes	—/____/____/____/____	mantenemos mucho secretos sobre asuntos importantes
nos escuchamos el uno al otro respetuosamente	—/____/____/____/____	siempre ignoramos al otro
entendemos todo lo dicho	—/____/____/____/____	me parece que nunca nos entendemos
trabajamos juntos si es necesario	—/____/____/____/____	nos peleamos cuando necesitamos cooperar
tratamos de usar ideas nuevas para resolver problemas	—/____/____/____/____	siempre lo hacemos de la misma manera
me ayudan si es posible	—/____/____/____/____	nunca me ayudan
nos tratamos como adultos	—/____/____/____/____	nos portamos como padres y niños

Por favor, ponga un círculo en la respuesta que describe su posición en la familia:
  madre/esposa   padre/esposo   otro:_____   ¿Cuál es la fecha? _____

Valoración Sistémica del Ambiente Familial

por Lynelle C. Yingling, PhD; traducido por Todd C. Smith

Instrucciones: Para cada una de las descripciones abajo, indique la respuesta que describe las relaciones en su familia en el momento presente: Ponga una "X" en la línea donde piensa la descripción coresponda a su familia (a la izquierda o a la derecha). Ud. tiene que pensar en su familia y como se relacionan los otros miembros los unos con los otros si hay un problema. También, ponga una "O" el la línea donde le qustaría ver su familia.

X = como es ahora cuando hay tensión

O = como me gustaría que fuera mi familia

A. Mis Padres/Padrastros

nos compartimos uno a otro ____/____/____/____/____	mantenemos muchos secretos el uno del otro
nos escuchamos bien ____/____/____/____/____	nunca nos escuchamos bien
nos comprendemos bien ____/____/____/____/____	nos malentendemos siempre
trabajamos juntos bien ____/____/____/____/____	trabajamos en contra del uno a otro
tratamos de encontrar otras opciones si la primera no functiona bien ____/____/____/____/____	nunca cambiamos la manera que tratamos de resolver algo
nos apoyamos el uno al otro ____/____/____/____/____	no nos apoyamos el uno al otro/a
trabajamos juntos igualmente ____/____/____/____/____	el uno/a controla y el/la otra/a es sumiso

B. Yo y mis Padres/Padrastros

soy libre de decir lo que yo quiera ____/____/____/____/____	nos guardamos muchos secretos
cuando yo hablo, alguién escucha ____/____/____/____/____	me parece que nadie escucha
todos entienden cuando hablamos sobre asuntos ____/____/____/____/____	nadie entiende lo que tenemos que hacer después de hablar
los miembros de mi familia trabajan juntos como un equipo ____/____/____/____/____	me parece que estamos jugando en equipos diferentes
si algo no funciona bien tratamos de hacer algo diferente ____/____/____/____/____	nunca cambiamos la manera que tratamos de resolver algo
todos se sienten apoyo adicional cuando lo necesitan ____/____/____/____/____	no tenemos bastante apoyo cuando lo necesitamos
ultimamente, los padres controlan a la familia ____/____/____/____/____	me parece que los niños tienen más control que los padres

C. Mis Padres y Mis Abuelos

nos hablamos de asuntos importantes ____/____/____/____/____	mantenemos mucho secretos sobre asuntos importantes
nos escuchamos el uno al otro respetuosamente ____/____/____/____/____	siempre ignoramos al otro
entendemos todo lo dicho ____/____/____/____/____	me parece que nunca nos entendemos
trabajamos juntos si es necesario ____/____/____/____/____	nos peleamos cuando necesitamos cooperar
tratamos de usar ideas nuevas para resolver problemas ____/____/____/____/____	siempre lo hacemos de la misma manera
me ayudan si es posible ____/____/____/____/____	nunca me ayudan
nos tratamos como adultos ____/____/____/____/____	nos portamos como padres y niños

Por favor, ponga un círculo en la respuesta que describe su posición en la familia:

hijo   hija   otro:_____   ¿Cuál es la fecha? _____

Valoración Sistémica del Ambiente Familial
por Lynelle C. Yingling, PhD; traducido por Todd C. Smith

Instrucciones: Para cada una de las descripciones abajo, indique la respuesta que describe las relaciones en su familia en el momento presente: Ponga una "X" en la línea donde piensa la descripción coresponda a su familia (a la izquierda o a la derecha). Ud. tiene que pensar en su familia y como se relacionan los otros miembros los unos con los otros si hay un problema. También, ponga una "O" el la línea donde le qustaría ver su familia.

X = como es ahora cuando hay tensión
O = como me gustaría que fuera mi familia

A. Mis Niños en la Edad de Majoridad y su Esposo/a Pasado/a

nos compartimos uno a otro _____/_____/_____/_____/_____ mantenemos muchos secretos el uno del otro

nos escuchamos bien _____/_____/_____/_____/_____ nunca nos escuchamos bien

nos comprendemos bien _____/_____/_____/_____/_____ nos malentendemos siempre

trabajamos juntos bien _____/_____/_____/_____/_____ trabajamos en contra del uno a otro

tratamos de encontrar otras opciones si la primera no funciona bien _____/_____/_____/_____/_____ nunca cambiamos la manera que tratamos de resolver algo

nos apoyamos el uno al otro _____/_____/_____/_____/_____ no nos apoyamos el uno al otro/a

trabajamos juntos igualmente _____/_____/_____/_____/_____ el uno/a controla y el/la otra/a es sumiso

B. Mis Nietos y sus Padres

soy libre de decir lo que yo quiera _____/_____/_____/_____/_____ nos guardamos muchos secretos

cuando yo hablo, alguién escucha _____/_____/_____/_____/_____ me parece que nadie escucha

todos entienden cuando hablamos sobre asuntos _____/_____/_____/_____/_____ nadie entiende lo que tenemos que hacer después de hablar

los miembros de mi familia trabajan juntos como un equipo _____/_____/_____/_____/_____ me parece que estamos jugando en equipos diferentes

si algo no functiona bien tratamos de hacer algo diferente _____/_____/_____/_____/_____ nunca cambiamos la manera que tratamos de resolver algo

todos se sienten apoyo adicional cuando lo necesitan _____/_____/_____/_____/_____ no tenemos bastante apoyo cuando lo necesitamos

ultimamente, los padres controlan a la familia _____/_____/_____/_____/_____ me parece que los niños tienen más control que los padres

C. Yo y mis Niños en la Edad de Majoridad

nos hablamos de asuntos importantes _____/_____/_____/_____/_____ mantenemos mucho secretos sobre asuntos importantes

nos escuchamos el uno al otro respetuosamente _____/_____/_____/_____/_____ siempre ignoramos al otro

entendemos todo lo dicho _____/_____/_____/_____/_____ me parece que nunca nos entendemos

trabajamos juntos si es necessario _____/_____/_____/_____/_____ nos peleamos cuando necesitamos cooperar

tratamos de usar ideas nuevas para resolver problemas _____/_____/_____/_____/_____ siempre lo hacemos de la misma manera

me ayudan si es posible _____/_____/_____/_____/_____ nunca me ayudan

nos tratamos como adultos _____/_____/_____/_____/_____ nos portamos como padres y niños

Por favor, ponga un círculo en la respuesta que describe su posición en la familia:
    abuelo   abuela   otro:_____   *¿Cuál es la fecha?_____*

Valoración Sistémica del Ambiente Familial
por Lynelle C. Yingling, PhD; traducido por Todd C. Smith

Instrucciones: Para cada una de las descripciones abajo, indique la respuesta que describe las relaciones en su familia en el momento presente: Ponga una "X" en la línea donde piensa la descripción coresponda a su familia (a la izquierda o a la derecha). Ud. tiene que pensar en su familia y como se relacionan los otros miembros los unos con los otros si hay un problema.

X = como es ahora cuando hay tensión

A. Yo y mi Esposo/a o mi Esposo/a Pasado/a

nos compartimos uno a otro	——/——/——/——/——	mantenemos muchos secretos el uno del otro
nos escuchamos bien	——/——/——/——/——	nunca nos escuchamos bien
nos comprendemos bien	——/——/——/——/——	nos malentendemos siempre
trabajamos juntos bien	——/——/——/——/——	trabajamos en contra del uno a otro
tratamos de encontrar otras opciones si la primera no functiona bien	——/——/——/——/——	nunca cambiamos la manera que tratamos de resolver algo
nos apoyamos el uno al otro	——/——/——/——/——	no nos apoyamos el uno al otro/a
trabajamos juntos igualmente	——/——/——/——/——	el uno/a controla y el/la otra/a es sumiso

B. Yo y mis Niños

soy libre de decir lo que yo quiera	——/——/——/——/——	nos guardamos muchos secretos
cuando yo hablo, alguién escucha	——/——/——/——/——	me parece que nadie escucha
todos entienden cuando hablamos sobre asuntos	——/——/——/——/——	nadie entiende lo que tenemos que hacer después de hablar
los miembros de mi familia trabajan juntos como un equipo	——/——/——/——/——	me parece que estamos jugando en equipos diferentes
si algo no functiona bien tratamos de hacer algo diferente	——/——/——/——/——	nunca cambiamos la manera que tratamos de resolver algo
todos se sienten apoyo adicional cuando lo necesitan	——/——/——/——/——	no tenemos bastante apoyo cuando lo necesitamos
ultimamente, los padres controlan a la familia	——/——/——/——/——	me parece que los niños tienen más control que los padres

C. Yo y mis Padres

nos hablamos de asuntos importantes	——/——/——/——/——	mantenemos mucho secretos sobre asuntos importantes
nos escuchamos el uno al otro respetuosamente	——/——/——/——/——	siempre ignoramos al otro
entendemos todo lo dicho	——/——/——/——/——	me parece que nunca nos entendemos
trabajmos juntos si es necesario	——/——/——/——/——	nos peleamos cuando necesitamos cooperar
tratamos de usar ideas nuevas para resolver problemas	——/——/——/——/——	siempre lo hacemos de la misma manera
me ayudan si es posible	——/——/——/——/——	nunca me ayudan
nos tratamos como adultos	——/——/——/——/——	nos portamos como padres y niños

Por favor, ponga un círculo en la respuesta que describe su posición en la familia:
    madre/esposa   padre/esposo   otro:_____   ¿Cuál es la fecha?_____

Valoración Sistémica del Ambiente Familial

por Lynelle C. Yingling, PhD; traducido por Todd C. Smith

Instrucciones: Para cada una de las descripciones abajo, indique la respuesta que describe las relaciones en su familia en el momento presente: Ponga una "X" en la línea donde piensa la descripción coresponda a su familia (a la izquierda o a la derecha). Ud. tiene que pensar en su familia y como se relacionan los otros miembros los unos con los otros si hay un problema.

X = como es ahora cuando hay tensión

A. Mis Padres/Padrastros

nos compartimos uno a otro	____/____/____/____/____	mantenemos muchos secretos el uno del otro
nos escuchamos bien	____/____/____/____/____	nunca nos escuchamos bien
nos comprendemos bien	____/____/____/____/____	nos malentendemos siempre
trabajamos juntos bien	____/____/____/____/____	trabajamos en contra del uno a otro
tratamos de encontrar otras opciones si la primera no functiona bien	____/____/____/____/____	nunca cambiamos la manera que tratamos de resolver algo
nos apoyamos el uno al otro	____/____/____/____/____	no nos apoyamos el uno al otro/a
trabajamos juntos igualmente	____/____/____/____/____	el uno/a controla y el/la otra/a es sumiso

B. Yo y mis Padres/Padrastros

soy libre de decir lo que yo quiera	____/____/____/____/____	nos guardamos muchos secretos
cuando yo hablo, alguién escucha	____/____/____/____/____	me parece que nadie escucha
todos entienden cuando hablamos sobre asuntos	____/____/____/____/____	nadie entiende lo que tenemos que hacer después de hablar
los miembros de mi familia trabajan juntos como un equipo	____/____/____/____/____	me parece que estamos jugando en equipos diferentes
si algo no functiona bien tratamos de hacer algo diferente	____/____/____/____/____	nunca cambiamos la manera que tratamos de resolver algo
todos se sienten apoyo adicional cuando lo necesitan	____/____/____/____/____	no tenemos bastante apoyo cuando lo necesitamos
ultimamente, los padres controlan a la familia	____/____/____/____/____	me parece que los niños tienen más control que los padres

C. Mis Padres y Mis Abuelos

nos hablamos de asuntos importantes	____/____/____/____/____	mantenemos mucho secretos sobre asuntos importantes
nos escuchamos el uno al otro respetuosamente	____/____/____/____/____	siempre ignoramos al otro
entendemos todo lo dicho	____/____/____/____/____	me parece que nunca nos entendemos
trabajmos juntos si es necesario	____/____/____/____/____	nos peleamos cuando necesitamos cooperar
tratamos de usar ideas nuevas para resolver problemas	____/____/____/____/____	siempre lo hacemos de la misma manera
me ayudan si es posible	____/____/____/____/____	nunca me ayudan
nos tratamos como adultos	____/____/____/____/____	nos portamos como padres y niños

Por favor, ponga un círculo en la respuesta que describe su posición en la familia:
    hijo   hija   otro:_____   ¿Cuál es la fecha?_____

Valoración Sistémica del Ambiente Familial

por Lynelle C. Yingling, PhD; traducido por Todd C. Smith

Instrucciones: Para cada una de las descripciones abajo, indique la respuesta que describe las relaciones en su familia en el momento presente: Ponga una "X" en la línea donde piensa la descripción coresponda a su familia (a la izquierda o a la derecha). Ud. tiene que pensar en su familia y como se relacionan los otros miembros los unos con los otros si hay un problema.

X = como es ahora cuando hay tensión

A. Mis Niños en la Edad de Majoridad y su Esposo/a Pasado/a

nos compartimos uno a otro ___/___/___/___/___	mantenemos muchos secretos el uno del otro
nos escuchamos bien ___/___/___/___/___	nunca nos escuchamos bien
nos comprendemos bien ___/___/___/___/___	nos malentendemos siempre
trabajamos juntos bien ___/___/___/___/___	trabajamos en contra del uno a otro
tratamos de encontrar otras opciones si la primera no functiona bien ___/___/___/___/___	nunca cambiamos la manera que tratamos de resolver algo
nos apoyamos el uno al otro ___/___/___/___/___	no nos apoyamos el uno al otro/a
trabajamos juntos igualmente ___/___/___/___/___	el uno/a controla y el/la otra/a es sumiso

B. Mis Nietos y sus Padres

soy libre de decir lo que yo quiera ___/___/___/___/___	nos guardamos muchos secretos
cuando yo hablo, alguién escucha ___/___/___/___/___	me parece que nadie escucha
todos entienden cuando hablamos sobre asuntos ___/___/___/___/___	nadie entiende lo que tenemos que hacer después de hablar
los miembros de mi familia trabajan juntos como un equipo ___/___/___/___/___	me parece que estamos jugando en equipos diferentes
si algo no functiona bien tratamos de hacer algo diferente ___/___/___/___/___	nunca cambiamos la manera que tratamos de resolver algo
todos se sienten apoyo adicional cuando lo necesitan ___/___/___/___/___	no tenemos bastante apoyo cuando lo necesitamos
ultimamente, los padres controlan a la familia ___/___/___/___/___	me parece que los niños tienen más control que los padres

C. Yo y mis Niños en la Edad de Majoridad

nos hablamos de asuntos importantes ___/___/___/___/___	mantenemos mucho secretos sobre asuntos importantes
nos escuchamos el uno al otro respetuosamente ___/___/___/___/___	siempre ignoramos al otro
entendemos todo lo dicho ___/___/___/___/___	me parece que nunca nos entendemos
trabajmos juntos si es necesario ___/___/___/___/___	nos peleamos cuando necesitamos cooperar
tratamos de usar ideas nuevas para resolver problemas ___/___/___/___/___	siempre lo hacemos de la misma manera
me ayudan si es posible ___/___/___/___/___	nunca me ayudan
nos tratamos como adultos ___/___/___/___/___	nos portamos como padres y niños

Por favor, ponga un círculo en la respuesta que describe su posición el la familia:
    abuelo   abuela   otro:_____   *¿Cuál es la fecha?_____*

B

D

A

C

Appendix E

Record Keeping Forms Including GARF Ratings:

Coded Research Case Notes
Clinical Case Notes
Therapist Periodic Assessment
Supervision Case Presentation Guidelines

CASE NOTES

(developed by Lynelle C. Yingling, PhD)

Client Number_____   Clients present_____

Session Number_____   Therapist_____ Team _____

Date_____   Next apt. date _____, time_____

GARF rating: therapist_____ [I = _____, O = _____, E = _____]; team members average global_____

[use attached code sheet for "interventions used" & "interventions planned" below; write in "other" as appropriate; check & explain "goals"]

INTERVENTIONS USED:_____

SYSTEMIC HYPOTHESIS [including extended as well as nuclear family system]:
 Organizational =

 Interactional =

THERAPEUTIC GOAL [check focus goal/s for next session]:
 organizational:
 ____ marital:_____
 ____ parental:_____
 ____ sibling:_____
 ____ former parent:_____
 interactional:
 ____ improve understanding needed to ___solve problems /___negotiate boundaries through speaking/listening skills
 ____ increase supportedness outcome of communication through greater ___togetherness /___autonomy

ASSIGNMENT:

NEXT SESSION INTERVENTIONS PLANNED:_____

SIGNIFICANT FAMILY EVENTS OF THE WEEK:

RESEARCH CASENOTES CODE FORM

JOINING:
1. confirm family members with empathic responses
2. absolve individuals from personal responsibility for the problem
3. track information as a neutral listener
4. understand and use the family's language
5. emphasize the expert position to create a therapeutic context and engender hope

ASSESSING:

Strategic [macro lens] = tracking interactional patterns around the symptom/presenting problem which are a result of the family's attempts to get fundamental needs met by responding to the stress of the necessary change
6. problem solving enactment/reenactment [videotaped]
7. circular questioning
8. clinical rating scale family assessment models [GARF/Circumplex Model/Beavers Systems Model]

Structural [50 mm lens] = defining how the family organization maintains the ineffective patterns by identifying the family rules about boundaries which define power bases/decision-making authority and consequently inhibit the system's ability to use more effective interactional patterns for meeting their needs
9. sculpting/choreographing
10. listing nuclear family rules
11. self-report family assessment written instruments [FACES/SFI/SAFE]

Family-of-Origin [wide-angle lens] = identifying loyalties which inconspicuously lock in the ineffective family organization which supports the interactional patterns which perpetuate the symptom and rigidify the patterns
12. genogram construction
13. listing family-of-origin rules
14. tracking reactions to "parent firing" assignments

STRATEGIZING: [formulating, executing, & evaluating interventions based on the hypothesis]
15. focus on solution of the presenting problem in a way which will provide a systemic change that will strengthen future problem solving capabilities
16. reframe the motives of the interactional patterns as an attempt to make the structure more functional
17. reframe the stuckness into hopefulness through metaphor
18. use paradoxical/straightforward directives to help the family experience new interactional patterns
19. reduce anxiety about change by giving "go slow" directives
20. coach the family on improving problem-solving skills
21. use videotape playback of enactment for family self-assessment of organization/interaction
22. join effectively before beginning stroke-kick approach to facilitate restructuring
23. interrupt & redirect communication interchanges to redirect power bases/alliances
24. use rearranging of family member seatings to imply alliance shifts
25. help set boundaries by defining who attends sessions
26. use genogram construction/referencing to help family identify extended family patterns consciously
27. refer to extended family members by given names vs. role names in session
28. use practice exercises (unmailed letters, etc.) to help client identify desired changes in relationship with extended family member/s
29. give assignments to begin changing interaction patterns with extended family members to adult-adult interaction, using the nuclear family as the support resource to help protect from regression to child-adult interactions
30. invite extended family members into session & coach a renegotiation of interactional rules for an adult-adult relationship; include the spouse as co-therapist if possible
31. other:_____

CASE NOTES

Clients present_____

Session Number_____   Session Duration_____   Date_____

Next apt. date _____   time_____

GARF rating: [Interactional_____, Organizational_____, Emotional_____] Global_____

SIGNIFICANT FAMILY INFORMATION:

INTERVENTION TECHNIQUES USED:

SYSTEMIC HYPOTHESIS:

THERAPEUTIC GOAL:

ASSIGNMENT:

NEXT SESSION PLAN:

THERAPIST PERIODIC ASSESSMENT

Therapist_____ Date_____

Family Name_____ Client Number_____

1. Presenting problem/s of each family member:

_____
_____
_____
_____

2. Family's attempted solution(s) & results:

_____
_____
_____
_____

3. Life cycle stage: ___Young Adult ___Married ___Young Children ___Adolescents ___Launching ___Later Life
   Family Structure: ___Married   ___Separated ___Divorced ___Remarried ___Never Married ___Widowed

4. Therapist Conceptualizations:

   A. Organizational & interactional 3-level hypothesis:

_____
_____
_____
_____
_____

   B. External stressor/s

_____
_____
_____

   C. External & family strengths:

_____
_____
_____

   D. Family typology (from SAFE/other assessment instrument):

_____

   E. Family of origin influences: genogram in file

   F. GARF: Initial = _____   Current = _____   GAF: Initial = _____   Current=_____

   G. DSM IV Diagnosis: Axis I_____ Axis II_____

                        Axis III_____ Axis IV_____

5. Therapeutic goal/s & intervention plan:

_____
_____
_____
_____

SUPERVISION CASE PRESENTATION GUIDELINES

_____, *Supervisor*

Being prepared for supervision appointments with well organized case information will help both of us function more effectively. For each case you choose to present in supervision, please complete this sheet and bring to the appointment. Or you can bring a copy of your case notes from the session if using the comprehensive form provided by me.

1. Family genogram with *structure, significant events information, & relationship mapping*
   [**draw on back of page or bring from case file**].

2. Presenting problem as defined by client:

3. How clients have attempted to solve problem and results of attempts:

4. System Assessment: GARF = _____ [I_____, O_____, E_____]; SAFE = _____

   Beavers CRS: Competence_____, Style_____; SFI Competence_____, Style_____

5. Therapist hypothesis about system functioning which blocks problem resolution.

6. Goal/s for therapy session: clients/therapist.

7. What specific kind of feedback would you like from supervision?

8. Supervisor's feedback [completed by supervisor during session]:

_____   _____   _____
Supervisee   Supervisor   Date

Appendix F

Clinic Research/Clinical Forms Not Including GARF Ratings:

Clinic Client Intake Form
Intake Form
Contact Summary Sheet
Duty to Warn
Permission for Consultation/Taping/Research
Consent for the Release of Confidential Information
Parental Release Form
No Suicide Contract
Contract for Non-Violence
Termination Form
Family's Evaluation of Services

CLINIC CLIENT INTAKE FORM

A. *Initial contact information collected by office staff:*

Date of initial call/intake: _____   Staff doing intake:_____

Name: _____   New Client [   ]   Former Client [   ]

Spouse:_____   Home Phone: _____

Address: _____   Work phone: (Her)_____

_____   (Him)_____

Employment: (Her) _____   Insurance: (Her)_____

             (Him) _____   (Him)_____

Social Security #: (Her)_____   Combined annual income: $_____

                   (Him)_____   Assessed fee: $_____

Date of birth: (Her)_____   1st appointment: _____

                (Him)_____   Appointment written in book [   ]

Referral source:_____   Appointment not scheduled because:

     [probation officer:_____

      phone number:_____]

Information reviewed with caller: Ethnic Origin:

     [   ] 1st appointment arrival time   ___1. Black

     [   ] Payment w/Services   ___2. Anglo

     [   ] Insurance statement   ___3. Hispanic

     [   ] 24-Hour statement   ___4. Asian

                                                 ___5. Other:_____

Assigned file number:_____

Family Members Attending 1st Session: _____

B. *Therapist assigned:*_____

C. *Intake information collected by therapist at 1st session*
    [date:_____]

    FAMILY STRUCTURE: [check one]
    _____Married
    _____Separated
    _____Divorced
    _____Remarried
    _____Not married: living alone
    _____Not married: living with extended family
    _____Grandparent and child with absent parents
    _____Cohabitation with unmarried partner

    Total number of marriages of male head of household:_____
    Total number of marriages of female head of household:_____

NAME OF ALL FAMILY MEMBERS	AGE/DOB	RELATION	IN HOUSEHOLD
1._____			
2._____			
3._____			
4._____			
5._____			

PREVIOUS EXPERIENCE WITH therapy:

_____MFT:_____, date_____, outcome_____

_____other:_____, date_____, outcome_____

PRESENT MEDICATIONS [WHO, WHAT, WHY, MONITORING PHYSICIAN]:

_____

_____

PROBLEM/S AS DESCRIBED BY FAMILY:

PRESENTING PROBLEM/S [*identify session # in which each becomes known*]:

____ chemical dependency   ____ anxiety
____ child abuse/neglect   ____ depression
____ divorce issues   ____ disability stress
____ incest: __child __adult survivor   ____ eating disorder
____ marital stress   ____ grief
____ parent-child conflict   ____ school problems
____ sexual disorder   ____ suicide threat
____ spousal abuse   ____ work stress
____ other family:_____   ____ other individual:_____

FAMILY'S IDENTIFIED PATIENT:_____

SUBSYSTEM FAMILY BELIEVES INVOLVED IN PRESENTING PROBLEM:
____ individual   ____ marital   ____ parental   ____extended

FAMILY'S ATTEMPTS TO SOLVE PROBLEM:

D.   ***SUMMARY ASSESSMENT INFORMATION COLLECTED IN FILE:***
[   ]   all relevant informed consent forms
[   ]   SAFE
[   ]   Beck Inventory
[   ]   10-minute research videotape segment of what family wants to change
[   ]   Goal Attainment Scale completion and evaluation
[   ]   Genogram
[   ]   Therapist Periodic Assessment
[   ]   Casenotes for each session
[   ]   Contact Summary Sheet complete
[   ]   Family's Evaluation of Services

[3/96: LCY]

INTAKE FORM

A. Initial contact information:

DATE OF CALL_____ 1st APPOINTMENT DATE_____, TIME_____

NAME OF CALLER_____

ADDRESS OF CALLER_____

PHONE # OF CALLER: WORK_____ HOME_____

FEE ASSIGNMENT:_____ INSURANCE:_____ CLIENT NO:_____

B. FAMILY STRUCTURE: ____married ____separated ____divorced ____remarried ____cohabitation
_____unmarried, alone _____unmarried, extended family _____grandparent with child

NAME OF ALL FAMILY MEMBERS	DOB/AGE	RELATION	IN HOME
1._____			
2._____			
3._____			
4._____			
5._____			
6._____			

C. MARITAL HISTORY:_____

D. PREVIOUS EXPERIENCE WITH COUNSELING:

_____MFT date_____, outcome_____

_____other:_____ date_____, outcome_____

E. PRESENT MEDICATIONS: [who, what, amount, for what, monitoring physician]

_____

F. ASSESSED PROBLEMS: [indicate session number identified]

___ chemical dependency   ___ anxiety
___ child abuse/neglect   ___ depression
___ divorce issues   ___ disability stress
___ incest: __ child __ adult survivor   ___ eating disorder
___ marital stress   ___ grief
___ parent-child conflict   ___ school problems
___ sexual disorder   ___ suicide threat
___ spousal abuse   ___ work stress
___ other family:_____   ___ other individual:_____

G. PROBLEM/S AS DESCRIBED BY FAMILY:

CONTACT SUMMARY SHEET

[attached to front of folder]

Client no:_____   Family name:_____

Therapist:_____   Insurance carrier:_____

Date	Interview #/ phone contact	family members present	client fee check #/cash	insurance fee: amount	authorization #	date billed	date received

DUTY TO WARN

Confidentiality and privileged communication remain rights of all clients according to state law. However, some courts have held that if a client intends to take harmful or dangerous action against another human being, or against himself/herself, a therapist has a DUTY TO WARN A) the person who is likely to suffer the result of harmful behavior, B) the person's family, or C) the family of the client who intends to harm himself/herself. In cases of suspected child or elder abuse, the therapist has a responsibility to notify the appropriate authorities of such allegations. Court orders, especially in cases involving children's safety, can sometimes require disclosure of records. Third-party payment from an insurance company will require some level of disclosure as covered by specialized release forms.

The therapist will, whenever possible, share with the client the intent to notify relatives or authorities. In cases of threatened homicide or suicide or exposure of a spouse to AIDS, every effort will be made to resolve the issue before such a breach of confidentiality takes place.

_____
Therapist

I have read the above and understand the therapist's professional responsibility to make such decisions where necessary.

Date_____   Client_____

Date_____   Client_____

Date_____   Client_____

Date_____   Client_____

PERMISSION FOR
CONSULTATION/TAPING/RESEARCH

In order to provide the best quality of services possible, it is sometimes helpful for the therapist to consult with other supervisory therapists regarding a particular client's difficulties. It is necessary to receive your permission in order to discuss your situation with other professional therapists. Video or audio taping of sessions is also helpful for the therapist to review in order to gain more insights regarding the clients. These tapes can also be helpful for clients to review themselves by making special arrangements with the therapist. Research efforts can improve the quality of services offered.

AGREEMENT:

We understand that our privacy will be treated with utmost professionalism and respect. We realize that permission for consultation and taping is extremely helpful to the therapist to constantly improve the quality of services, but refusal to give permission will not in any way interfere with receiving professional services. Permission for research is voluntary and means that information about our family will possibly be used anonymously and confidentially for research purposes only.

This agreement will remain in effect until 1 year following termination of services with J&L Human Systems Development.

I give permission for (initial each):

consultation _____

taping _____

research _____

Client_____ Date_____

Client_____ Date_____

Therapist_____

157

CONSENT FOR THE RELEASE OF CONFIDENTIAL INFORMATION

I understand that my records are protected under federal and state regulations and cannot be disclosed without my written consent unless otherwise provided for in the regulations. I also understand that I may revoke this authorization at any time except to the extent that action has been taken in reliance on it. I also understand that permission to release records must come from all members of the family participating in treatment. This authorization automatically expires 6 months following termination of treatment with _____.

• •

I/we authorize therapist [_____] TO OBTAIN INFORMATION FROM:

      name:_____ phone:_____ fax:_____

      address:_____

Check all which apply:

Purpose: ___ Treatment planning
              ___ Monitoring of treatment progress
              ___ Other (must specify):_____

Content: ___ Information regarding attendance at scheduled apointments
              ___ Status with program: admitted, discharged, etc.
              ___ Assessment of treatment needs
              ___ Treatment progress
              ___ Other (must specify):_____

• •

I/we authorize therapist [_____] TO RELEASE INFORMATION TO:

      name:_____ phone:_____ fax:_____

      address:_____

Check all which apply:

Purpose: ___ Treatment planning
              ___ Monitoring of treatment progress
              ___ Other (must specify):_____

Content: ___ Information regarding attendance at scheduled apointments
              ___ Status with program: admitted, discharged, etc.
              ___ Assessment of treatment needs
              ___ Treatment progress
              ___ Other (must specify):_____

• •

Client name:_____ Signature:_____ Date:_____

Client name:_____ Signature:_____ Date:_____

Therapist name:_____ Signature:_____ Date:_____

PARENTAL RELEASE FORM

_____

Child/children names/s

has my permission to participate in the therapy services offered by _____.
It is my understanding that all client material is confidential and will not be released to any agency or person
without the written permission of all family members participating in therapy, with some legal exceptions.
Work with an individual child is generally more productive if parents voluntarily agree to not request
information about the child's private session. The therapist agrees to share with the parent/s any information which is necessary for the safety of the child.

_____

Parent's/legal custodian's signature

_____

Parent's/legal custodian's address

_____

Parent's/legal custodian's telephone number

If divorced, my divorce order identifies me as a managing conservator:

_____ yes or _____ no

_____

Date

NO SUICIDE CONTRACT

I _____ agree that I WILL NOT attempt suicide and that I will work in therapy towards the goal of reducing and eventually eliminating any suicidal thoughts/feelings that I may have. Furthermore, if a crisis develops that I believe I am unable to handle alone, I will do the following:

1. Contact one of my family members for assistance. If I am unable to contact them, I will:

2. Contact my therapist _____ at _____. If I cannot reach my therapist, I will:

3. Call the Dallas Suicide and Crisis Center at 828-1000 (service is available twenty-four hours a day). If I am still in need of assistance, I will:

4. Call the Parkland Psychiatric Clinic (590-8761) for assistance and then present myself, in person, to the Psychiatric Emergency Room at Parkland Hospital on Harry Hines and Inwood in Dallas.

In return, my therapist agrees to do all that is reasonably possible to assist me in helping myself to overcome my suicidal thoughts/feelings.

_____
Client

_____
Therapist

_____
Date

CONTRACT FOR NON-VIOLENCE

The following parties:_____ and

_____, husband and wife, do

hereby agree to enter into a Contract for Non-Violence. Terms of the contract shall be:

I. During the period of time that each party to the contract engages in therapy services with _____, neither party will exhibit violent behavior toward the other party. Neither shall strike, hit, nor threaten the other party.

II. If either party to the contract shall break Condition I above of this contract, the other party to the contract shall proceed to an attorney and file for divorce from the party who behaved violently.

There shall be no exceptions or mitigating circumstances to this contract.

_____   _____
contracting party signature   date

_____   _____
contracting party signature   date

_____   _____
witness signature   date

TERMINATION FORM

client no:_____   therapist:_____

date:_____   family name:_____

1. Summary of case to date: [no. of sessions, issues addressed, family members participating in therapy, degree of progress made]

2. Significant information regarding the last session, including date and reason/s for termination:

3. Recommendations for further treatment:

FAMILY'S EVALUATION OF SERVICES

form developed by Lynelle C. Yingling, PhD, J&L Human Systems Development, 570 E. Quail Run Rd, Rockwall, TX 75087; 972/771-9985

Family name/number:_____ **Therapist:**_____

Dates of therapy sessions: 1st = _____ **last** = _____; **Total number of sessions:**_____

Please help improve future services by the family answering the following questions together after you have finished your work with the therapist. Check one response for each question and write in additional explanations where asked:

1. Therapy was concluded by:
_____(a) the therapist & our family decided together that
       we had finished our work
_____(b) our family
_____(c) the therapist
_____(d) our insurance ran out
[If (b) or (c), please explain briefly:

_____
_____]

2. Did your therapist understand your problem/s:
_____(a) extremely well
_____(b) well
_____(c) somewhat
_____(d) not so well
_____(e) not very well at all

3. How well were you able to relate to the therapist:
_____(a) extremely well
_____(b) well
_____(c) somewhat
_____(d) not so well
_____(e) not very well at all

4. Did you and your therapist work together as a team to make changes needed to solve your family problem/s:
_____(a) completely
_____(b) yes, mostly
_____(c) somewhat
_____(d) not very much
_____(e) not at all

5. Were you able to establish clear, realistic goals for therapy:
_____(a) completely
_____(b) yes, mostly
_____(c) somewhat
_____(d) not very much
_____(e) not at all

6. Were the goals of therapy met:
_____(a) completely
_____(b) yes, mostly
_____(c) somewhat
_____(d) not very much
_____(e) not at all
[If (c), (d), or (e), please briefly explain:

_____
_____]

7. Do you believe the family changes will last for the next 6 months:
_____(a) completely certain
_____(b) mostly certain
_____(c) unsure either way
_____(d) mostly doubtful
_____(e) completely doubtful
[Please list the changes that your family has made since therapy began:

_____
_____
_____
_____
_____
_____]

8. How satisfied are you with the services you received from your therapist:
_____(a) very satisfied
_____(b) mostly satisfied
_____(c) indifferent
_____(d) mildly dissatisfied
_____(e) quite dissatisfied

9. If a friend were in need of similar help, would you recommend the services of this therapist to them:
_____(a) yes, definitely
_____(b) yes, probably
_____(c) not sure
_____(d) no, probably not
_____(e) no, definitely

Thank you for your comments. Please add your suggestions for improving the quality of services on the back of this page.
[3/96]

Index

165